Translated by
Au Chung-to
Tom Rendall

The Collected
Poems of LOMEN
: A Bilingual Edition

ISBN 978-957-549-693-7

*first edition *1000 copies*

Additional copies auailable through
The Liberal Arts Press
4,LANE 72,ROOSEVELT ROAD, SEC. 1
TAIPEI, TAIWAN, REPUBLIC OF CHINA

The Collected Poems of
LOMEN :
A Bilingual Edition

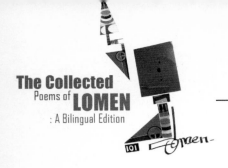

The Collected
Poems of **LOMEN**
: A Bilingual Edition

Contents

III Nature

The Collected Poems of LOMEN
: A Bilingual Edition

IV Self

V Other

Lomen's Poems in Chinese

（三）　自然

The Collected
Poems of **LOMEN**
: A Bilingual Edition

The Collected
Poems of LOMEN
: A Bilingual Edition

Acknowledgements

The completion of this volume would not have been possible without the assistance of our friends. Barbara Rendall, as a poetess herself, gave us a lot of poetic inspiration as well as suggestions. Thanks also go to Kuok Hio-cheng and Chan Sok-han who helped us prepare the typewritten copy and designed the lay-out of the book. Above all, we are also indebted to Professor Wong Tak-wai for his generous help, especially with Lomen's biographical notes. As usual, any errors that remain are our own.

Introduction

Lomen (Han Jentsun) was born in 1928 in Hainan Island, on the mainland of China. His father was a merchant who frequently traveled throughout South East Asia. Lomen dreamed of becoming a pilot during his early years. In 1942, when he was fourteen years old, he went to Sichuan to attend the Air Force Elementary School, and when he was twenty entered the Air Force Pilot's Academy in Hangzhou. In 1950 after the defeat of the KMT, Lomen moved to Taiwan. Having broken his leg in a football match in 1951, he left the air force and went to work at the Aviation Bureau. Although Lomen tried his hand at verse when he was sixteen, he never expected to become a poet. According to Lomen, his serious interest in poetry began when he met his wife in 1954. Rongzi (Jung Tzu) was already a well-known poetess in Taiwan, and under her influence and inspiration, Lomen began his career as a writer. The two married in 1955, and in 1974 Lomen retired from his job at the Aviation Bureau. Since that time he has been able to dedicate himself entirely to poetic and theoretical writings.

Lomen has been awarded many literary prizes during his career. To name only two, he received a gold medal from the President of the Philippines for his "Fort Mckinly" in 1966, and he was crowned with Rongzi as "Laureate Poets" at the 3rd World Congress of Poets in 1976.

Lomen is a member of one of the most important Taiwanese poetry clubs to have sprung up in the sixties -- the Blue Star Poetry Club (Blue Star). Others that developed at that time were the Epoch Poetry Club (Epoch) and the Modernist School (Modernist). The goals of these poetry societies varied. When Ji Xian organized the Modernist School, he advocated a horizontal transplantation of Western themes and styles from the works of Baudelaire onwards. The Epoch Poetry Club promoted surrealist poetry. Blue Star, in contrast, was a revolt against westernized poetics and advocated continued cultivation of the traditional Chinese lyric.

Although the Blue Star poets advocated Chinese style, elements of Lomen's work are reminiscent of Western writers such as Rimbaud, Rilke, Yeats,

and Eliot. These resemblances make Lomen different from his fellow Blue Star poets such as Yu Guangzhong and Rongzi, whose debt to the traditional Chinese lyric is more easily detected. However, Lomen's works go far beyond mere imitations of the Western Modernists' masterpieces.

In fact, it is difficult to categorize Lomen and his works: he is a nonconformist in all senses.

For example, although Lomen's works, especially his city poems, share similarities with his Western counterparts, his nature poems remind us of the traditional Chinese lyric. In "Thinking of the Moon," Lomen utilizes an age-old combination of the motifs of moonlight and longing:

Late at night

the moon stitches a ray of light

on the carpet

Mother is still busy with my new-year's clothes

      under the lamp at my old home

      She is putting stitches on the last pocket

I move closer to the window

The pocket on my clothes

is actually a piece of moonlight

My hands feel for the lucky money inside the pocket

and find a glittering coin

      It is the moon which is thousands of miles away

Mother   how can I get it?

Your hands draw back forever

      under the countless pointed guns

After you leave   no one tells me

your face and the lucky coin you gave me

      still dwell in the moon

Likewise, although Lomen's poems are often thought to be abstract and sometimes even obscure, many are easily accessible. "Four Strings of a Violin," for example, presents four similes describing the appearance of a person's eyes in four stages of life. At first, the similes are traditional, even cliched, "In childhood your eyes are like an azure sky. . . ." But the final simile is hauntingly effective: "as old age approaches they are home to melancholy / as quiet as a midnight theater, its curtain fallen." A stanza describing a woman businessman in "Snapshots of Women" is another example of vivid simplicity. Here the subject is the personal emptiness that often accompanies professional success. After returning home from the office where she "deposits the world in a bank," the lady executive takes off "her precious Longines." Turning off the light, however, "only her silk and transparent pajamas / embrace the night which is getting colder and colder."

Some poems are not only accessible but also contain richly comic elements. Consider, for example, the single line summing up bitter disputes, which "are more irritating than a saw asking the way from a tree" ("The Tower of Death"), or this stanza from "Works of Social Installation Art":

5. The Incident of Rubbish

In front of A's door   rubbish lays in piles

In front of B's door   rubbish lays in piles

In front of C's door   rubbish lays in piles

In front of D's door   rubbish lays in piles

In front of E's door   rubbish lays in piles

You point out in front of ABCDE's doors

                rubbish lays in piles

                polluting the scenery

When you wake up next morning

all the rubbish

        blocks the door where you can see the garden

The police fine you at once

without asking any questions

Lomen's eschewing of traditional meter and rhyme places him clearly with the modernists. On the other hand, his poems are nevertheless highly structured through the devices of shaped stanzas and verbal and syntactical parallelism. "Seven Visions of the Poetic Eye" and "Café" are examples of rigid structures of this sort. Lomen's most effective use of the techniques, however, is found in the poems where he mixes pattern and flexibility, as in the following, which treats one of the poet's most pervasive thematic motifs:

Window

I fling it open   my hands follow the flow of a stream

> always mountains and rivers

> always eyes with no return

Being seen in the distance

you become a bird with a thousand wings

Leaving the sky you no longer have your wings

Being heard

you become a flute with a thousand holes

The road of music is as deep as my eyes gazing at the past

I fling it open   but I am locked in an inescapable

> transparency

True to the modernist injunction that poets must exhibit "unified sensibility," Lomen treats unpoetic subject matters such as washing machines ("Church"), air travel ("Soaring to Thirty Thousand Feet. . ."), photocopiers ("The Wilderness"), and blue jeans ("The Space-Time Sonata"). He also writes movingly about the experience of classical music, heard not in a concert hall, where we would expect such a poem to be set, but on a record player ("The Undercurrent of the Ninth Day"). In fact, Lomen's inclusion of non-traditional themes verges on the postmodern in his obvious admiration for popular culture. He celebrates the music of Debussy, the sculpture of Henry Moore, the dance of Paul Taylor, but also the goals of the Argentinian football star Maradona ("Watching the

World Cup)" and the singing of Michael Jackson ("Michael Jackson is Running with fin de siecle"). A particularly memorable poem describes MacDonald's, with a group of young men blowing through the automatic door "like a rushing in and out of strong wind." Their unhesitating embrace of fast-food culture is poignantly contrasted to an old man sitting in the corner "wearing a wrong size / ready-made suit / finishing a not-to-his-taste / hamburger" ("Lunch Hour at MacDonald's"). Perhaps also postmodern is the whimsicality of such poems as "Using Film Shots to Write the Poem 'Tranquility'" and "My Shortest Poem"-- a one-line work accompanied by no less than three pages of prose commentary.

Although there are frequent references to religion in Lomen's works, it is also clear that for this poet as for most modernists and postmodernists, God is dead, or at least indifferent to human concerns. Lomen's "Melancholy Symphony No. 921," a response to the devastating Taiwan earthquake of 1999, reminds western readers of Voltaire's famous questioning of divine providence on a similar occasion ("Poème sur le désastre de Lisbonne"). One of Lomen's best-known works, the long "Fort McKinley," commemorates the American soldiers who were killed in the Asian theater, and ends with the bleakest of comments on their present situation: "There is no door on the seabed of the ghastly Pacific Ocean." Like many twentieth century writers, however, Lomen finds solace in art. In "The Undercurrent of the Ninth Day," listening to the phono stylus drawing a spiral tower as it plays Beethoven's Ninth Symphony transports Lomen into a state of near-religious ecstasy, "as silent as snow scenery flashing in winter time."

Last but not least, judging from the ways he incorporates different kinds of media such as paintings, installation art, dance, music and so forth into his poems, Lomen not only moves away from modernism but also seems to want to transcend the boundries of poetry itself. In fact, Lomen is also a visual artist and theorist. In addition to composing poetry, Lomen also makes installation art work -- lights. Lomen calls his home the "House of Light" because of the more than thirty lamps which he has made to decorate it. Lomen considers these lights a kind of installation

art which serves an artistic rather than functional purpose. For example, the first lamp he made is approximately six feet tall and resembles a lighthouse. The poet states that the inspiration for this work – the "Lighthouse" – was his marriage with Rongzi. On the day of their wedding, Lomen noticed that the cross on the top of the church looked bright and shiny, like a lighthouse. This lamp not only triggered the later additions to the "House of Light," but also contributed to the development of Lomen's poetic theory of the "Third Nature".

Broadly speaking, Lomen's poetic world is based on the "House of Light." Lomen created the "House of Light" and decided to dwell in it because he noticed the drawbacks created by urbanization and the rapid change of living tempo in the modern world. According to the poet, the speed of our city life has quickened due to the invention of motor vehicles and other types of public transport. As a result, time expands while space contracts. These changes have resulted in a chaotic conception of time and space. In the modern world, past, present and future are compressed together. Consequently, modern people are especially indifferent to the conception of time and space. Lomen further elaborates that in order to free themselves from a limited, suffocated, blockaded as well as gloomy reality modern people naturally indulge themselves in surrealistic and abstract worlds. However, Lomen surmises that it is not very easy for the spirit of an artist to sustain itself in a boundless and abstract world. Consequently, in order to fix the unstable and flowing self, the soul looks for something solid to grasp. In response to this situation, Lomen created the "House of Light" as both a refuge from these changes and a statement of resistance to them.

All of Lomen's creative works – poetry, assemblage art and installation art -- are related to his theory of the "Third Nature Spiral Structure". The "Third Nature" refers to the imaginative world of artists and poets. Poets and artists work hard to transcend the external world, the natural world, such as fields, mountains, streams (the "First Nature"). Eventually, cities (the "Second Nature"), and, finally, the transcendent beauty of the "Third Nature" emerges. Lomen's poetic theory is as complex as it is important for a full understanding of his poetry, and it is therefore discussed further in the Afterword of this volume.

This English version of Lomen's poems has been prepared at the author's suggestion, and the translators hope that it will serve a useful purpose in aiding those who do not read Chinese or who read it only with difficulty. Of course, as Robert Frost remarked, "poetry is what is lost in the translation," and this is particularly true of a translation between languages and cultures so distant as Chinese and English. The process of compiling this book was a long and arduous one. It began by the preparation of an initial version of the poems, which was then smoothed for English expression. Then problem areas (many) were discussed and debated, attempting to find English wordings which would fulfill the target language's requirements of grammar, idiom, and style, while remaining as true as possible to the artistry of the original texts. Some lines and passages cycled back and forth many times before even tentatively adequate solutions were found. For us, however, the task has been a satisfying one. We hope that readers of this volume will find similar interest and pleasure in the poems of this important modern writer.

I

Fort McKinley (1967)

*Things which can surpass the greatness come about when
human beings are at a loss in the face of the greatness itself*

For whom does war sit here to cry?
Its laughter　has made seventy thousand souls fall into a realm which is deeper
than sleep

The sun turned cold　　the stars turned cold　the Pacific Ocean, which was boiled by
gunfire, also turned cold
Smith and Williams:　　the firework festival's glory cannot bring you home
Your names were taken back to your country　which is colder than winter's sea water
Inside the noise of death　you were not saved　　Where were God's hands?
The great memorial has already been rinsed by blood
Even war weeps　　why doesn't the greatness smile?
Seventy thousand cross-flowers　　crowd around to make a garden line and make a
forest circle and make a lily village
They move neither in the winds　　nor in the rains
They are silent for Manila Bay　　they are bleak for tourists' cameras
Smith and Williams:　　on the chaotic lens of death　　　I only want to know
where do your childhood eyes always visit?
where are the recorded tapes of spring and the colorful
photographic slides hidden?

Fort McKinley:　　birds do not sing any more　　leaves dare not move
Any sound will make the silence here bleed
Space is isolated from space　　time escapes from watches and clocks
Here is quieter than the gloomy horizon　　forever soundless
A beautiful silent room　　a garden of the dead　　a tourist spot for the living
God has been here　　reverence has been here　　cars and cities also have been here
but Smith and Williams:　　you can neither come nor go
You are as still as a handless watch　　you cannot see clearly the years' face
through the night's sunlight　　through the starless evening

Your blind eyes fall asleep in all seasons
waking a dying world
lulling Fort McKinley into a deeply gloomy lawn

Death packs and offers his sacrifices on the shouting marble
showing them to the hoisted American flag　　showing them to immorality　showing
them to the clouds

Fort McKinley is the Pacific ocean on the land whose sea spray has already been
carved as a forest of pillars
A relief sculpture bemoaning the universe, hung against the
darkest background of death
Seventy thousand stories have been incinerated in the white restless trembling
Smith and Williams: when the setting sun burns a forest of mangos to red in the
evening
God will leave in a hurry   all stars fall
You can go nowhere
There is no door on the seabed of the ghastly Pacific Ocean

Notes:

1. Fort McKinley is a war memorial to the seventy thousand American soldiers who died during the World War II in the Pacific Ocean theatre. Americans used seventy thousand marble crosses which bear the names and places of birth of the dead to exhibit the tragedy of the Pacific war and the ill fate of humanity. The crosses spectacularly and sadly line up on a vast lawn. Seventy thousand colorful stories are forever buried by death. This world is beyond the artillery range of the cities' noise. The emptiness here embodies the trembling of greatness as well as its restlessness. The forest birds are too threatened to sing. The tranquility here is frightening. Even God can feel this kind of loneliness and dares not stay. Manila Bay glitters in the distance. Mango trees and phoenix trees are everywhere. The scenery is so beautiful that it makes us feel sad. The blue sky and the waving flag fill us with deep veneration. The dark sky and the still flag lull the whole area. We are pressed by the shadow of death....I have visited the Philippines for business recently and took a picture in front of Smith's and Williams' crosses.

2. War is a tragic and a great theme which human life and culture has been facing for thousands of years. During war, human beings grasp "the greatness" and "sacredness" on the one hand. On the other hand, we grasp blood. Even God cannot bear to direct and watch this tragedy. However, human beings have no choice but to accept war bravely for the sake of freedom, truth, justice and survival.

Based on human beings' intelligence and conscience, we certainly feel that war is the most difficult dilemma of our existence. This is because it is a binary opposition of "blood" and "greatness." Its byproduct is an indifferent and terrifying "death."

The Meaning of Tea (1975)

"Tea! You are close to nostalgia"

The afternoon sun weakly
       leans on the sky
The weary heads, one by one
     droop on the chair backs
The setting sun and the eyes sink together in
               the dim horizontal line
Vision silently enters the cup of tea
       Years are sleeping in it
        Blood and tears are sleeping in it
        Hearts are also sleeping in it
Smoke draws a sword out of the mouth
       accidentally pricking the distant place
            a cry in fear
The sinking tea leaves are awakened at the bottom of the cup and become shrapnel
If they are flower petals   spring should return
               home should be here
The floating tea leaves
       are actually a blood-dripping begonia
Even in a dream, it must return on the river

Panmunjom, 38 Degrees (1976)

1

A knife
passes through the wings of the bird
The sky splits open
Eighteen colorful flags
turn into a line of bandages
Should we put the blame for the scar on God?
If this scar splits open again
will the fire which comes up from the crater
      truly be magnificent blood?

2

A healing land
lives inside the wound
God is too far away to visit it
Even fields and animals do not visit it
An American solider has been keeping guard over it
            for thirty-six months
After he goes home   he also will not come back to visit it

It lies on its wound
and cannot go anywhere
All doors and windows are opened by guns
        and they are all closed now

3

Where can it go?
The bridge has one end
      but is without the other*
even the road cannot find itself
God, can you walk across it?

A disabled wilderness
      pulls the blind sky
One cannot move   One cannot see:
where can it go?
The horizon is a heavy chain
        which tightens around its legs

Birds fly   the sky escapes
Wind blows   trees flee
If you stand there and do not run away
lines of gun shots will come over
               from silence
vomiting smoke lightly
The distant clouds   are echoes and turn into the roar of guns
The sky is covered by the wings of aircraft
Forests are lined with guns
Fallen leaves are scattered by shoes
Valleys are dug by wounds
Mountain slopes are undulating tanks
Mountains are piled up bodies
The starry night is studded with bullets and eyes
          When the moon rises   blood sheds tears
          When the sun rises   blood flows

4

What is the color of the gunfire?
And what is the color of the blood?
What are the colors of roses and wine?
And what are the colors of lips?
When legs and skyscrapers
          raise the pillars of heaven
asking the bodies and bones to pile into a steel structure
does this mean that the small conference table
      is as heavy as the two hemispheres?
       There sit two lines of chariots
            two lines of guns
            two lines of daggers
            two lines of blood
            two lines of tears
            two lines of eyes which will never see each other
            two lines of hands which will never grasp together
            two lines of cigars which help each other work
Is that clouds drifting over the bridge
or smoke vomited from the guns?

5

The line on the conference table
is not the rope the children play with
but a dagger blocking the wound
pulling it out   blood flows outside
leaving it there   blood flows inside
Who will think of the one being punished?
  Pushing him into the fire   his head droops
  Throwing water on him   his head still droops
Who will think that the wire-netting fence is made of veins?
  Whether you make or destroy it you must break the veins
Who will think that inside the garden where bombs open into flowers
   babies are the flying butterflies
   nuns are the whitest blooming lilies
   and God can never grasp the catchers' and the pickers' hands?
Who will think that on the distant road
  a sergeant who abandons his gun and a ruffian who discards his dagger
  are handcuffed together
  by a chain without a key?

6

Walking towards the end of the bridge
is also towards the mountains' and the rivers' end
   the rivers' and the mountains' end
the winding mountain path and the twisting road
When we leave the bridge
all escaped eyes
  try to look from the blind sky
Being so nervous   the hands stick inside the pockets
    and dare not say goodbye
    the eyes hide in the gaze
    and dare not look

A few feet away, where shooting is not necessary,
a couple of absentminded soldiers
  laugh foolishly for some reason
God, can you make a guess
  whether it is a star shell arcing here from the midnight
  or a spot of light flashing in the funeral parlor?

* There is a bridge at Panmunjom, 38 Degrees, which is named "A Way With No Return." After you cross the bridge, you can never come back.

Thinking of the Moon (1981)

Late at night
the moon stitches a ray of light
on the carpet
Mother is still busy with my new-year's clothes
     under the lamp at my old home
     She is putting stitches on the last pocket

I move closer to the window
The pocket on my clothes
is actually a piece of moonlight
My hands feel for the lucky money inside the pocket
and find a glittering coin
     It is the moon which is thousands of miles away
Mother   how can I get it?
Your hands draw back forever
     under the countless pointed guns
After you leave   no one tells me
your face and the lucky coin you gave me
         still dwell in the moon

The Space-Time Sonata (1984)
— Looking at the Canton-Kowloon Railway from a Distance

1   A triple jump which only has a hop and a step

The whole world
stops breathing
    at the starting line

Before trains arrive
eyes have already run away
jumping over the first and the second mountains
reaching the third*
They hang in the air without coming down
stretching ahead   is a boundless sky
looking back   Kowloon has already boarded the train
                    scurrying for the border
which makes me look back to Taipei,
to the windows at Tai Shun Street

2   Waiting for thirty years

The old man who sells flowerpots at the street corner
is still looking at the flowers and earth of
                    his hometown

The glass buildings along the street
                    open rows of
                    beautiful nostalgia
Under the buildings' giant shadows
he sits until under a great banyan tree, his childhood returns
An imported Japanese motor car Wild Wolf,
with speed as sharp as a warrior's bayonet,
pierces Hepingxi Road through
                    Hepingdong Road
Passing through memories
a spasm of fear
the whole earth falls into blood
The mountains and rivers which are more obscure than splash-ink
are his distressing tearful eyes
Looking at the bombs' marks on his body which are like

        the river rushing to this place
       the cold wind and chilly water
    the fallen leaves and drooping branches
On the highway which is built of machine guns
on the flyover which has shells above in the sky
each direction has already cried
Heaven's entrance and exit
are wounds never healed
Looking at his own eyes
for thirty years
his weary vision
can only drag an old cow home
        from an evening field
It can no longer move the busy street scenes
A western baby carriage
pushes a new era by
A row of high-rise buildings tower on
        the great noises of pilings
He wakes up from a roar of bombs
and still finds the foundling who cannot grasp the milk bottle
      lying among the ruins where shell fragments shatter everywhere
In the smoke the whole sky
    cannot be blue anymore
When the Wranglers turn the whole street
          into blue
a group of people rush to the churches
      to see the Virgin Mary
a group of people flock to the department stores
        to see the years
He cannot think too much
When he sees the Roman tiles
  he asks for the cobbled road
  When he sees Sunkist
  he asks for well water
  When he sees the new arrival fashion
  he asks for his mother's aged face

Sirens are everywhere on the street
Their wailing calls for birdsong and whistles
He longs to fly, to jump
Thirty flowerpots peer around and
       look at the sky
asking him to sit down quietly together

To sit until it gets dark
his legs which have difficulty walking
are handed over to the washbowl
              returning to his childhood
          to the little pond where he liked to play with water
He feels so excited   the water drops splash on his face
                              All laughter becomes tears

Teardrops are stars
The starry sky of his hometown
sparkles on the television screen
              and comes to visit him

When all the stars are glittering
how can they be a group of singers?
The earth rolls against the bombs' direction
Singer Feng's beautiful eyes
                      are diamond lamps
          which laugh all the way to the luxury hotel's
                  ten-storey, high-rise building
His eyes are a rapeseed oil lamp
      which gets dim at the corner

Before going to sleep
      a young man takes out an architectural design of 007
                      having a look at tomorrow
                  using a computer to calculate tomorrow
Nights always make him sit on the wounds of his memories
              to check the years which are getting less and less
                      in his savings book and on the calendar
He has never heard any literary goodnight
              before embracing his single bed and falling asleep

Sleeping until one day he cannot wake up
Yet the sun will rise as usual
Clocks and watches will stop running
Roads themselves will walk
Whether guns will boom or not
whether the Security Council will hold a meeting or not
newspapers will tell us someday
As long as the earth is still there
wire fencing is still there
day and night are still there
White milk powder and black dynamite
                  will also be there

3   The line which passes through God's pupil

The line
which travels from Panmunjom
to the corridor between East and West Germany
reaches into this place
It is farther than where the clouds go
but is closer than legs and soil

Whenever eyes
touch this line
even the sky wants to go home
When the line looks at and merges into the horizon
even God misses his home

Who throws the line
        on the ground?
Along the line
mother   where is your hand holding the sewing needle?
Where is my childhood falling broken with the kite?
Mother   had this line
stitched the wounds of the earth
I would have already boarded the train which just set off
            running along the painful lines on your forehead
                returning to the days without the roar of guns
                                    to visit you

If this line
  is a one-stroke painting
when it moves it will become the thousand mile long Yangze River
when it keeps still it will become the Great Wall
These icebergs and this ice-water which freeze
                    in memories and freezers
all flow back to great mountains and rivers
flushing the wire fencing and shell fragments away
Motherland   you swim with the sunshine of Jiangnan to this place
                you ski in the snowfields of the north to that place
Then   you open the giant tea table of the field
        holding the tremendous teapot of the blue sky
        which is not inside a small teahouse
You drink from "the running Yellow River rushes to the sea"
to "the lonely sail is lost in the boundless azure sky"

You drink from "the moon emerges from the running river"
to "a lonely pier where a boat floats on its own"
Let the cameras imported from
  Paris, London and New York
be loaded and return with first-class mountains, rivers and culture
Let the Tang dynasty come back to say
this is the oriental flower
    which is most beautiful and has the longest blossoming

Motherland   after six days' labor
          cities will think of weekend's countryside scenery
          birds will tell the planes in the sky that
          the lofty Imperial Tower
            is never higher than you
          the carefree south mountain
          does not worry about the number of astronaut seats placed in space
Motherland   you are still the biggest rocking chair
                              on earth
As long as the years sit on the chair
opening the Tang poetry and the Ci-poetry of Song
Without the thunder of any guns around
the world will be as far as
    the distant hills which float and fade out by turns
It is difficult to say
    how long it will take the spacecraft to reach that place

If the spacecraft cannot reach there
I can only look at my heart
Taking a few glances at it
how can I look back again to this line
          which is the train heading for the border
                              it comes back
                    with compartments of nostalgia

After the train leaves
even earth forgets
where to get on and off the train
The railway
lashes across the sky
The echoes are
    spasms of pain

* The third mountain is fenced with barbed wire.

The Music of the Years (1987)

— Some thoughts upon listening to the performance of Huang Anyuan, a player of the two-string Chinese violin

When you ply the bow of the violin
the Yangtze river and the Yellow river
           run with no return
The two strings of your Chinese violin
are the shores of the rivers
are also the double track of the years of the Chinese people
        which transport endless miseries and sufferings

Each of your bowings
shows the scratches of swords and the marks of bombs
        on the body of our earth and our people
Each of your pauses
is millions of sighs with regrets
When you play quickly   you hurry the turmoil and chaos of war
When you play slowly   the pains are drowned out

Drawing blood and mountains
        teardrops and rivers
           together
how does spring return to the south of the Yangtze with flowers?
how does winter return to the north of the Yangtze with snow?
Whether the years are laughing or crying
even the music cannot say clearly
Waiting for a reply
      culture keeps its glory
      mountains and rivers keep their splendor

On the stage   the music is crying for home
Below the stage   black hair is looking at silver hair

Postscript:
After having listened to the music of Huang Anyuan, I found his bow has been pressing the grieving heart, the years and the earth of Chinese people.

The Global Political Game (1988)

He uses his left eye to hit <u>his</u> right eye
           weeping
<u>He</u> uses his right eye to hit *his* left eye
           weeping
He uses his left atrium to hit <u>his</u> right atrium
           bleeding
<u>He</u> uses his right atrium to hit *his* left atrium
           bleeding
Many *his* and <u>his</u>
     left and right eyes are weeping
     left and right atriums are bleeding
As a result, *he* and <u>he</u>
 are the same person

II

The Collected
Poems of **LOMEN**
: A Bilingual Edition

Death of a City (1961)

City, your construction is
almost higher than god's heaven

1

The layers of the buildings   hold people's faces upward
The displays of the food hall   carve people's stomachs
The show-windows flash with the seasons' sharp eyes
People buy the years' appearances with banknotes
Right here   footsteps do not transport the souls
Right here   priests cover their eyes with bibles and by falling asleep
                all restricted areas become markets
                all eyes become hawks' eyes in the blue sky
It is like the running cars clinging to the roads at high speed
people seize their own shadows rushing off
                to look inside the changes which are too rapid to understand
                to think inside the cyclotron which is too rapid to understand
                to perish inside the death which is too rapid to die

Speed controls the circuits   God cannot grasp the megaphone
This is a busy season   Between pressing a button and a switch
city   the thick net you weave stops our breathing
Within its anxiety, the station cries for a journey
within its exhaustion, the road is covered with tracks
everything slides down the slope without any resistance   dashing at the terminal
No one knows when the sun will die
People bend over the overlapping negatives, never able to recognize themselves
                                never able to see their eyes

Everything returns to the wind
        Which is like a banquet killed by a cleaning cloth
                Holidays die under the motionless wheels

2

Sundays   people return after getting away for six days
The houses of their hearts   having been cleansed by pastors
tomorrow   they will again go to smell the rosy scent on women's skin
                will go to see the seven suns squatting in front of the bank counters
When people are sitting, standing or walking
                they are like waves in the wind
Tobacco holds the days   liquor floats the years

Eden never has a door
On nylon mats   on soft or hard beds
civilization is a flowery belt which has been taken off
A beautiful beast   becomes as wild as the nude wilderness
When tomorrow comes   it will resume its clothes again
                return to its decorated hair and face
And the world under its waist   is always a moon rising in a tranquil night
                an ivory counter
                only nothingness can be exchanged for hope

City   the crossroad on your neck clamors all day,
God does not believe in God   God is even more restless than the sea
Although the spire of the church   takes in the tranquil blue of the sky
                that color cannot be injected into your rosy veins
The Cross is then used to make your half nude breasts glimmer
Your half nude breasts   as naked as the square where the moon takes a walk
    elevates the Eiffel Tower
 guarding the nights of Paris, the mist, the heaven which prays with the loins

3

Gazing at the rippled pond
the shaking shadows are those clouds which cannot grasp the sky
Breaking the mirror urgently   still what is wished for cannot be retrieved
City   when you vacillate now to the left and now to the right
        all pulling rings are broken
        all hands droop and become broken branches in the wind
        A sound always flees inside the crack of the broken glass
People hurriedly sow seeds with their shadows   collecting themselves on the ceiling
To chase after spring   the flowering season has already gone
To watch the tidal water   the storm has already subsided
Life is last year's snow   is the fallen flowers in a woman's mirror case
Death stands on the old sun's chariot
    crying silently to the sound and the soundless
    crying lowly   to the consciousness and the unconsciousness
Clocks and wheels gnaw the scenery on both sides of the road
The leftovers soften the path for Death
The hour hand is a generous yet an agile guillotine
The term of imprisonment is more lenient than a sound sleep
To die with wide-open eyes is like a body covered by a glass coffin
People conceal themselves   which is like hiding a ticket-stub inside the pocket
It is impossible to grow yesterday's branches   to make the sound of the dying wind
A tree then drifts to somewhere beyond the earth

4

City   daytime winds round your head   nighttime drapes over your shoulders
You are an ugly belly without a face
        a faceless beast which swallows lives without leaving any wounds
                        which gnaws the bones and muscles of God
Your glorious crown   always rises from the multicolored starlight
                        and breaks under the street cleaners' dawn
On a day of hunting   you are a dead bird hanging on the holiday
                        you are shot dead again and again
A hungry hawk from the wilderness   looks flurried
Laughter soars up from the entrance   falling down at the exit
The wind goes up and down   the wave comes and goes
Who can save the road from these tramplings?
Who can get away from the wound which is opened up by oneself because of the
                                            dull pain?
Who can keep himself away from the current when he is inside the rash sounds of
                                            the river?

On a day of shipwreck   only bed and cutlery keep you afloat
The struggling arms are a bunch of yelling keys
crying for the door   crying to escape the inevitable deadlock

5

City   before the bell of the terminus rings
all your fast turning wheels break   and run off the rails
Death will not scream   nor give a signal
You are like Death who dies with wide eyes
    dies in the wine bottles   dies in the ashtrays
    dies on the bed   dies under the Eiffel Tower
        dies of an overdose of civilization's drugs
When the lobe of the lung no longer transmits sounds to the stethoscope
when all veins become broken circuits
heaven fades away and becomes a shadow
God collapses amid respectful looks
City   everything dies quickly during Easter
And you are a bride just coming out from a sedan-chair
    you are the wedding night when lanterns are hanging
                the honeymoon which is made of fruit juice
                a nude beast   the most empty primitiveness
                a screen   hiding the shadows of the graveyard
                a carved coffin   loaded with moving death

A Vagabond (1966)

The boat, exhausted by the sea's vastness, is in the harbor
By the coffee table, he uses the lamp to bring his own shadow to heel
the animal he carries always with him
Besides it   Nana is only as close as what is far away

He drinks the wine until it becomes the moonlight of his home town
and looks at the empty bottles until they become a desert island
He carries the animal with him
walking toward his own footsteps
Far away, a star is walking
    and carrying the sky with it

Tomorrow   when the first roll of the blinds
        tugs at the sun and turns it into a ladder
he does not know whether he will go up   or go down

The City's Pentagonal Pavilion (1969)

He seizes the city firmly,
The city also takes a firm hold of him.

1 Newspaper Boy

Yesterday is not shot dead
Yesterday is smuggled back by the printing machine

Before the milk bottles' sounds can be heard
before Anna swims out of her arms
his bicycle rushes before the sun's one-wheel-car
Like a garden, Yesterday is brought back by him
People's eyes are polished until they become vases
waiting for different flowers' various colors
Civilization opens into flowers   bombs open into flowers
no matter whether God is willing to see or not

2 Shoeblack

He and his kit
sit together until they become a "L" shaped vacuum cleaner
sit together until they become a tiny desert

In a sand-storm
his hands are a durable rope
   While he pulls the boats which transport sun-shine
over to the roads
He is not sure whether his hands are
                        the sails
                        or the cactuses

3 Waiter

He always bends his body into a
      V with improper direction
and let the black butterfly rest on his white collar
   until it flies and becomes a numbered gentlemen

Amid the waves of brandy and laughter
the yacht and the spray leave him some beautiful bubbles
Facing a room of chaotic plates

he feels the black butterfly which can never fly into a garden
    feels the row of numbers before his chest which are irrelevant to the lottery
    feels himself
his face is invited to the back of the lamp

4 Woman Singer

When it gets dark
something will look for her either to do massage
                    or to receive electric treatment

In the flammable air
she is a Ronson lighter
Night is a hempen cigarette

When her vocal chords extend
they become the road where citizens always go to take a walk
Going ahead of the road is Fifth Street
Going ahead further   is her garden
Going ahead further   is the fountain in her garden
Going ahead further   is the ruin dying in the mist
                        it is as bleak as her face
                        which next morning is deserted by cosmetics

5 Rag-picker

In order to smell a piece of blue sky in the bright area
his nostrils are two underground drainpipes
In that place   there is no analytic study
which is better than his hands and able to analyze his tomorrow

Carried on his back is the city of excretion
Carried on his back is a blossoming graveyard
He is in a wasteland without sky
  walking until another kind of clouds comes out
  On the surface of a dead clock
    he wakes up another part of years

The Collected
Poems of **LOMEN**
: A Bilingual Edition

Mini-skirt (1971)

When we hear the sound of cutting, like a pair of tailor's scissors
        night is halved
One half is mixed by the eyes and becomes a palette
The other is already printed on a bed-sheet with a phoenix pattern

Cutting here
        cuts out the melodies of '72
Cutting there
        cuts out a heart-broken
        nostalgic
        horizontal
        line
        how many sunsets
        how many falling stars
        how many sinking moons

Video-recording on the Bed (1971)

The next morning
the bay is so quiet that it seems no boat has visited before
The sea is unable to awaken
My eyes are too weary to bear
   the light reflected on the windows

Looking outside, I see the tables of the restaurant opposite
                        have yet to be cleaned up
   a straw is bent inside an empty bottle
Looking further, I see a racing car
   on its way chasing after the scenery
   it breaks down at the car park   its hood remains open
Looking further yet, I see an oar
   withdrawing from the sound of the waves
             laid aside on the empty beach
      The sea bird has already vanished into the lowest
                        horizontal
                         line

Car Accident (1975)

He is walking his hands are searching the sky
He is walking his mouth is mumbling echoes of the bomb
He is walking his body is leaning to one side
He is walking he enters the sound of a sudden braking
He stops walking the road in turn steps on him
He stops walking the beautiful weekend in the city strides on
He stops walking the elevated advertisement board
                        freezes the whole sky

Café (1976)

A line of lamps
  line up a line of eyes
A line of cups
  line up a line of mouths
A line of chairs
  line up a line of shoulders
A line of dresses
  line up a line of legs
A line of brassieres
  line up a line of breasts

A line of eyes
  line up a line of moonlight
A line of mouths
  line up a line of bubbling fountains
A line of shoulders
  line up a line of broken bridges
A line of legs
  line up a line of torrents
A line of breasts
  line up a line of waves
      Night
      starts to move

Coffee Love (1976)

"City! This lens captures your boredom."

Coffee-colored, it
always focuses on him
as if it wants to shoot something
But he tries to escape
        crying out: "I am an exposed film"

It always happens in the afternoons
The buses with identical numbers
        pass outside the window again and again
The man who has an identical name
        sits inside the window again and again
When the window within and without is misted over
it will be impossible to see what a gear wheel is chasing after inside a clock
                                a car wheel chasing after in the street
                It happens the coffee-colored camera lens
                                        is blind
                        Except for the glittering lights
                                        the lustful eyes
                                the beautiful women
                                        the rippling nights
                        it sees nothing

Motorcycle (1980)

The hand of the Twentieth Century
    waves a whip
   and cruelly slashes
  the wild legs of the cities

The long scars
are the withered tree roots in the fields
 and the drying up rivers

A Young Man Carries a 007 Briefcase (1981)
— He dreams of 007, a crystalline mansion built on breasts

007, the secret code of time,
    it only opens tomorrow
007, the most handsome speed
        on the highway,
    it never looks back

Carrying 007
he is chased by the whole city
until three o'clock in the afternoon
Before the bank lowers its iron gate
He is either carrying a heaven
        or a graveyard

Be Alive! These Two Words (1982)

The city is a fast absorbing paper
Written on it again and again
are always these two words: "be alive"

The commuters go to work in a hurry
they write numerous lines in regular small characters:
"be alive"
The buses go to work in a hurry
they write numerous lines in regular script:
"be alive"
The motorcycles go to work in a hurry
they write in a cursive script too fast to be read:
"be alive"
Because of writing these two words "be alive"
we are within the inkstone of a clock
our hearts have almost run dry

City. A Square Existence (1983)

The sky is drowned in the square well of the city
Mountains and rivers wither outside the aluminum windows
What should eyes do?

Eyes look out
  from the square windows
  of the cars
They immediately are themselves looked at
     by rows of square windows
        of high-rise buildings

Eyes look out
  from the square windows
       of the rooms
They immediately are themselves looked at
       by rows of square windows
         of other apartments

Eyes look out but see nothing
All windows are blind and set into
      the square walls
With no choice, the eyes search for the square windows
          in the dining tables
         in the mahjong tables
They have looked them over   Finally
     through the square windows of
         the TV sets
       all eyes escape

Adjustments of Living Space: Twentieth Century (1983)

Apartments and cottages
sit at the ends of the highway
            glaring at each other

It is better to relax than to
come to a total deadlock
Because mountains have a peak
            buildings have a roof
The sky does not belong to anyone
            is not being tall for anyone
Everything does not seem to be right
Birds and planes say so
            when they pass by

In the future
as long as the highway is
            open to traffic
someone will take the garden and field to town
someone will drive the city to the countryside
Soil and carpet have already put on
the same pair of shoes
The beautiful countryside and the street scenery have already entered
the same pair of eyes
Everyone crowds into the television screen each day
even if they do not know each other at the beginning
they will get familiar with each other sooner or later

Lunch Hour at McDonald's (1985)

1.

A group of young men
      carrying the winds
      rush into the restaurant
They are attracted
to the shiniest place
    and sit together
with the whole city

Inside the windows, there is a plate of food
Outside the windows, there is a plate of scenery
The knives and forks in their hands
which are faster than the cars,
passing by:
a charming and handsome
    afternoon

2.

Two or three middle-aged men
dwell inside exhaustion
The knives and forks in their hands
stretch out slowly and become the legs of chopsticks
They return to thirty years ago to the old town and the small restaurant there
Six eyes stare
at six big flies
they go into a trance
The table suddenly gets dim, changes into
               an image of memory
Who knows where the afternoon is driven
by a bottle of red wine
and its drunken nonsense

When a gust of young men,
      like a rushing in and out of strong wind,
           blow in and blow out
         through the automatic door
Can you hear the sound of the fallen leaves
         amid the wintry woods?

3.

An old man
sits in the corner
wearing a wrong size
     ready-made suit
finishing a not-to-his-taste
         hamburger
It is impossible to surmise
where the Han dynasty fortress has gone
Those glass buildings could not be
       the shiny paddy field

The old man sits until he becomes
     a withered old pine, an interior decoration
It is better to keep silent
Once he talks to himself
he must speak with
the deafening noise of bombs
When he starts to talk
the afternoon just now
has already become evening in his eyes

The Alienation of Glass Buildings (1986)

Standing at the street corner
I look at the glass buildings
   They freeze the scenes one after the other
            and keep them in the glass windows

Going out of town by car
I look at the glass buildings
   outside, they are quickly dissolved
   by the speeding windows of the car
They fly until they become pieces of scenery
fusing into mountains and rivers
turning into mist and smoke
Eyes fail to catch up with the changes
and turning back inside the car
I look into a pair of empty eyes which
are gazing at another glass building
   The glitter inside the country boy's
                           pupils
            which will take me fifty years
                  to come close to again

Karaoke (1987)

Is there anything still not OK?
The whole city is trodden under your feet
By you the world is also trampled down
Starting from O
you trample yourself to empty until you
                          return to your origin

Your brain is empty and thinks of nothing
Your heart is empty and considers nothing
Submitting everything to the movement of your body
your limbs are a burning high voltage circuit

The city is beating on your radiant body
The uproar and the indifference of the city
are vomited from the throat of the speaker
To dance until life becomes only the body
Whatever you touch is bodies
Whatever you embrace is bodies
Is there anything still not OK?

The Book of Ethics is yawning in the Chinese classrooms
Karaoke is dancing vigorously underfoot
But even Karaoke faints from dancing
his mouth still throwing the beer foam up and
                          crying OK

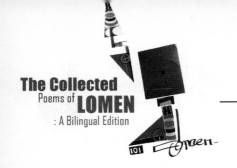

The Collected
Poems of LOMEN
: A Bilingual Edition

Eyes' Asylum (1989)

Following a traffic light, eyes run in relay with it
Following documents, eyes run to and fro
Following news, eyes run everywhere
Following the prices of stocks, eyes run after them
Following menu and stomach, eyes run with them
Following women's breasts, eyes run up and down
Following knife, gun and bloodstain, eyes run away with them
Following prayers, eyes run toward heaven
Whether you are shortsighted or farsighted
whether you wear glasses or not
after running all day
you are exhausted and look for
television's asylum

Robbery and Rape (1989)

Under the dim street lamp at midnight
the swaying curve of her body
    connects to his sight
The pearl necklace hanging around her neck
                  strikes his eyes
The breasts towering on her chest
are like his territory
    Mt. Chang Bai
The whole visual space
enters a fearful, primitive, barbarous place
Once the church, the court and the police station are out of sight
          he can do whatever he wants

Bank (1989)

This is the place where money takes a rest and sleeps
When she wakes up and
goes out
all directions focus on her
Smiling faces point to her
Guns aim at her
The meters of the cabs mount up on the way when
       they are running after her
Years bear the salary bag
following her all their life

Wherever she goes
the world follows her
Department stores open their doors to wait for her
Restaurants open their mouths to call for her
Lounges and hotels open their red doors to grab at her
Offering bags open their charities to greet her
Thousands of people open their hearts, their brains and their eyes to look at her
          to think of her
She is beloved by all She is a charming and beautiful woman
       who gives birth to a dandified
         pleasure-seeking city
         which is truly awful

The Disease of *fin de siecle* in the Cities (1991)

To start with, bronze leaves the statue and returns to the hardware store
    A moustache is painted above Mona Lisa's mouth
Then, God asks himself where he is from
Finally, shoes ask the way
    The way asks for directions
The directions ask and enter an almost extinguished lamp
        which closes the door and falls asleep
           waiting for the dawn
The past of the past of the past   falls sound asleep
The future of the future of the future   falls sound asleep
The sandwiched present   has a sleepless night
It slips out
and follows the insomniac city
smoking and drinking together
watching nude pictures together
singing karaoke together
They open their eyes wide together
    slipping into drugs and sleeping pills
        tossing from side to side

A boat drifts on the undulating sea
without reaching the shore

The Mole Growing on the Back of "Postmodernity" (1991)

Between the symphonies of hero and destiny
Nietzsche follows the earth's axis
climbing up to the roof of the sky
    He wants to exchange his heart   for that of the universe
                        and to sign a contract with eternity

Numerous eyes
look up for a hundred years at Nietzsche
When the eyes get tired   they climb down from the sky
The world lies on the ground
The sky and the earth look at each other   both of them not tall at all
which puts the sky in trouble because it cannot fly
In fact, flying, running and going
                    are walking
Wherever we walk   we will find your
popularity which both PhD holders and movie stars admire
Pop singers and Mozart enter the same studio
Poets and legal clerks use the same desk
*San Mao, Si Mao** grow on the forehead of Maugham
              put down their roots on Bacon's head
A tailcoat wears a pair of jeans
Bars and churches have their own foods
Being pressed by masseur's hands and powder   buildings cannot move
In fact, both upper class and lower class are classes
        both sewage water and sea water are water
those cannot be separated   will enter the sewage
those cannot leave   will crowd into the yellow light
        All directions are stir-fried on the steering wheel
                until they become chop-suey

* Translators' Note:
"San Mao" is the name of a leading character in a Chinese comic book, namely, the
Adventure of San Mao. The literal meanings of " San Mao" is three hairs and "Si
Mao" four hairs. The name of " Si Mao" is made up by Lomen. The poet plays with
the Chinese pronunciations of "Mao" as in "San Mao" and "Si Mao" here. This is
because the Chinese translation for Maugham is "Mao Mu." Lomen obviously makes
a pun on the word " Mao."

A Classical Tragedy (1992)

The recreational center cannot be the cultural center
The flyover cannot be the magpie bridge or the maple bridge
The stock exchange cannot be the peach blossom valley or the mandolin ballad
The karaoke cannot be the place where people sit watching the clouds
The traffic jam street corner cannot be the place where
                              all people vanish

He looks for the road   the road also looks for him at the intersection
He looks at his watch   he does not know when the watch stopped
He looks for himself   his upper part is going up
                  his lower part is going down
Going to and fro,
he consciously or unconsciously
      wears a Chinese jacket   entering a European steak house
      dresses in a Western suit   entering a Chinese teahouse
After eating and drinking
he sees a lot of Mercedes
      passing and polishing a row of glass buildings
He quickens his paces on the red brick pavement
A few days ago   a Boeing 747 jumbo jet
carried him and the kitchen in the air
        to another glass building which is three-million-feet high
                          to have dinner
He did not know whether he should order the goddess Chang'e flight to the moon
                        or the spacecraft's escape to the sun
In a sudden burst of chaotic currents
he loses his balance in the air
After vomiting
he falls into
the mountains and rivers of nature
the sounds and sights of the city
He leaves his body to enjoy in the city
changing his brain into a shop of fake antiques
in order to go back to the ancient emptiness
He also carries scholars' writings with him
  in order to go back to look for the brush pots of the eight great writers
                    to wear Du Fu's old shoes
                    to put on Li Bai's old cap
Drinking the dregs in their cups
      he also gets drunk and forgets himself
      staining himself with a few spots of history and eternity

Even the wine cannot imagine
that only a bottle of *shu pao*
    in the international refrigerator
can wake him up at his luxurious apartment
    which costs two hundred thousand for one square meter
He looks at the mountains and the rivers painted on the carpet and the tiles
watching the micro-nature of the bonsai
sitting opposite the buildings
which whirl in the air, on and on
He suddenly discovers that he
    is only a copy of the Taoran Pavilion
            inside an urban garden
which is surrounded by artificial mountains and rivers
allowing a look into the city's holiday

Michael Jackson is Running with *fin de siecle* (1993)

1.

The city paralyzed in its material center
      is deafened among machine noise
If you did not come here to dance, to shout and
to give the city an injection
          it would not feel so good
          and it would not immediately become excited

It is a kind of drug reaction
    another way of love making
        To love blindly
      in the homeland of sensations
the upper part of the world   is tranquility
the lower part of the world   is uproar

Your screams
    pierce through the city's lean, hollow heart
          its empty private parts
The out-of-control madness
      is a burst open brewery
No wonder the whole city gets drunk and crazy

2.

You are a source of action
The energy of ten-million hands
          are in your hands
The power of ten-million legs
          are in your legs
When you wish to have an earth-shaking change
     wish to fling the audience up into the air
             into the sea
so long as you open your mouth
millions of hearts   are willing
millions of affections   are ready

When you open your mouth
except for the crowd's cries
the loudest sounds will fade away
When you lift up your hands

the whole city sways in the air
When you kick up your legs
the city becomes a ball
You chase it and come here
The world is made vacant
    and watches you cry, shout,
make a beautiful *fin de siecle*
    nail ten million eyes to the screen
 Let the most popular news shows watch you

Tonight
the television station finally broadcasts
the world's biggest music explosion
which takes place continuously in many public squares
The quietest place in the world
 is the Imperial Palace which sits amid mountains, rivers and ancient jades
 is the city of Vienna which falling asleep, embraces a symphony

Postmodern Channel A (1993)

Postmodernity   grins cheekily
        following stern modernity
           and comes here
which makes all upward-looking eyes
            look downward
    The world becomes shorter
    Idols fall to the ground

Crowns and ancient Roman domes
    are put on buildings' heads
Acrylic-made transparent roof and sky's roof
           are placed together
Driving a Mercedes to the countryside
    bringing trees from the fields to the high-rise buildings
        and having a meeting with the city*
Wearing a pair of "Yuppie" shoes
    walking on the whole city and stepping on the luxurious carpet
dragging a pair of sloppy slippers
    tugging the whole city round the streets and lanes
where should the direction go?
    As long as there is a road
where should the direction take a rest?
It depends on how tired the direction is
  Ashtrays, empty bottles
  recreational centers and churches
    all are good places

On time square which is open 360 degrees
someone enters *Xin Dong Yang Lao Dai Chang*
someone rushes to McDonald's and KFC
someone pours coffee into *Longjing* tea
someone squeezes lemon into milk
someone raises his left hand, his right hand
someone raises both his hands
someone hugs the stock market's buttocks
someone hugs a women's buttocks
someone hugs a classical eight-part essay
someone strips culture of her clothes
someone makes sublimity
    tower aloft on women's breasts
someone makes wine bottles, women's legs and guns
    heaven's pillars

someone piles copper and cement
          into eternity
As long as you are happy
everything is up to you
the value is fixed by you
the years are chosen by you
the world is selected by you

* The architecture of the Taipei restaurant "Xiandai Qishilu" embodies the concept of postmodern installation art. It not only has a transparent roof but also encloses a planted, age-old tree. The juxtaposition of the city with the countryside within a single space makes a dialogue between the two possible.

The Fuse of "People's" Living Space (2000)

The beautiful earth
the winds, the clouds, the birds   fly and bring freedom and vastness
Nature   beautifies the earth and brings out its original beauty

When human beings drive the first stake into the ground
many small and large maps arise
The borderlines shown on the map are drawn by knives
                    which separate you from me
and also draw paths of blood stains
which make crowds of people   walk upon bullets

The earth is round
   Eyes are round
  Silver dollars are also round
It seems all of them eventually become silver dollars
The perfect circles which rise from our hearts are no longer seen
The sun and the moon when they come here can only follow silver dollars
On their way they pass on a saying: "people die of money"
                which is our unwritten biblical creed
Walking along the road of wealth   we can only see that profit is running
which is leading the way all the way
which is shouting "Bravo" all the way
which is saying "amen" all the way
From international sea routes, land routes and air routes
       to the streets and lanes in the cities
       to the apartments' staircases and lifts
       to HOME SWEET HOME
       the most peaceful home
       God watches with his own eyes that
           a son stabs his father with a knife
               and draws a
                  bloody
                   road
                    of
                 wealth

Note:
In an era when money and profits are people's main concern, we recently learned from the media that a father and son killed each other for the sake of money. This and other news reflect that human nature, humanity, human relations and the value of life

are being destroyed, which gives us food for thought about our world. It seems that no matter whether we are a collective or an individual, we are destined to chase after money and benefits. We continuously plunder and get far away from the metaphysical, transcendent world in our hearts. As a result, a quickly ignited fuse is hidden within the living space of human beings which is waiting for the beauty of art's rescue.

Tracing the Whereabouts of Human Beings (2001)

In an era when all values are on sale
in an era when the center has no heart
in an era when bodies are most important and spirits are no longer a concern
in an era when people are only interested in sex and no one cares for marriage
human beings   where are you?

In an era when the upper parts of our bodies separate from the lower
in an era when materialism topples metaphysics
in an era when digestion dissolves culture
in an era when spirituality disappears
human beings   where are you?

In an era when everything becomes relative and everybody is right
in an era when God disappears and everybody becomes god
in an era when every minute rushes to become eternity
in an era when guns rush to connect with heaven
human beings   where are you?

In an era when coins roll with eyes
in an era when pockets and brains only have cards and bank books
in an era when media and advertisements speedily dump goods
in an era when rubbish mountain, spiritual mountain and Mount Nan are all
                                        considered mountains
human beings   where are you?

In an era when cars race through yellow lights when all traffic signals are out of
                                        order
in an era when roads ask for directions   and directions ask the way
in an era when chairs should hang in the sky
in an era when the earth has already sat in the spaceship heading to somewhere we
                                        don't know
human beings   where are you?

Human beings   where are you?
Since legs cannot ignore the hour hands
people sit inside themselves
embracing poetry and art
and meditating until they cannot think of anything
Which is also kind of existentialism

The Collected
Poems of **LOMEN**
: A Bilingual Edition

Ecstasy (2002)
— Shaking into the vortex but saving mountains and rivers

Heads are shaking when things go right
Heads are shaking when things go wrong
Hugging the whole city to shake their heads
The sky and earth follow to shake their heads
shaking off the crown and laurel on their heads
shaking off the cross on their heads
to shake the world until it arrives at the place where God and Caesar cannot reach
(It seems Baudelaire has been there before
but he did not shake so vigorously)
                    shake
            shake   shake
        shake   shake
            shake   shake
                shake   shake
                shake
To shake the earth until it becomes a cradle which God and spirits have never before
                                                                used

a new-born, foundling in his dream
    visits a garden which angels never imagined
    The flowers blooming in the garden are not fragrant carnations and roses
    but poppies sniffed at by police dogs along the way*

Ecstasy, glue, morphine and opium all are drugs.

The Slanting 21st Century (2004)
— A Postmodern Beat

1

Nietzsche opens chain stores   at the top of the sky, of the mountain and of the heads
                                to sell aloofness and arrogance
Rilke opens chain stores   at the bottom of the sea, of the mountain and of the hearts
                                to sell aloofness and loneliness
After having visited and eaten the foot of a hill and the seashore
                        the beautiful and delicious scenery
                                tourists fly away
The skyscraper built by "modernism"
                    has to close down
All capital is transferred elsewhere (1)

2

The round silver dollars
seize the eyes and the earth
   pushing the 21st century downtown
and shout "Bravo"
The sun is shattered and twinkles on the ground
The world illuminates several beautiful and
                    flower-like fireworks
which are brightened and dimmed within its lightspeed
Shadows remain on the screen at the stock market
            they become the sunrises and sunsets of our city
            The visual order is reestablished

3

This is an era of food and sex
Culture is beaten by digestion
If you want to eat postmodern
   you will go to a chafing dish restaurant
            pouring all edible flesh, plants and sources into the dish
            and flushing your stomach and belly with coke and beer
If you want to have a sound postmodern sleep
you will rush to the network
  spreading prostitution, one-night-stand and 3P on the bed
  and under the bed there is a mud-rock flow no one can shut out
If you want to enjoy yourself and play with postmodernity

you will make the electronic toys consider you a toy
and play with you
until both your and the computer's brains become a synthetic brain
When your desire has no limit   you are the god who has a gun
When your desire cannot be fulfilled you desert your body as if it is an empty house
Even you do not want to live in it

Hollowness   you are watching the wheels' shadows and footprints running on the
streets
you have become an autumnal fallen leaf swept by a speedy
whirlwind
Aloofness   you are watching thousands of people shoulder their ways through
the streets and they do not know each other
Loneliness   you are watching people and the world walking within their shadows

4

This is an era when scales have no digits shown on them
It is difficult to tell lightness from heaviness, genuineness from fakery
because fresh flowers, plastic flowers and the flowers' shadows on the network
are all considered flowers

It is difficult to distinguish right from wrong, true from false
because the lights on the table are switched off
The switch is left in the hands under the table
Who wants to buy culture from a famous brand
Money is always on its way
going up
Who wants to sell out human history
in order to see the biggest flower of nostalgia
He will embrace machines
and let life leave its homeland, his body

5

This is an era when shooting cannot find its target
Ecstasy will shake its head no matter whether things go right or wrong
it is an aimless missile going to different targets
Directions flee in every direction
"god" is missing
Traffic lights are broken

The world hides itself in the yellow light
The grey zone
is the home of dust and sand storm

whoever enters the zone will have trachoma
        will have a grey head, grey face and never see the daylight
unless you sit on the "metaphysics" built up by Heidegger
darkness sinks at the bottom of the valley   You will never see
                          blue sky and green field
unless "poetry" uses the horizon to pull at the sky and earth
                to straighten them up (2)
      The sun and the moon pass in and out regularly
           Height goes up and down regularly
The tilting and falling 21st century
      is not be able to climb up

Notes:
(1) "Modernism" has become "Postmodernism's" quality controller and financial
    controller.
(2) The most beautiful nation and community in the world will be made by poetry
    and art instead of by machines.

III

River (1973)

If only I could return to the sound of your welling up first
                   I would recognize your original face
Following with my eyes
your music-like figure
   is a primitive song
which makes   the mountains become higher
                 the woods become deeper
                 the wings of the birds fly farther

Until the soft cloud
   is rubbed by the sky and
   the sound of water is rubbed off
Through the collision
you understand your own body

A beautiful "S"   whether it is a saw
                   or a corkscrew
Those delightful threads   upon twisting
their drifting sound turns into a parabola   which is grasped by the birds in the sky
The whole wilderness is shivering amid the whirling
                        music

All the slopes   grow melodies
All the bends of the rivers   become sensitive
                 become very smooth
   There are many whirlpools
   Numerous mountains and rivers that cannot be saved
Besides the earth who can let you travel like this
Besides the bottom of the sea   who knows you are coming
Besides the horizon   who saw you had already been here

Sea (1973)

If only the piano notes could enter the deep midnight
I would be able to go into your blue tranquil distance

That transparent vastness
has already changed into wind
The
horizon
is
the
last
string
Even if we use the whole sky to pluck it, no sound will be heard

In the grasp of a hand, the whole tranquility
stretches out   Rivers follow the lines on the palm and flow
                The sounds of water fill my eyes
Mountains are coming one after another   and your form is shaped by them
Wings pile up one upon another and fly away   until they become your remoteness
In a distant place   the seed has already formed the order of a forest when it passed
                                                                              by

            The drop of water is also a seed
               it moves until it becomes you
                  moves until it turns into your waves
                               the layers of your wings

Who says flying is not the sky
     the sky is not sitting on your swing
        which is as light as a cloud
When it drifts   in its dream it will not descend
When it undulates   there will be a piece of rope in the bleeding palm
                    which is like a vein holding a tree tightly

Sailing into a thousand sails
     the sail is your face which braves wind and rain
Sometimes it is as soft as a tongue
licking the lips of water and sky
A
distant
place
spreads
until
it

becomes
petals
You think of seeding stars
                    seeding moons
                    seeding clouds
                    seeding birds
                    seeding winds
                    seeding waves
    but so many breasts are seeded unexpectedly
No wonder when the sun kisses affectionately
                            you become a blue graveyard
When the dusk arrives treading on the lowered sails
you withdraw from the last net

Mountain (1973)

If only my eyes could step into a gaze
I would be able to enter into your dark green chanting
                                The lowland is water
                                The highland is tree

Clouds and seas go far away
You stay behind alone
leaving the whole sky overhead
        the wilderness underfoot
Let the thousand-year wind and rain twine round that ancient pine
coiling the eagle's wings up to the thousand-mile vastness
When your loftiness   falls into the horizon
                        it becomes a distant place
When your meekness and geniality   fall asleep
                one night becomes deeper than the other

Night is your door
        your window
        your House of Light
        your sleeping eyes leaving everything behind makes you see things more
                                                    clearly afterward
The sun falls asleep and becomes rock
The river falls asleep and becomes roots
The bird songs fall asleep and become metals

The sky and the wilderness fall asleep and become marble's variegation
Who can wake you up?   Except the eyes which never return from the gaze
except the smoke which is pulled apart by the eyes and becomes a broken rope
whether you go or not   you are eternal

A Wild Horse (1974)

Raising your forelegs until they become a flash of lightning
                    your neigh is like thunder
Putting your legs down
    they turn into
                    a
                    gust
                    of
                    wind
                    chasing
                    after
                    the rain
    rushing to mountains and rivers
    leaving for mountains and rivers
Except for the horizon
    the horse never sees a rein
Except for the mountains which are the seats for clouds and birds
    it never sees a saddle
Except for the rainbow which is holding in the sky's mouth
    and the river which is holding in the earth's mouth
    it never sees a bridle
Except for the smoke in the desert
    it never sees a whip

When the horse thinks of a stable
even the wilderness will be torn apart
When the horse thinks of the vastness of nature
its legs will become wings
    mountains and rivers will fly together
    Wherever its hooves step   flowers are everywhere
    Wherever its hooves lift   stars are everywhere

In the Car (1977)

A car is at full speed
Its open windows   are a piano's white keys
Its closed windows   are a piano's black keys
The car is at full speed
My open eyes   are scenery
My closed eyes   are bygones
When I look back   the car has already left the ground
                          My body is inside the clouds
                          My dream is outside of them

My gaze melts into the landscape
The landscape changes into the hazy clouds
The hazy clouds have no choice but to come to an end
Things always come to an end like this
The car at full speed   wants to pursue something past
Both eyes always grind the car windows into confusion
                                    into depression

Clouds (1977)

Clouds (1977)

Because of me
    the azure sky is as soft as lovers' eyes
I go for a stroll with the sea
        and rove over distant places

When I walk   the earth follows
When I fly   the sky pursues
When I smile   the sun is there
When I am angry   wind and rain come
My far-reaching feelings   cannot be exhausted by the words of the river
My outstretched mind   is infinite to the eyes of the sea and the sky

My route is   only perceived by a few birds
    When they are flying here along the mountains and rivers
        I drift there along the mountains and rivers
            We meet with each other

My route is   mostly on the other side of the horizon
    Sunset and the sinking stars   clouds and mist are buried in oblivion
        Amid the boundless sky
          the vast earth
        and the immense eternity,
          I alone remain

Watching the Sea (1978)

After finishing the last drop of the rivers
you get drunk and become the stormy sky
When waves are petals   the earth becomes colorful
When waves are wings   the sky starts flying
When waves undulate   the mountains beat their hearts
When waves come and go   when waves go and come
you swallow numerous setting suns
and vomit many bouquets of rising suns

Tomorrow is ever glowing
The distance is ever echoing back the sound of music
The far-reaching rivers are your hands
Grasping the snow from the peak and the flowers from the woods
you bring the scenery to this place
It happens the most beautiful and durable thing
is not the views
but the immortal emptiness
        which blossoms on your forehead

The unheard   becomes audible
The unseen   becomes visible
The inaccessible   becomes present
You therefore become a kind of
        boundless vastness and completeness
                full of sunshine
                full of moonlight
                full of wave sounds
                full of sail shadows

Where exactly can the horizon
                stop you?
When you cannot suppress your excitement
                you become a violent storm
                        millions of waves
cracking the gigantic stones on the cliff   opening them one by one
    releasing the imprisoned sunshine and rivers
Actually whatever you meet
    you always open your arms and follow it
lying down quietly without paying much attention to which shape you take
You are still the carefree running river

flowing away with March, at which winds keep calm, waves become tranquil
flowers blossom and birds sing
All go without any traces
All come and go without any tracks

Since where you come from is also where you go to
where you go to is also where you come from
whether you go or not
you are always walking
leaving the horizon
returning to it
Your beautiful silhouette
cannot tell the flash of dawn
from the slanting setting sun
Let the sun and the moon come or go to ask
Your floating face on the sparkling waves or in the misty rain
is always the surface of the watch on which no inscription can be engraved
What can you remember?
If anything came before
winds and waves have already left it on the cliff
until it has become the years' original look
time's earliest appearance

If vastness can trace out everything's original appearance
the pure sway or
the everlasting upsurge
will be the hearts of watches and clocks
the hearts of time and space
It is also your heart
which collects the sun, the moon, the wind, the rain and the rivers
fills millions of abysms
is burnt to blue color with fire and ice
Let evenings and nights paint here in layers
Let the sun pour down all the paints
Let the wars violently sweep over this place
Let the cannons continuously pour down blood
they can never change your blue indomitability
blue profundity
blue gaze

Even though you gaze until the wisp of smoke is broken
by the distance

all wandering eyes
   look back to the horizon
they still cannot understand your eye
    which is looking at a kind of nostalgia
they still cannot understand where your wheel
   is heading
From the boundless daytime
       to the indistinct evening
if you can return in triumph
       you will come back with the moon
The starry sky is your crown
All stars revolve around the crown
The incomparable majesty and glory
make the lights of the lamp, the smoke, the bomb which illuminate the air
                                      all return
And you climb up to the pinnacle of the light, on and on
lifting yourself up until you become the dawn of tomorrow
Let all doors and windows open for you
    the sky is free for you
    the earth becomes boundless for you
    the rivers flow to you
    the birds fly to you
    the flowers are fragrant for you
    the fruits sweeten for you
    the views look at you
    whether you sit until you become mountains
        or lie until you become fields
           flow until you become rivers
           Whether you are awake or asleep

as long as the puff of clouds drifts by this place
you will flow farther than eternity

The Wilderness (1979)

*— Keeping watch over the original vastness until the end, the wilderness
surveys all perfections and sends them to eternity.*

1

Giving gentleness to the clouds
giving bounce to the hoofbeats
you follow the endless sky
   and take the distance to tranquility
The earth goes around, on and on
It offers you its most gorgeous view
makes you become the most beautiful poster
announcing the performances of spring, summer, autumn and winter

Being a river, you run yourself
Being a lake, you stop yourself
Being the scenery, you beautify yourself
Being day and night, you grow light and dark yourself
Time is neither inside the clock nor inside the watch
The sky is not within the cage
Your widespread chest
  which is under the sun's millstone
    is ground into light's echoes
        flowers' fragrances
         fruits' sweetness

2

When the first pile is driven into the ground
the world follows your rift crack
   fleeing in chaotic directions

In the wind, there are shadows of all kinds of flags
In the rain, there are shadows of all kinds of stray bullets
In the river, there are shadows of all kinds of blood
In the lake, there are shadows of all kinds of wounds
On the mountain peaks, there are shadows of all kinds of tombs
In the woods, there are shadows of all kinds of wire fencing
On the cliff, there are shadows of all kinds of walls
Taking with them the sky   birds escape to the horizon
Bringing with them their passports   people flee to the border
Carrying the clouds and mist   you return to the origin
Let all guns and arrows   be submerged in a pool of blood
        growing into all kinds of bonsais

which embellish the staircases of history
You send the four seasons' scenery   to God's garden

3

The high-rise buildings crowd around
   which force the sky to hide itself until it becomes a ceiling
Driving you to reduce your size with the Xerox machine
 until you become a piece of curtain
 which still provides flowers for the windows

Within a frame, a blind deer
stares at the four walls
The lines of vision pierce through the wall
On Yanghui road   no sheep appears
On the road   no horse appears
A motorcycle becomes a dashing whip
It lashes and drives all animals howling and running

A green-light is the boundless grasslands
A red-light is the setting sun
        resting on the horizon
Wishing to run   all rivers are in the reservoirs
Wishing to fly   all wings are in the markets
Panting between the accelerator and the brake
drinking Glucose makes you tired
Coffee flushes you into the weariest afternoon
Your loneliness piles up at the mid-night car park
When the morning bus driver presses tomorrow out of the accelerator
who knows whether you are busy looking for the road or
                the road is busy looking for you

People flock together under the billboard
The eye is a slicing machine
   cutting your mountains and rivers into pieces
                which are the buildings' layers
                   The display window's order
                        is marked with prices
If the money in your pockets is your clouds
following the waist down   you will find your rivers
climbing up to the breasts   you will find your mountains
Between the ups and downs
you become a lift through circulation
limited by the closed sky, the restrictive height
            Birds fly in a uniform manner
                   sing in a uniform way

The bed condenses all your vastness
Cutlery invades all your movements
When the sewage and rubbish collectors walk on the ground
                brains and advertisement balloon wave in the air
You are a piece of unfolded blank paper
on which a brush and a pen are writing the New Great Harmony

High-rise buildings sit with mountains
Streets run with rivers
Smoke drifts with clouds
Markets wave with seas
Eyes and waves have the same shape
Display windows and scenery have the same face
Restaurants and garden fields have an identical ancestor
Hotels and wilderness have an identical tribe
Man and the sun have identical last names
Woman and the moon have identical first names
Bedding and the four seasons sleep together
Lips and petals open in the same way
Alcohol and dew ripple in the same way
Pregnant women and dawn radiate in the same way
The crematorium and night dim in the same way
Squares and the sky walk together
Watches and the earth go around together

4

Temples prefer mountains' aloofness
The Cross matches the coordinates of heaven
You burnish emptiness and remoteness into a mirror
    looking at where the light starts to flow
        where water spring starts to gush
        where flowers start to blossom
        where birds begin to fly
Allowing all the roads to see the starting point
        all the sounds to merge into your stillness

The wisp of smoke
has already told the distance about your vastness and bareness

has already given your roughness to the primitive tenderness
Wind and rain go there in the same direction
The sun and the moon come here from opposite directions
Time and seasons change places gradually
You always stand above the horizon
taking in lines of distant vision

Rising at Dawn (1981)

I stand on the roof of dawn
taking a breath
    flowers redden, foliage becomes verdant
    the sky turns blue, mountains change to green
looking further
    my feet have already trodden on the clouds
opening my arms
    the sky and my chest meet
    It turns out they are lighter than wings

If I do not fly at this moment
what makes a bird a bird?
how can my hands touch the distance?

Soaring to Thirty Thousand Feet Above the Clouds (1986)
— Reading Poetry, Looking at Paintings

The world only leaves
the last space of the layout
to the sun, the moon and the stars
All else has already faded into the mountain of clouds

Even chimneys and cannons
organize lines of poems under the clouds
                        which life must read
but when these poems are read above the clouds
they change into an infinite, distant look
until the boundless vastness
turns into nothing but transparency
The world will keep
the last gallery
        for its own use
All else will be buried in the mountain of clouds
Who has been here to paint
                    to exhibit
And those paintings which cannot be drawn
are fiercely
        rushing into the gallery on their own
My eyes are forced
to kneel down to look at them

A thousand mountains and rivers
                where are you going?
A thousand soarings and hoverings
                where are your wings?
Ask pens,
ask ink
all say that nature is inside the frame
which is as skinny as an imprisoned bonsai

How much sky
and vagueness
can a spaceship send back to us?

Inside the endless chaos
ask time   spring, summer, autumn and winter are sleeping
ask space   the east, the south, the west and the north are missing

The whole world remains empty there
If you still want to paint
whose eyes can be the palette?
whose visions can be the clear-cut lines?
The cosmos looks at me
I look at the cosmos
no picture is painted
but all are paintings

The Collected
Poems of LOMEN
: A Bilingual Edition

The Sky and the Bird (1990)

If the bird is not on the wing
what will it be above the sky

In fact, he is the sky
        not a bird
It is the sky which always can fly
           and not the bird

The sky saves various kinds of cages
           for the morning parks
Saves thousands and millions of nests
           for the evening woods

He flies along the horizon continuously
The sun and the moon are his wings
Days and nights are his projecting shadows
All birds are flying intermittently after him
Who knows how high he flies
        how far
        how long

Grand Canyon Sonata (1992)
— A world where poetry and art take care of each other

1

Millions of abysms sink from here
      Numberless ↓ ↓ ↓ are running
            downward after death
Stone houses disintegrate on the cliff
       and their original blueprint cannot be found
         Millions of paths have no human in sight
Grand Canyon:
the buildings and corridors on your sides
have been constructed for millions of years
by the sun, the moon, the stars, the thunder, the lightning, the wind and the rain
The two doors opened by the cliff connect with heaven's gate
              They are always open
          The world can come if it wishes
             can go if it likes

Was Whitman here
      with his western wagon?
Was Liu Zongyuan here
       to fish the snow capped river?
The silent barbaric fields and loneliness
           never find out
No one bothers about the sky
Birds fly here with mountains and rivers
Planes fly there with cities
You are the line
     which leads birds' and planes' wings to fly
You fly until you are close to the East where the sun rises
Another line
then darts out from
the Great Wall
The line carries the scenery of nature and
     the undulations of history
       to fly in the sky
The line flies until birds' and planes' wings
        can fly no more
The other line
will drift out from
the boundless sky and earth

resting there at leisure

You grasp these three lines   in your hands
which are the longest whips
If the earth wants to protrude at the top
                        be hollow at the bottom
                        become a O
all these can be fulfilled by the long whips

2

Looking at the contract signed by the sky and the wilderness
you make many hard and soft
                layers and colors
built into a magnificent and grand structure
If water and ink want to flow over
it would become an oriental landscape painting
If there came geometric figures
it would become a work of Western sculpture
If the Colorado River, which runs through the bottom of the gorge,
                                            were a string
whether it were installed on a erhu or a violin
it would play the most primitive
                        notes
                        intervals
                        and echoes
    The world would pull
        the sweet-sounding and visually beautiful things together
            Where does the rumble and the quarrel come from?
            Everything is in chaos
            which cannot be seen or heard
            Our sense of vision and
            our sense of hearing are everywhere raped

3

Grand Canyon
your depth is amazing
Even if the Empire State Building and New York's commercial buildings were
                                            joined together
                        they still could not reach your bottom
Down below is a kind of serenity without any staircase

Even the majestic Arch de Triumphe
would not be able to escape from your mysteries
Forever lost in their thoughts
the still surfaces of the rocks
                        are mirrors
All reflections
cannot escape
The most curious thing is that
eyes start to speak first
then silence itself makes sounds
asking the surroundings to empty themselves out
to become the blank space in landscape paintings
How to say it?   It is better not to speak

4

Grand Canyon
even the biggest earthquake
could not make such a huge crack
You hold the sun in your mouth by day
    have the moon between your teeth by night
Light is always with you night and day
The years forever walk in the light
                        with beautiful faces
transforming all visible and invisible fragments of shells
                        into hard rock strata
                            soft leaves and petals
Let pictures and structures be renewed
tanks and rubbish collectors
change into coaches
                        driving through the scenery

Rows of buildings of the city sandwich
                        a red-light district
The cliffs of the Grand Canyon also sandwich
                        a red-light district
No matter whether there are gaudily dressed men and women
                        or red flowers and green leaves on the street
they all return to nature
                showing themselves to their origins

5

Grand Canyon   in order to show the naked truth
you tear your chest open   digging out your heart
                    to show it to the earth and the sky
When you talk about love
if your long, wide mouth
distributes kisses all around
        it will become the longest love river
        it will become the farthest Boai Road in the world
When you talk about pain
all visible and invisible
large and small wounds
will come to you
However words cannot explain everything
Finally they become numberless car windows
                which rush off on their journeys
                under Henry Moore's carving tool

6

Grand Canyon
If you are the world's
            biggest burial ground and incinerator
only the lyrical rivers
    the sensible lines of the cliff will be buried
Burning up the whole world   results in
                            only clouds
                    not dense smoke
When everything is over   the scenery is still beautiful
                            the blue sky
            has never been polluted

Even in the stormy and chaotic moment
everything loses its sense of direction
when wind slants and rain slopes
Looking around
        the fence is about to fall down
You endure all these
        with the cliff's steadfast steepness
giving the most beautiful skateboard
            to a world which cannot stand steadily enough
                                to slide down

Grand Canyon
You show us your depths and uncover your recesses
You are not a feigned trap
but honesty in your world
Every dangerous cliff
warns the eyes in advance
When you get close to its edge, the warning bell will ring
which is safer than your entourage
Adventure and wonder
are two of the most beautiful flowers
blossoming at the bottom of the gorge
You can only see them
　　from the edge of the cliff
If you are afraid of high and deep places
you can follow a guide and other tourists
and walk only within a safe distance
you can stick to tourist maps
　　　　　　and routes in tourist guidebooks
　　　　　　walking back to the town
　　　　　　crowding into shopping malls
You can pass through the sea of strangers
　　　　　to look for your hotel
　　　　　locking yourself inside a room
　　　　　lying down on your bed
There is also a grand canyon underneath
　　　　　　Although it is less than half an inch deep
　　　　　　it has already buried a lot of people

8

Passing to and fro
the world always travels
Between the hour hands　　　there is a moving bridge
Between the legs　　　　　　there is a moving bridge
Fin de siecle is also a moving bridge
　　　　　hanging between modernity and postmodernity
　　　　　walking while swaying
　　　　　swaying while flashing
Grand Canyon　　　what about you?
You fix the whole sky between your cliffs
Someone says
it is an empty bridge

    no one ever walks on it
Someone says
the visible and invisible
are walking in all directions
In fact   it is a roof which is made of acrylic
covering the world inside its transparence
   to open it naked in order to have a look
It sees people
who
carry
the cities
the fields
the wilderness
walking in the vastness

9

Going down along the depth
following the slope and coming up
Grand Canyon, your vertical line of vision
joins together with the earth's axis
Your bottom bumps into the earth
Your top touches the sky
As long as you go around with the earth
numberless changing round faces
start to whirl until they become a ceaseless spiral tower
in vertical and horizontal directions of space-time
All eyes rest on the tower
    looking at the progress of eternity
            and heading for it

Passing Through the Three Gorges (1994)

1

Rivers bring boats and mountains along with them
                          walking towards the vastness
Winds bring faces and waves along with them
                    running to the mist and emptiness
     How far away do roads lead?
     Thousands of mountains and ridges
                         from the high and far
          from the deep and distant
                               walk
                                to
                               the
                            flatness
                             and
                        remoteness
How old is time?
The aged cliff will answer you
          Millions of years ago
all clocks and watches stopped ticking
          to listen to the heart of nature
                              beating

The nearby mountains look at the distant rivers
The rivers close by look at the remote mountains
                    Mountains and rivers
                    rivers and mountains
which consider us the empty space on
                    landscape paintings
Let all heavy mountains around us
drift to the clouds lightly
If being carefree is too leisurely and deliberate
we will then turn back to look at the passing water by the stern
                              chasing after our memories
running into the historical rivers inside our hearts
Rivers once ran with tears and blood
Looking inside the cabin which is still crowded with poverty
our ship is in an adverse current
          dragging the heavy years
it must slow down

2

One gorge after an other
                    and another
forcing open the solid womb on either side
grasping the balanced tension of both sides
along the safe central line
breaking through difficulties and coming out from the bottle neck
the bow is heading for a bright remoteness
Looking far away   it rolls and roars on and on for a thousand *li*
entering the distant mountains
                    the remote rivers
Then all in one, the sky and the earth flow together

Time   Space
become empty and return to their origins
Painting brush and carving tool cannot move anymore
The eight great painters' splash-ink
Mondrian's installation art
Chirsto's land art
all vanish from sight
Only the mountains and rivers are left behind
      One is strong and the other is graceful
      One is moving and the other is motionless
They are painting landscape pictures
                    which are impossible to be painted
They are carving sculptures
                    which are impossible to be carved
                              an exhibition for nature
Nature watches until the setting sun above the long river becomes round
                                    until mountains die with the river
                                    until mist and clouds vanish

A boat lamp far away
  lights up the whole river
  reading at night
Reading until the setting stars and wide fields come
                    the moon emerges and rivers run
Reading until dawn
  then the horizon reminds us of the Chinese character yi
People, boats and scenery all wake up
            reading with the sun
            reading until millions of mountains and rivers come
                  mountains are high and earth is remote
                  the south and the north of the Yangtze

which has a distant source and a long stream
If we look at it from a two-dimensional perspective   it is like a picture
If we look at it from a three-dimensional perspective   it is like a sculpture
All things belonging to eyes   are carried back by the camera
All things belonging to hearts   are transported by poetry
Traveling by water   you find a million miles of the Yangtze River
                           Let the scenery walk for you
Traveling by heart   you find the road is longer than history
                           Then let the winds, the clouds and birds fly for you

The Collected
Poems of **LOMEN**
: A Bilingual Edition

A Beautiful Metaphysics (1991)
— Some thoughts on flying at thirty thousand feet

Leaving the ground and rising
flying across the clouds
a beautiful metaphysics
reaches the sky at thirty thousand feet
the plane is already a real
                castle in the air
floating across the sky

People are sitting in the plane
The world is sitting outside the plane
A pure dialogue
a transparent look
becoming selfless is the longest
the farthest
the smoothest
road

Numerous mountains and rivers
numerous scenes and images
are rushing at the horizon
until the world is emptied
or the eyes will not return

A mountain of clouds, a sea of clouds
Illusion has taken shape
            modeling a form
On the clouds   nothing remains
Even where there is something   it must be found out of nothing
Under the clouds   only chimneys remain
Cannons
crosses
make an iron triangle of the years
Cities and fields are two toy cars
dragged by the wings of the plane
You cannot loose your grip
If you let go   the world will become lighter than the clouds
                                It can never come down

On the journey
the wings of the plane sometimes will prick the remoteness

and the memories
The only things that can come closer are:
the house of light which has already transformed into poetry
the blue bird which flew across the church with laurel leaves held in her mouth
The rest is a wilderness of vastness   which is left to the sky
This is good enough   very well
matching with the blue glass building of the cosmos*
and all these become a trinity
You had better not ask
eternity   it will come
if it wants to come

* *When I travel abroad with Rongzi by plane, we have to fly across the clouds thirty thousand feet above the earth. There is a vacant "blue glass building of the cosmos" up there. Nothing can remain in the building. When time, space and I are dissolved in "purity" and "transparency," everything can be expressed in words as well as not in words. I am reminded of poet Valery's words: "Poetry is a grand ceremony of awakening."*

Melancholy Symphony No. 921 (1999)

*The earthquake in Taiwan has brought us tremendous disaster. All people, no matter
whether they live in Taiwan or in other parts of the world, feel shock and sadness.
After having recovered from humanitarian concern and the bleeding wounds, we naturally reconsider our ideas of life, of the world and of the universe. We also realize
the latent limitations and fatalism of life.*

Creator
you settle us down on this beautiful island
Your kindness   our gratitude
are parallel to the rails of years
In the fields   the tough lines
                carved by the sun and sweat
have already been beautified by urban civilization and access to the global village
                        The diversified and unimpeded network
            is running for the sake of improvement and prosperity

Creator
can you tell us the reason why
before you have time to prevent this violent anger
there are landslides and earthquake?
Death has no time to recognize death
Blood, tears and rain
irrigate the gloomy graveyard
Fields lie on the ruins panting
The blacked-out cities are watching with blind eyes
In addition to crying "Help"   there is crying
In addition to praying   there is kneeling
No response is heard from lamentation to heaven   God does not understand at all
We escape from the bleeding wounds with tears in our eyes
                        standing firmly before life
Sympathy rushes to us from every corner of the world
On the darkest land of death
a spot of warm light is ignited
reading human beings' care and hope

Creator
can you tell us the reason why
you change so abruptly?
You crack your kindness and turn it into cruelty
At the moment even God does not know you are in anger
the world is frightened and hides under the table

Time and space draw back
We are in such emptiness that nothing can be touched
obeying your orders   shaking on the swaying line of life and death

Surviving the earthquake, we return to the pain
we realize the weakness of human beings: we cannot conquer nature
we are unable to question you
We are made by you
we are your works
How can we stop a sculptor
      who destroys his sculptures
from San Francisco, *Tang Shan*, Turkey to *A Li Shan*?
You became filled with anger on your way here
Bronze statues, museums, banks and national treasuries
            fall down like rocks dropping from a peak
The world hopelessly becomes a monk's bald head
Atomic energy becomes impotent
Police dogs, excavators and ambulances
      only wish to find a dying sound
The United Nations and Red Cross can only
donate some kindness on your behalf afterwards

Creator
after having used our blood, our flesh and our bones
                  to satisfy your burning anger
after having experienced pain after pain
we are still living in the bodies and on the land of the earth which you bestow on us
we are still living in the chronological order in which spring comes after winter
the sun rises   and then sets
We cannot forget you have designed us
      as part of nature's structure
We walk   the land follows
We fly   the sky follows
Our remote love   rivers speak endlessly
Our far away hearts   the sky and the land watch infinitely
When we are happy, flowers bloom and birds sing
When we are sad, clouds become dark and rains become bitter
When we yearn for each other, yellow leaves fall
When we feel lonely, the clouds in the sky become alone
When we are in the vastness, there comes the horizon
When we have hope, the sun rises tomorrow
We certainly live in your kind right hand
            and in your cruel left hand

leaving you to manipulate us and to order us about
Our senses of hearing and seeing come from your ears and eyes
Our movements cannot leave your hands and legs
Our life and death are both inside your body
You take one second to destroy the world
which takes us months and years of labor to repair

Creator
if you are a kind father
how can you mix up the jigsaw puzzle a child is happily playing with?
How can you cut with your cracked earth
        every single hair on the head and every single blade of grass on the ground?
After suffering your disastrous anger
both the land and we are tired by pain
Death is still enveloped by the lingering chill
Aftershock and fear are still inside the tick-tock of clocks and watches
Years still cannot sleep well at night

Creator
please grant us your greatest love
to bury the fuse in the broken layers
falling asleep quietly
        becoming only a warm electric current underneath
Let the recovering earth and us
regain our warmth
in the frozen night when death passes through
Let us chase after tomorrow's sun
replant our green mountains, blue water and fields
                            our colorful cities
                            our comfortable life
            our future which is sung, listened to and praised by poetry

We Come from Nature (2000)

We come from nature
    but are not natural anymore
Nature is locked inside a bonsai
From the aluminium windows we see the forest of the cities
                the river of the streets
                the sea of people in the city center
When the sky and the wilderness compete with each other for the wings' width
we are jammed together between the traffic lights
When lakes, rivers and seas
compete with each other for the blue
our pipes continues to drain the sewage
              away
When the white clouds on the peak float and become
              beautiful metaphysics
the grove of chimneys
line up numerous black forests

We come from nature
    but become more and more unnatural
When the flowers blooming in the green fields
      become plastic flowers in an engine room
      leaving shadows to the internet
we are eager to open the electric door
         floating to the weightless
            cyber world
talking with each other across a layer of glass
Looking at nature
it is still natural
  it walks along the routes of birds and clouds
         to grasp rocks' patterns climbing to the mountain
         to grasp waters' patterns entering the sea
         to grasp trees' roots going into the earth
         to return to its origin

The Collected
Poems of **LOMEN**
: A Bilingual Edition

IV

Four Strings of a Violin (1954)

In childhood   your eyes are like an azure sky
and as you grow   they are like a garden
In middle age   your eyes are like an unruly sea
and as old age approaches   they are home to melancholy
as quiet as a midnight theater, its curtain fallen

Light is in Black Pajamas (1958)

Under the violet circular lampshade   Light is flowing
Under the azure circular sky   Light is flowing
Under Churchhill's circular top hat   Light is flowing
Only under the girls'spinning flower-patterned skirts
          only at spring's hunting ground   Light is dancing
However, under the domed-shaped graveyard   even the priest, who is
                                                         the support of heaven,
        also frequently complains that light is in black pajamas

The Undercurrent of the Ninth Day (1960)

Beethoven, as unrestful as the sea, rests forever with Symphony No. 9 under earth. I live with wide eyes on earth. Except for this kind of quivering beauty, what else can reach to eternity?

Prelude

When Toscanini's baton
        chops off the chaos
you are a running car   I am a road
I am the road   you are the remoteness which is persistently pursued by the road

Saint of Music   my old housekeeper
When you are away   the living room's lamps remain dim at night
                the fire is extinguished   the door is heavily locked
                the world falls asleep with its back to the light
When you return   tramping up and down the record player's immortal growth ring
I will follow you and become a spring day, whirling
        amid the sounds of rushing water in the forests

In the attic where you weave the melodies
        everything is beautifully adorned
When days smile as if there is a Leica:
I will be on the sensitive paper of your sound
                and become a kind of visible echo

1

When the phono stylus draws a spiral tower
all buildings vanish from sight
The spiral tower rises until it becomes the sky's pillar
Height and remoteness are led by boundless blue
The perfect roundness and pureness are busy with the beauty's modeling
Through a glazed window   scenery is flowing like wine
Getting drunk with the profundity   I fall asleep and become the undercurrent
Inside the quiver where boundless tranquility enters deeper and deeper
only this kind of shouting is soundless
Inside the glorious realm of your tower
pure time is still squeezed by watches' hands
After things return to their own positions   they still can look at each other with a
                                lovely face

My mood is as beautiful as an exquisite fabric   entering your transparence
which is as silent as snow scenery flashing in winter time

2

Time is calling with the sunny sky of March
Sunshine strikes up a tune of harmony through the latticed windows
A steadfast gaze finds its object in the bright, distant scenery
Tranquility is a kind of audible echo
The blue sky sits on the churches' spires
All eyes enter the respectful looks
Directions are like children's expressions which gather in astonishment
Bodies flock towards Sundays to change into clean clothes
because the rest of the week will make them dirty again
At your no. 9 revered circular room
all structures imitate light's pattern   clock's pattern
My Sabbath day is a soft sponge   it is embroidered with osmanthus flowers
    having the anxiety removed like a bloody nail
        Pains take a rest under your layered bandage

3

Eyes are shot by vastness
Time is still turning around and becomes clocks' round faces
The garden is still drawing seasons with branches and leaves
During dark winter   the poinsettia is a torch reaching towards heaven
People preserve the best myths on a small card
The hunting car which is pursued and attacked by the snowy night
eventually breaks the lights of the town into pieces   and meets the Sabbath day
Doors and windows remain open like the cover of a bible
At your holy house no. 9
the furnace is burning   the contents are roasted
Nothing will copy river's rashness again
The iron rings, shooting gun and stick hanging on the wall
will join in the chorus with a harmonious expression
will enter a profound steadfast gaze together

4

Always meeting around the corner of the corridor in astonishment
views facing into nights like lamps   you calm down my perspective
two cars move crisscross and pass hurriedly
two roads then die in the intersection
When the winter sun visits the garden's fallen leaves
I am also observed by a date on the calendar which died long ago
While the doors of yesterday and tomorrow are pulled open from both sides
all arms hurry to have different kinds of contact within the vastness
"The present" still uses its flower arrangement shape in exchange for
                                        people's appreciation
And the continuous disappointments help to build up the house of death
Using the corridor's silence to connect the verandah with the noisy living room
using the satisfaction of the bride's brimming eyes to stumble on the red carpet of
                                        the church

On the ninth day, your voice is the Virgin Mary's eyes
which guides people's inward marching

5

Passing the ancient castle of history and the flyover of metaphysics
man is an emaciated bird getting lost in a barren field
No green color will come to confirm something is a tree
He is imprisoned in a blurred mirrored room   hanging by light and darkness all the
                                        day
His body spins rapidly   like the sounds of waves in a typhoon
Facing the mirrors for a while   like a monument built on a torrent
                                        reflected by the sun
Between the moving and fixed halves of a shell-fish
man is a dead butterfly pinned into the book of time
To imprison the black torrent and winter's bleakness inside the body
to turn the mirrored room into light's graveyard   color's prison
at this moment   you must flee from those crisscross reflections
to sell out the whole working morning and afternoon
then burying your head in a plate in order to recognize your God
And at the moment of echoing   another hand has already touched the forehead of
                                        eternity

6

Staring in this way   the face of death in front of a mirror is like a garden field in
                                               profound thought
Inside a dark square house   you are guarded by an invisible light all the day
The curtain falls   the eyelashes lower
The boundless vastness   is in fact a touchable soft body
That kind of mystery is always like a ray passing through blind eyes for the first time
The remote scenery stands with a posture of still buildings   injected with the
                                               eyesight of the first meeting
using continuous obsession to make the heart fall in, forever following
Nothing will throb with terror   when tides flow over the typhoon season
Being in a ruin after burning   condolence is like a bird flying out of
                                               clasped hands
When a voyage enters the ninth day   the quarrelsome stories fade from the
                                               background of the sea
And the world is as quiet as your gaze
connecting with heaven's corridor from far away
On the stone staircases   respectful looks walk into reverence
On the red carpet   footsteps search for stability

7

A chandelier looks over the tranquil living room   echo is soundless
Delightful movements are like roving steps which kick awake the flying birds at the
                                               historic site
Reflections in a mirror are looked at in astonishment
To drag the lake for a tower's posture   to catch the sun's shadow under the light
to slide over the blue sound waves   the river leaves the sound of waters behind
Before and after the harvest seasons   hope and fruit take the same course as
                                               the burning of a match
Numerous anxious heads fall forward on the broken pillar of time
A severe pain even a blade cannot reach always emerges from the bloodless wound
When time flows off as a broken kite in a child's eyes
      a patient seizes medicine and coffin with his hands
      a prisoner sees a released prisoner off
Those silent cries   are as thick and heavy as childhood's memories
      They are supported by a gesture which is sinking into a whirlpool
And "finale" always falls as gradually as prelude

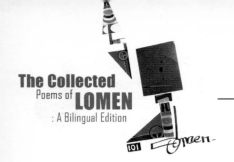

The Collected
Poems of **LOMEN**
: A Bilingual Edition

8

When green falls into pieces from a tree's top   spring is a stalled pulley
At the bottom of a still abyss   only the fallen leaves are sounds
Hanging on by the eyelids   seasons escape with a frightened face
To imprison a hunting season inside a window which is dampened by winter's mist
Let the movement of the sawtooth find out the blood type
let a river see itself when it cannot flow
Somewhere deep inside the years, the belly keeps walking until it becomes a road
walking until it becomes a constant direction
Looking out of the car   the vanishing distance is like a thread rolling into
the remote scenery
The whistle leaves behind a waving handkerchief at the station
let the turning heads peep at the years' elegant tailoring and stitching under a lamp
Everyone is the clouds   who chases under the drifting clouds
following stillness
The tower climber has already sensed the inverted coldness on the pinnacle
After going downstairs   the door is waiting for you to go out

9

My island   is embossed by soundless waves all day long
With the speechless primitive affection and the mountains' deep thoughts
in the calm season   a voyage sleeps under the curl-like folding sails
my distant looks are the sea within the remote sea   the sky beyond the sky
Looking out   things which are looked at will not turn around
Driving a winged car on the pathless path   wheels' tracks are buried in the snow
Both hands barred by the vastness rest on my chest which is like the closing door of
a church
My island spends the Sabbath day quietly   it is as idle as a garden after the harvest
In the mirror   the bustling city   the city's lights will never be seen again
The stars and the moon exhaust themselves by running   whose legs can be the sun?
The horizon becomes deaf and dumb forever
When the sunset glow's flowing light   cannot flow back to the East in the morning
my eyes get dim on the last crossbar
listening to the car sounds coming closer   going far away   going far away

The Tower of Death (1969)

*It is supposed to be God's job to understand life through death. I do not
know who has made me God's assistant after the death of poet Zihao.
Actually, the oppression of time and the vastness of space bought by
death is tremendous, which forces Rilke to say: "Death is the
maturity of life." I am also compelled to say: "The enormous echo
of life will be heard only after it meets death." Standing on the
Tower of Death, I come to a profound understanding of life.*

1

When the setting sun lowers the black curtain
        all shadows of sails die in the sea
Your hand is like a broken oar
        sinking in the torrent which cannot be fixed by the eyes

It cannot seize the fire burning day
  cannot grasp the sun's square city
    nor row Rimbaud's drunken boat

The threshing-floor sifts out all mature grains
Death is a forever shiny reaping-machine
No one knows which season one belongs to
and heaven is only a boat without harborage
When the boat casts off its cable   shores are unable to follow
A tree falls under the last sound of chopping
          it is exiled to buildings until it dies
And inside the everlastingly sleeping space-time
God's artificial arm never reaches the baby in the Virgin Mary's hands
Life is like those muddling footsteps
which are forgotten on the forgetful platform
When hopes and prayers all arrive
if a pair of scissors cuts the ribbon   what breaks in will not be
                               laughter
All hands flock to grip a disconnected plug
Let the layers of night surround you   embracing you
The years have already stared at the hollow eye-sockets   looking
                       where there is no window
The world is like a mirror which is broken into pieces   light goes away
                          shadows run away
Eyes are compelled to lose sight of what escapes around the corner
  It will be difficult to retrieve the line of vision

In the past, you planted your manuscripts with eucalyptus
   and your mill was built on it
The gears which grind your watches into pieces   still cannot break your
                                       sinking vision
Throwing yourself into the current in which the hour hands rapidly turn
                       you try to whirl in an opposite direction
Those clashes   know more than a sword about a fatal wound
Those disputes   are more irritating than a saw asking the way from a tree
Your uneasiness has already become a serious stormy season
On a night which is burnt awake by nicotine
your face cannot escape from light's watch
   It is buried in your manuscripts
   which become the vast scenery   turning into the sleeping fire
   above the clouds   under the strata
When winter arrives   harbors become dim wave-sounds turn cold
Cold currents also bring a message
urging what is left behind in the gardens to go away as soon as possible
You go home too the earth also returns with a tearful face
My friend   if the blindfold is taken away when playing hide-and-seek
those familiar faces will not emerge from the surroundings
How can we push open the fence which is lowered by your eyelashes
      entering it and tearing open the night   having all the loss
                   recovered from the misty current?
During the fifth season of the year   all ringing bells remain dumb
A river dies in which the tape-recorder can play music no more
The river dries up   and windmills cannot turn the scenery around
Inside the boundlessness   the display of tranquility   covers a remote exit
     from which birds cannot fly back   from which wind cannot return
We will draw shadows with the sun   decorating your journey

2

The morning sun holds dawn's silver white milk bottle in its mouth
                         running to the afternoon
          It falls from the cliff of light
        The blood of the setting sun dries up in the western sky
My friend   under the pillar of the evening corridor
the loom's handle is unloaded in your eyes and lines of vision cannot be woven
   the postures of sitting leave the chairs   lamps also die under their lampshades

The sun's shadows following the floating season change their positions in the garden
The changes are traps   things always slip
After the reaping day   nothing can point out wind's direction

A gaze also cannot penetrate the darkness of the fields
You become the grain in the barn   soaring up in the fire
O, God   on the mass day   prayers have already been chewed until they become the
scent of olive
Why do people smell something burning in the Holy Communion?
When an incinerator is more reliable than a post box
an express letter is sent through the fire
and we can read clearly   O, God
you repair heaven with ashes
O, God   if you are an open and closed Venetian blind
between the two strings' pull from side to side
there is a sun rushing out of the lying-in room
a night is nailed into a coffin
The wooden horse dies   and the bluest sky is buried there
A veil is dropped   flowers' faces ask their fading date through the flashes
Trembling on the cliff   your shoes will be recognized by one of the broken stones
The years are like a fountain drifting down on its return which is incapable of rising
Speaking amen is like a doorbell yelling at things' chaotic doorplates
 Sawing sounds cry for forests   shooting sounds cry for birds
 Fire cries for a smoky current   which wakes up somewhere beyond the boundary
Out of the border   even the returning clouds fall asleep
My friend   when the burning scenery extinguishes in the eyes' burner
 the gorge's bottom rises up   the rock's bottom rises up   the seabed rises up
 light and darkness quarrel no more
 trees and winds quarrel no more
 tides and waves quarrel no more
On the smooth slope of night   even shadows cannot steady themselves
How can your searching steps grip the slipperiness?
Being surprised at stumbling
the palette of the blue sky is broken into pieces   even the sun cannot press any color out
of it
The world is pushed to enter a vastness which has no picture nor frame
Let everything have only a single miserable name in the blind eyes —
Death! It becomes everything's sealing shell
 It becomes a tremendous shadow which swallows God's robe
Days cry out in surprise because a lock cannot make a copy of a key
As long as the window is open   even the ceiling will run away
My friend   when the sounds of collapse noisily run down along the broken pillar
you are a spasm of silence after the event
When the everlasting holiday is written on a monument
you are a broken watch   which is dismissed by time forever
 freedom leaves its nurse, the wire fencing,
 a storm cannot find out the mirror of its woods
 the subsiding tides cannot carry away the shore they once embraced
And you step out of yourself escaping from your footsteps   running away from the path

The days on which the stairs are built up by French poetry rest peacefully
The days on which the sea is made by Beethoven rest peacefully
The days on which the bodies of banquets are dragged from the bottom of glasses
                                                              rest peacefully
The days on which girls and pregnant women disclose flowers and fruits rest
                                                              peacefully
The days on which two different kinds of blood circulate through the guns and the
                                                      pens rest peacefully
When the fire has already jumped out of light's corridor
and the stylus has already finished walking its splendid route
your face is as dim as a screen which is moved away from a projector
     It will never be embossed by light   never produce scenery
                                    never recognize eyes
During the holidays when Jesus is also on vacation   you bring the clouds
to skip   to skip the rope of the horizon which will never finish turning

When the building with a Cross is completed in front of the breast
the sun's gold donkey also dies in the earth's black mill
O, God   even you become jobless and starving
How can we claim back your borrowings from the dedication?
How can we dig out our babyhood cries from a broken doll?
How can we gather from the boulevard the sounds belonging to our childhood of the
                                                      rolling hoop?
How can we lay down on the railway to recollect the days of escape?
O, God   when a pair of empty shoes is like an abandoned ship which is deserted
                                                      on the shore
     it will never load the uneasy sky   never transport the everlasting remoteness
Inside the tide-less returning tide   we think of seas
Inside the motionless returning current   we think of rivers
Inside the soundless echoes   we think of valleys
Inside the mist we miss the outline of a cigarette end   the outline of mountains
                                                      the outline of birds
Inside the noises of grave digging we miss the postures of walls   the postures of
                                    doors   the postures of windows
Inside a burned-away rainbow   we search for a rainy scene in the sunlight

3

The years' lumberjack   makes clearings in the forest of hair
     which are used to play hide and seek   or to gaze on heaven from far away
When the pigeon-gray autumnal sky   cannot spread its wings
we gradually become aware of the drooping silence
     which is like the shadow of the cross   fire sleeping amid the ashes

The genial sun eats up all spring flowers
and makes the long summer drunk and as red as a corridor
The sky is scorched   seasons fall into the ruin with sedate faces
Snow becomes the most basic color and sound
talking about the forever sleeping face

The order of time cannot run away from the four seasons' square cities
the eyes cannot see millions of mountains and rivers again
Even vases cannot recreate spring
Life is like a rope cut by a knife
Eternity is the receiver   which is compelled to release on the deadline
Everybody is destined to be a phonograph record which must end
        It is as strange as a tower whirling by a whirlpool
        which collapses when the circular current becomes still

Like grain satisfies villages
people are the food piled into a clock's gears
                                to satisfy its hunger
O, sea of time   because of you
fate determines that we are a river drying out because of you
When the dam in your womb is opened during festival   we rush to you
Until all waves die in your deafness
        all lights dim in your blind eyes
we still do not realize that we also belong to a wandering wind
Upon departure   we will leave our shadows on a negative
Mountain groves emboss the earth's graveyard
Coral reefs carve the sea's graveyard
Clouds and birds draw the sky's graveyard
        through a Chinese pavilion's distant view point
        through a windless harbor's protection
        through a velvet quilt's waiting
On that night   the world is exhausted like a banquet having been hunted by cutlery
                        eyes sleep behind the back of a lamp
                        mirrors look behind the back of an image
After having taken part in the green leaves, flowers and fruits' relay race,
everyone becomes too tired to hold the sun's rugby ball
                rushing to the years' Arc de Triumph
Separated from the coffin's cover   priests cannot always splice the broken cassette
                                                                        tape

Only let part of the news be sent to Sundays
        the rest is sent to no address

Inside a square house   echoes bump against the walls
 When they are under control

121

they become as meek as a river running along the shore
We silently meditate on the world which has risen from our clasped hands
   we sense death   become slaves of death
     We are as humble as a cup passed at Communion
         waiting silently for a gesture from the breast to approach
         to arrange the flowers into a white round window
         to blur the remoteness
         to blur also the homeless steady gaze
  Let the eyes become blind in deep thinking
  which is like flowery tiles becoming blind in the dark living room
      They still know the loneliness of night   the gaze of the lamp from above

4

No matter where the sunlight falls
a half face always flows in the light
a half face freezes and becomes a glacier
The florist is busy everyday
     selling two kinds of flowers for two different festivals
Let the eyes become a garden where roses quarrel with the white chrysanthemums

Glancing in the mirror, it rings and becomes an alarm clock
            it rings and becomes a kind of time measurement
The razor gradually senses a certain resistance from growth
Tomorrow always comes here to make yesterday become something forgotten
        always persistently leaves half of the entrance ticket outside the arena
          leaves the other half drifting and becoming the shape of fire
Saving the left leg with the right one turning into a monument eventually
             and becoming a landmark of wilderness

Man is destined to roam around with all kinds of bottles
  He cannot experience the same kind of drunkenness he had before
  He also cannot experience the same kind of sleep and awakening after getting drunk
He has no choice but looking at the horizon
  His vision becomes a driverless car
    It is like the clouds which do not apply for a license It is like the winds
                      which do not see any road signs

When the terminus wakes up at the sound of the brake
although footsteps say that a road has multiple faces   a road is still a road

Although scenery makes millions of colors which drift from vision
    only one of them becomes eyes

Staring eyes and bullets cry out stillness
    which is as beautiful as a sleeping night
The visionless wide eyes   are a kind of shadow which is made by putting out the light
Everyone will become nobody   when scars can no longer recognize the sharpness of the
                          knife
Those fatal eulogies and smiling faces
are always as tender as the scattered food within a shooting range
Man is a kind of bird which is tempted to build another kind of wild desert

5

A house of light pushes me down on the wall
  forcing me to speak the name out of the shadow
And the thought which thinks of nothing
    is a further remoteness

Using an association from cartoons   you still cannot guess the answer of the riddle
                           hiding inside the blind eyes
Using a night of Southern Europe   you still cannot brew such a matured sleepiness
And it always becomes a kind of sincere hospitality
        becomes a woman's smooth breasts
        becomes a mirror which shelters all countenances

On the memorial day   the face of my deceased friend is no longer a shiny gold coin
Who will wait forever under the cold wind in order to recognize yesterday's wind?
Who can hold the shadow steadfastly after putting out the light?
When the twelve months of a year come down from the wall
the hour hands run on a clock which has no inscription
Life is only layers of sky colors   folded inside a black umbrella
      a burst of waves   folded inside the wind
At the end of a banquet   servants are the busiest grave visitors
On the wedding night a musical note from the Aegean breaks upon a beast's roaring
We have used applause to polish a row of medals
    have rushed into a black alley with which the Virgin Mary is not familiar
    have spoiled days and nights because of a rumor and a world of praise
And we always grasp the palm but never know where the hands are
    always cannot surmise when the birds will fly out from their wings
In order to save themselves from the night   the setting sun carves it's shadows in
                        the daylight
We release a road from a pair of damaged boots allowing the wilderness to return on its
                        own
When our backs are like footsteps walking far away
how can we reunite the forward footsteps with the backward ones?
how can we make baskets of display flowers recover spring?

When the scars of bullets seal an ancient battlefield
   and a single armed man wraps it with a nylon cloth
even if we were the bullets we would never recognize the wound
Who can still hear 1969's boom of guns
     in the Paris spring of 2969?
When a coffin hammer and a long nail squeeze in a mournful cry
heaven looks down   a broken rope on a precipice
Even if we stand inside our eyes   we still cannot see what the eyes are looking at
    If we sit on our hearts   we still cannot ponder what our hearts are thinking of
If it is light   we will be the glasses through which it passes
If it is a glass window   we will be the scenery which is brought into it
If it is a tower which is built on the scenery we will be the sky being looked at

Window (1972)

I fling it open   my hands follow the flow of a stream
       always mountains and rivers
       always eyes with no return

Being seen in the distance
you become a bird with a thousand wings
Leaving the sky   you no longer have your wings
Being heard
you become a flute with a thousand holes
The road of music is as deep as my eyes gazing at the past

I fling it open   but I am locked in an inescapable
                       transparency

The Collected
Poems of **LOMEN**
: A Bilingual Edition

Shoes (1972)

At the bottom of the stairs, a pair of shoes
       is surprisingly a cloud in the sky
Distant mountains and far-away waters   a cloud is not a tree
Far-away waters and distant mountains   a cloud is not a cloud
A cloud is only an
ever
impossibly
identified
road
So are the shoes
so is the distant place
so is the falling leaf in the sky

An Invisible Chair (1974)

Everyone is searching for a chair which forever hangs in the air.
Damaged clocks and blinded eyes pile up around it.

1

Fallen leaves are the chair which is used by the wind
Flowing water is the chair which is used by the wilderness
Birds and clouds are the distant chair
    which is put far away in the sky
The cross and bronze statue are the chair
    which is put farthest away in the sky
The nearest chair
  is your shadow
     his shadow
     my shadow
    our shadows

2

The forest uses millions of images
          to frame a blue sky
Tranquility is a mirror
If only bird songs fly across
there will be a diamond knife
        scratching it
    cutting out numerous doors, numerous windows

Scenery flows across both eyes
Both eyes drift to gorgeous colors
When the gorgeous colors flow and become the mist
the river in the eyes
    will flow and change into smoke

3

The cigarettes in the pack
are twenty rivers
When they flow and become the sea   shores will disappear
To grasp the bottle of alcohol
is like grabbing God's legs
You insist on being first to go to heaven

Whether Mona is sleeping upstairs or downstairs is now not important
because when you enter   you will either gaze at the blue sky
                                      or look at the green fields

4

Midnight

A car park is a sleeping distant place
Roads stop when the brake is set

When the brake is released
The distant place will go around until it becomes a
                                      circle
One world turns around and enters along the centripetal force
The other world turns around and leaves along the centrifugal force
                              Going out and coming in
                              coming in and going out
                                 until you become a
                                      piece of
                                        pure
                                       white
                                       space

5

Early morning is made of glass
Bird songs illuminate its resonance
Windows, eyes and the sky work together and produce
                                 the vastness
          in which even scenery, mountains and rivers
                      will divert your attention

This is because you stand on the roof at this moment
               seeing a piece of cloud drifting
                      a bird flying
                   the remoteness blossoming

6

Light surges over
and surrounds him
What is inside the smoke
                outside the mist
they are all magic
        performing within a crystal ball
He prefers being nude and grasped by the light
        being locked forever by the light's heart
                                the stars' heart
                                the moon's heart
                                the sun's heart

7

It is hands which touch
It is feet which reach
All that can be grasped is not in the hands
All that can be reached is not under the feet
If both hands and feet return separately to
                        both shores and roads
mountains will be at the end of their rope when they are called upon
rivers will be at the end of their tether when they are called upon
Then we cannot see with our eyes
        we cannot watch with our eyes
who knows which color the eyes will die in at the end?
                        how the bird flies across the sky?

8

A river runs across her waist
thought of as
        a waterfall breaking through the mountains
People say that it is
        a sudden change of spring

Two knives
extend from her flattering eyes
sticking in the atriums of the heart
in which grow two acacias

9

The gun muzzles open a row of windows
It is very quiet in front of the windows
especially when those windows are
            closed after being opened

The praying priests also open a row of windows
It is extremely quiet in front of the windows
especially when those windows are
            opened after being shut

10

Under the lamp   there are some drafts of his poems and
            an empty chair which he has just used

Is better for night not to look outside of the windows
      When it takes a look outside   the empty chair
                              becomes the sky
            The man has gone   the stars are still there

Escape (1975)

1

The first shot from the bow
makes the wilderness scream
  and wings cannot recognize the sky

Wings which cannot escape from the sky
        hide inside the clouds
        lowering the crystalline curtain
        looking at the autumn moon through the delicately wrought carving

Actually   escape is your reflection in the mirror

2

If cages do not
emaciate the wilderness
how will wings consider themselves
                        the doors of the sky
and eyes will not be looked at and become the scenery outside the windows

Actually   escape is a kind of flying
                is the kind birds call vastness
Even clouds, in order to drift afar,
        shove the mountains' ladders open
they are only undulations and drifting which
never pass beyond the wounds

This kind of escape does not deserve to be thought of
if it does not pass beyond the wounds
   Are those iron bars the same as that leopard's lines of vision?
   Can the arrow recapture the wilderness?
When spring escapes from the petals of flowers
        summer escapes from the bursts of waves
        autumn escapes from the sounds of leaves
        winter escapes from the mountains of snow
        distant places escape from an eyeful of enshrouding mist
Whenever you think of the clouds and birds
the sky will grasp and transform you into
                        a beautiful metaphysics

3

Actually   escape is a beautiful naked body
                                              very lovely
Adults, having clothes in their hands, chase after
    their children who, grinning, run away with bare buttocks

4

Actually   escape is the bird
When the scenery is naked in the mountains and rivers
    the sky is naked above the clouds
    the sea is naked under the stormy waves
    the river is naked between the shores
    you are naked inside the body
    Eyes are naked when they look afar
    Smoke is naked in mist
The bird   when it flaps its wings
    will be a thousand miles away

Running Away (1984)

Inside the mirror polishing room of the sun and the moon
I see clearly that
roads run away from streets
    and the wilderness comes to pick them up
trees run away from bonsais
    and fields come to pick them up
birds run away from their wings
    and the sky comes to pick them up
people run away from their name cards
    and misty clouds come to pick them up
Roads and trees   people and birds
    run away together
and the horizon leads them back

2 to 2 . 20 to 20 (1986)
— An Incomplete Caprice

1

A door is outside the window
A lock is outside the door

Beyond the mountain is a river
Beyond the river is the boundless sky and earth

2

Man wears clothes
A passport is put inside the pocket of the clothes

Birds wear the sky
Nothing is put inside the pocket of the sky

3

Numerous pots of trimmed bonsais
    look handsome when they come out from the barber shop

Graceful long hair   is showered by the sun and becomes a waterfall
                is blown by the wind and becomes a grove

4

Roads draw lines, one after another
Railways fix the wheels which run on its sides   ·

Fields draw rivers, one after another
Wings never ask how the sky flies

5

Birds
fly to mountains and rivers

Fowls
fly to markets

6

If you want to look for the addresses of winds, clouds and birds
please call loudly to the sky and wilderness   and listen to their replies

However, where you live   must be no farther than your legs
                              the alley   the street

7

When you take a lift   no matter how tall a skyscraper is
                              it is no taller than a roof

When the sky sits on the clouds   who knows how high the eyes are
                                        how far the remoteness is

8

If you throw a fishing line into a brook deep inside a mountain
                              all of nature will sit quietly there

If you wind round her waist with vision lines
  and give a pull at the eye lines   rock music shoots people dead

9

Birds' songs and spring waters' music
      have made the forest fall into a deep slumber

Pop music and the wheels' noises
      have made the city toss restlessly

10

There are so many wheels
   but they can only move a few streets

The sun has only one wheel,
      nevertheless, everything follows its motion

The Collected
Poems of **LOMEN**
: A Bilingual Edition

11

When the sun's mouth kisses the sea
        sea-spray is in full blossom

When your mouth kisses her
     her eyes are full of amorous looks

12

When you stand upon the peak   the sky bumps against your head
          It is so close that you can touch it with your hands

When you cling to a woman's breasts   the sky slides down to
                    the bottomless abyss

13

Both shores embrace the rivers   embrace the vista
   falling into sleep until they reach the remote sea

Both your hands hug a woman   hug the night
   also falling into sleep until you reach the remote sea

14

The shells listen to the seas' calling
     listen to the sun's and the moon's chatting next-door

The ears listen to the guns' shouting
     listen to woman's and banknote's laughter within laughter

15

A flute is a river
     pouring out milk-like rays of dawn and wine-like sunset clouds

A gun is also a river
     pouring out white tears and red blood

16

The flowers on the trees   are windows
The fruits on the trees   are windows covered with curtains

The windows of the apartments   are flowers
The windows covered with curtains   are sweet fruits

17

If years are lowered sails
they will fold on your forehead, layer by layer

And the sun's shiny carving knife   grasps tightly the waves
                    grasps tightly the lines of marble and metal

18

The legs of the sky and the earth join together on the horizon
   transformed into wings and flying

Your legs are a pair of rusty scissors
   joined together in the shaky hands of your old grandmother

19

The body hair is inside the incinerator
                it is burnt to smoke

The mountains, the rivers are inside the sun
      they are boiled and become a pot of scenery

20

Nature
   is a bank

Human beings
   are banknotes with different denominations

The Magic Line Connecting the Doors, the World and I (1989)

Flowers push the door of spring open
The burning sun pushes the door of summer open
Fallen leaves push the door of autumn open
Cold winds push the door of winter open
(Time has doors everywhere)
Birds push the door of the sky open
Spring water pushes the door of the forest open
Rivers push the door of the wilderness open
The sea pushes the doors of the earth and sky open
(Space has doors everywhere)

The doors of the sky and the earth are pushed open by the sea
The sea cannot go out by itself
All people stand at the seaside
    staring blankly
They only see a puff of cloud
   drifting quietly through the crack of the door
Eyes run after to ask
until the gaze cannot reach any further
The eyes turn out to be two locks
which lock up the doors of the earth and the sky
Everyone outside the doors cannot enter
Everyone inside the doors cannot leave
Chen Ziang hastily reads his poem:
    Looking back, no sages can be seen
    Looking ahead, no one is coming
    I ponder over the boundless universe
    Bursting into sorrowful tears

Wang Wei also cannot help reciting his poem
    Rivers flow beyond the earth and heaven
    Colours play upon the mountains by turns
Amid the vastness
the doors still cannot be opened
until the sun sets, the stars sink, everywhere darkens
The priests and pastors who wear black and red gowns
      suddenly appear
They ask everybody to clasp their hands together which is like a door (door again)
       in front of their chests

Then all say amen (door again)
The door of heaven and all doors
   open accordingly

Although I am Lomen, the door collector
who wants to gather all doors around me,
amid the endless noise of opening doors,
I am still afraid of Solomon's hands
    which grasp the key and lock to imprison me — the door collector*

Postscript:
1. *Twenty years ago I said that human beings, especially poets and artists, were living in their excellent imagination; otherwise doors there were only wooden doors, leaden doors, iron doors, glass doors, front doors and back doors or no door in the world. However, imagination helps us push open the temporal door, the spatial door, the door in a philosopher's head, the door in a poet's heart, the door in god's heaven. As a result, we hear the noises of opening doors everywhere.*
2. *After having finished writing this poem, I suddenly feel that this poem clearly manifests the significance of imagination in composing poems. And my explanation is spontaneous notes rather than some substantial regulations.*

* Translators' note:
The literal meaning of Lomen's Chinese name is to collect doors.

The World of Windows (1991)

A window is the frame of nature
It is also the bird flying amid the scenery

Windows in the fields   automatically install a wide-angle lens
Windows in the cities   become short-sighted
Windows in remote places   are wings growing from the flying of birds
When windows feel happy   mountains and rivers do not turn their heads
When windows feel angry at being closed   bombs pass through thick walls
When windows feel lonely and empty   a mirror is polished by solitude
When windows close their eyes silently   deep inside the mountain, there is an
                                        ancient well. Someone nearby is meditating

Watching Time Who Is Running On His Own (1991)

The earth is running in space
A train is running on the earth
We are sitting motionlessly on the train
  and watching the scenery running outside of it
until speed is running
       upside down
the scenery then comes to a standstill
  and looks inside the coach where we are running
   the train then comes to a standstill
     and watches the earth running
  the earth then comes to a standstill
       and watches space running
    space then comes to a standstill
  and watches time running on his own

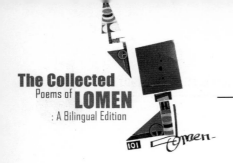

Who Can Afford to Buy the Horizon (1992)

I pull the sun's, moon's, stars' and lamps'
flashing lines
all over here
I pull the cars', the ships' and the airplanes'
routes
all over here
I pull the drawings in the painters' hands:
the curves and the straight lines
all over here
I pull everybody's eyes:
the aimless lines of vision
all over here
I gather them all together
until in the end
only the boundless horizon remains
it leads the sky and, walking, pulls the earth

The Different Designs of the "House of Light" (1993)

The House of Light is designed to be located
    in the light without any enclosing wall
You do not need to climb the staircase   or to take the lift
No matter how high it is   as long as you see it, you are already there

It is not like the Empire State Building
Even if you reach the one hundredth floor
you still cannot escape the walls on all sides
When you continue to climb
to the balcony on the roof
the walls disappear
If you are grasped by the sky
you are not the birds
When you fall you cannot hear anything
because there are railings on all sides

The Collected
Poems of LOMEN
: A Bilingual Edition

The Installation World of the House of Light (1993)
— a postmodern work of installation art and also a visual poem

It is a transparent building
   which is constructed with light
and all materials come from the world of installation art
Lamp shops' lights cannot pass themselves off as one of them
Thirty odd lamps with different appearances
play the symphony of light
crowding around a garden of light
The flowers of lights have been blooming for thirty-odd years
they have been transplanted into television's screens
they have been transplanted into the magazine's covers
   they have been transplanted into interviewers' eyes
             entering various kinds of memories

At this moment, the pillars of all internal lives
become a visible and substantial lamp post
supporting the whole glowing space
Light spirals upwards
     along the spiral staircase of light
The clouds go down
The sky goes up
The glass building of the universe is up there
except for the pure light of the sun, the moon and the stars
even a mirror cannot glow with light
     only the universe can light on its own

Looking around at 360 degrees
lighting up the ancient, the modern, the Chinese and the foreign all together
let all art schools
   follow the light and enter
Except for art and human beings
no shadow and noise
can enter
the transparent circle of light

Inside the spiraling lights
the house of light transcends and becomes a spiral tower
   grasping the basis of the eternity of the universe
raising the world up to the pinnacle of beauty
       spiraling it downwards to the profound, bottomless mystery

My Shortest Poem (1997)
— "The horizon is the last string of the universe"

Preface

Although this is my shortest poem, it has the longest postscript. In fact, the postscript is itself an essay which combines poetry, prose, philosophy, criticism and so forth. If we examine the essay from the postmodern point of view of "genre deconstruction," it can be considered as a poem, an essay, as well as a critical essay related to the exploration of life and space-time. At the same time in my mind's eye, this essay embodies land art.

In the postmodern era when value and center can no longer be counted on, most people are like bats rushing to the walls. Fortunately, poetry helps to show us a special line in our snobbish society which is beyond "noodles," "gold bars" and "pimps." The line is the "horizon" which always carries the rising and setting of the sun and the moon. It is also the final echo left by the universe's last string.

The horizon is the last string of the universe

Postscript

A "meta" poetics or explanation for this short poem is indeed necessary, because poem and explanation match each other very well.

I have written several poems which are extended in length and deep in meaning such as "The Undercurrent of the Ninth Day," "Fort McKinley," "The Death of the City," "The Tower of Death," "Panmunjom, 38 Degrees," "Watching the Sea," "The Wilderness," "An Invisible Chair," "The Space-time Sonata," "Grand Canyon Sonata" and so forth. I have also composed a lot of short poems, namely, "Window," "A Vagabond" and so on…. However, I believe this short poem is the shortest among all of my poems. I can never write any poem shorter than this one. Ezra Pound says that if a poet can write a unique and fantastic image, he should be very happy. Now, I must admit that I have found myself a unique and fantastic image and have turned it into a complete poem through my poetic eye. When I examine the contents and the structure of this poem, they become notes on my creative writing.

Although this poem is particularly short, my soul and thought have spent a long time on it. To me, in the vast expanse of space-time, "it" is the last echo to everything that exists. When I write "I fling it open   but I am locked in an inescapable / transparency" in the poem "Window," what I try to express is exactly what I want to say in this short poem. Deep inside my heart, I feel that I fall into an infinite vastness.

I remember when Rongzi and I flew across the Grand Canyon; I suddenly realized that there are only three lines left in the whole world, in the vastness of the universe:

(1) The first line refers to the Grand Canyon which is drawn by nature's primitiveness.

(2) The second line refers to the Great Wall which was made by human beings' flesh and bones. Human beings not only invade nature but also fight with each other for power and benefit.

(3) The third line refers to the horizon which is drawn by the universe's "vastness" and "tranquility." In fact, this line sometimes seems to exist, sometimes not; sometimes it is real, sometimes illusive.

These three lines are considered by my poetic eye the three lines of space-time and the activities of life. When I enter poetic meditation, I will unconsciously think of human beings' existence in the life structure of nature. On the one hand, we long for the freedom the birds, wind and clouds have; on the other hand, we are restricted by all kinds of things visible and invisible, new and old frames in our real and cruel world. Our hands and feet wear handcuffs and chains and are led by "existence" reluctantly. The life span of human beings is very short. From cradle to grave, we spend one third of it in sleep. If we live and betray our "true selves," we again waste our time. How much time can we really live? What can we accomplish and achieve? The assistants of death – the irresistible "time" and "space" — are on both sides of the cradle from the very beginning. All of us are abducted to the funeral home. Nevertheless, it seems that we are not aware of the abduction. And this case always remains unsolved. This fact naturally makes human beings, especially poets who are more perceptive and sensitive, explore the mystery in depth. It is undoubted that these poets will discover the following tragedy which is repeated everlastingly in their quest for the truth —

The truth is: "Human beings are destined to be eliminated by space-time. After having been eliminated by space-time, human beings imagine that they will bring back their lives from statues, memorial halls, encyclopedias and heaven. However, if we think deeply, we will see that statues, memorial halls, encyclopedias and heaven can only comfort those who are still alive. The dead man is at a loss. He does not even know from which direction the sun rises. He again falls into an infinite vastness. All he can grasp is the illusive "horizon" – "the last string of the universe" which echoes to everything's illusive sounds…."

At the moment, we are flying thirty thousand feet above the clouds. And there is a blue glass building of the vast universe above the clouds. However, no chair can be found. In fact, nothing can stay. Neither the scenic Grand Canyon nor the Great Wall can be seen. Even a sea of clouds and a mountain of clouds turn into a visible "vastness." The whole world has no choice but to enter the realm of "vastness," "emptiness" and "tranquility" which reflects that "emptiness" embraces everything in the world; "tranquility" in reality embodies all motion. In a world like this, except for turning the vast "horizon" into "the last string of the horizon," where can we find something to sound echoes for mystery and eternity? In fact, the erhu's strings, guzheng's strings, violin's, cello's strings and the heartstrings of our grandfathers, great grandfathers, great, great grandfathers are all broken in the vastness of space-time. Even the route from our coffins to heaven is only a broken line in our prayers. At last, only the illusive "horizon" remains and stays in the vast universe's space-time.

However, the "horizon" – "the last string of the universe"— is hung in the distance. People (such as writers, artists, philosophers, politicians, scientists and even priests) who want to play it will find it impossible. Even if they gather all legs, shoes, car wheels, wings of aircraft, birds' wings and clouds' wings together, these people still cannot get close to the "horizon." No one can play this "last string of the universe" except itself. It also becomes the inaudible echo of everything and the shortest poem in my life: "The horizon is the last string of the universe."

After having written this short poem, I was inspired by "visual poetry" and tried to transform the poem into a work of land art according to the conceptions of creative visual art.

Land art master Christo releases natural scenery from frames and painted canvases to nature. He uses "packaging" as a means to reconstruct and exhibit the authentic beauty of nature. If Christo's works are taken into account, I think it is also appropriate to consider "the horizon" (an illusive line in the universe) a work of my "new" "land art." In fact, my work is different from Christo's in terms of the ways we deal with meanings and symbols. Christo's works tend to be "expressive" and "explain themselves." On the one hand, I intend to use a minimal and an absolute conception to make the visual effect of my work as simple and pure as possible. On the other hand, my poem embodies many symbols and surrealistic elements which enrich its internal meanings and its consciousness of existence.

In fact, after having transformed the "horizon" in the poem "The horizon is the last string of the universe" into a work of land art and given it another title "No One Can Afford to Buy the Horizon," we face two questions: we can neither play nor buy it. I have already explained the reason why we cannot play the horizon. Why can't we buy the horizon? I have playfully discussed this issue with some artists: "As an artist, how many lines did you draw in your life? You must be very tired. Since "land art" has become popular, you can leave the whole business to "poetry" and make it buy the "horizon" for you. It can help to save your time. Besides, you can never underestimate its value due to its durability…."

Moreover, if we examine deeply and scan the things around us in 360 degrees, we will find an interesting fact which is: the light of the sun, moon, star, lamps, the routes of footsteps, cars, ships and aircraft, the parabolas of wind, clouds, birds, the vision of eyes, the straight lines and curves drawn by brushes are many uncountable lines. Nevertheless, they are all blocked by the longest and untouchable "horizon." Or we had better say that the "horizon" takes in all these lines, because this makes us feel better. In addition, this saying can also mollify our tragic situation.

Actually, when the "horizon" finds the genetic origin of its internal thoughts in the poetic eye it creates this work of land art. "No One Can Afford to Buy the Horizon" and the short poem "The horizon is the last string of the universen— these poems exhibit one thing: in the space-time of the vast universe, the poetic eye con-

siders these two poems two visible and invisible routes. One connects with the eternal realm of reality which is inside and beyond the universe in Toynbee's heart; the other connects with the boundless, soundless "emptiness" which leaves tremendous echoes as well as many questions. Whenever we try to answer these questions, we feel puzzled and weak –

First of all, the kings who could afford to buy a country in the past and the millionaires who could afford to buy a city have died with sorrow due to the fact that they could not buy the "horizon." Second, although scientists try their best to design and build spaceships, the spaceships will never be able to transport the endless "sky" and the "vastness." Third, the poet Chen Ziang chants continuously: "Where are the sages of the past / And those of future years? / Sky and earth forever last, / Lonely, I shed sad tears" [as translated by Xu Yuanzhong, 300 Tang Poems]. Fourth, monks discard their high positions as well as great wealth and shave their heads. They try to compare their bald heads with the empty sky. Lastly, priests lead the crowd to pray: "the Eternal God, the eternal heaven" and try to surmise their future lives.

This paragraph is almost the end of my short poem and its "meta" poetics or explanatory notes. I do not have much more to say except a few words. Through this poem, I have again realized that poetry is a minimal art which uses language as its means. It tries to use a minimum of linguistic symbols to release a maximum energy of life and thought. If you ask whether poetry belongs to the past, the modern, the postmodern and the post-postmodern, or belongs to classicism, romanticism, realism, surrealism, symbolism, abstractionism, neo-realism and so forth, I will say that although these questions are significant, poetry is beyond all of them. This is because when we create poems, we consider "space-time" and all kinds of "isms" to be materials. And they are transformed into the organic substance of the poems. In other words, poetry passes beyond the restrictions of "space-time" and "isms" and equips us with the power of "everlasting progression." Meanwhile, we also learn from transforming this short poem into "land art" that writers and visual artists are close neighbors. The partition between writers and visual artists in the past should be eliminated. As a matter of fact, especially in the postmodern era when deconstruction, pluralism and diversity are emphasized, if there must be a separation we must not use enclosing walls but transparent glass. We should have a chance to see each other in order to broaden our creative horizons.

A Unique Love (2001)
— Poets, artists and Mona Lisa's wedding

Mona Lisa
You are a splendid spring
     a passionate summer
     a magnificent autumn
     a pure winter
You bequeath a perfect appearance   to nature
You bequeath an eternal image   to the universe

Passing through the fragrant hair forest of the beauties
flowing through the smooth breasts of the beauties
in the Aegean sea beyond the Aegean sea
you are always my direction
     my final destination
Using imagination which is longer than the horizon
I pull the sun and the moon up to me to make you a ring
 Using everything beyond everything
     I transport all beauty here
     to build a beauty
     in a world beyond all the worlds
Following musicians' ears
     painters' eyes
     poets' hearts
I wave and scatter the light of the "Nine Major Arts"
to spread a red carpet for the kingdom of art
to switch on all the lights of heaven
Standing before the goddess of beauty among other deities
I vow that my love is beyond all kinds of love
Our eyes meet each others' our hearts connect with each others'
My right hand grasps your perfection
   My left hand grasps your eternity
Our kiss makes the door between the sky and the land open
Our wedding night is a magical, wonderful
               infinite space-time
Holding the passports and credit cards
        bestowed by the creator
we are honeymooning
     everlastingly

Postscript:
The living space of human beings has various aspects: where can we find them? Some of them can be found in the materialistic world; others can be found in the pure and metaphysical world. The idea of the so-called "nine major arts" mentioned in this poem is based on the familiar eight major arts. The eight major arts are considered as the "fuel" and all are put into the furnace of internal beauty. As a result, a kind of beauty which can be only felt by our souls and hearts emerges from the furnace. This kind of beauty is close to religion and to an invisible as well as absolute world. This world is omnipresent, which reflects the essence and the spirit of art. This world is constructed from and presented by the "ninth major art" of beauty. As I have pointed out elsewhere, "poetry" and "art" are not only something beyond the knowledge of philosophy, science, politics, history and even religion, but also create a knowledge of the life of beauty for human beings. In fact, my opinion has a solid basis.

V

The Beautiful "V" (1958)

Cramming into a bus, the primary students are joking
Their voices like a flock of birds
    whirling round the tree-like grown-ups beside them
A fairy land and a generation suffering from serious heart disease
    are sitting on the bus without disturbing one another

All of a sudden the bus puts on its brakes
The long leg of the road seems to be seized with cramp, followed by a sharp cry
The eyes of the passers-by converge to a beautiful "V"
      like a bouquet of flowers thrown there
In any case, someone will or will not be coming back from the border

"The House of Light": The Love of Spiral (1969)

In the House of Light, a record player plays and makes spiral tree rings. Music spins and turns into a spiral spiritual world. The spiral is deep and bottomless. When you get inside, you cannot easily come out. In this case, spiral nails are things which are unshakable and cannot be easily pulled out. What kind of love does this love belong to? Is it about lovers, life or the world and the existence of the universe? I will leave this question to you!

The tightly closed doors and windows   express a steadfast refusal
The drawn curtain   completes the tranquil isolation
Outside is like the wind which disappears far away
Inside is like the waves going ashore
touching after the completed isolation
Inside is like a ringing bell suddenly born in the air   the lightening of electricity

This is the purest space
raising a forest of birdsong   drawing a whole sky of clouds
beyond the eyes   beyond the coordinates   beyond the house number plates
Marble and crystal patterns are drawn by the diamond stylus
     Even Jesus' straw-made shoes do not know where they will go
It is as transparent as a mirror   as bright as a mirror
I am as dedicated as a lover   walking along the rhythmic spiral staircase
                                        falling into the whirling track
until my heart grasps the happy death   I wake up
Bird eyes wake up in a tree of green
A villa sits in a bright and beautiful summer garden
Let the light lightly shine through the leaves
let the scenery silently beautify our eyes
let the sound   soundlessly echo there
I have already felt the fog horn ashore
The searching expression in my eyes has already found the diamond along the red
                                                                    carpet
The sweetness of the vineyard will never run out
   The colors of the fountain will always be in my eyes
   The purity in an awakened baby's eyes will be always there for you to pick up
This kind of happiness is like a water bird catching spray with its wing tip
This kind of satisfaction is like the grain-gilded manor approaching autumn
When the musical meteor shower lowers a twinkling curtain
the world will become naked   will have no more illusions
     which is like soft eyes becoming naked in a fixed gaze
  is like a green shade without illusions in a forest interwoven with light and leaves
What a luxurious secret meeting

during that particular dinner party at which Caesar and God are absent
my gorgeous God   uses my eyes as his chair
The electronic pickup continuously chews the immortal tree rings of the record
                                                                                player
A nail drills a sound   in order to hang a picture steadfastly on the heart
A whirlpool spins continuously   in order to break the hands of the watches and clocks
A tranquil light flows   falls from the lampshade
My face is a rock looking upward from the forgetful river
it is as transparent as a mirror   as bright as a mirror
collecting a forest of birdsong   reflecting a whole sky of clouds

Paddling towards the blue lake of eyes
light enters the lampshade   a face covered by a veil
scenery becomes as smooth and tender as milk in order to accommodate my
                                                                        eyesight
Using a thousand oars, Rondo still cannot wake up my drunken boat
Waltz swings water and makes ripples   circles flowers and makes rings
I fall faint into the circle and curved spaces   neither circle nor curve can be seen
        which is like the sun sleeping deeply in the continuously spinning galaxy
I no longer see clearly the flowers of Christmas tree and fireworks
I only feel the distant place which is following boundlessly
                it is still a flying bluebird even when asleep
                it is the sea where spray becomes wings

In the boundless, bottomless spinning space
which is so pure that even air must leave   eyes are hidden in the deep gaze
Eternity needs no contrast at this moment   it is not made of copper and concrete

Neither is it a rainbow bridge, mortal or immortal, which is made over a blood river
It is only an unblocked whirling direction
                a road which belongs to violin and piano
                a distant place which eyes cannot exhaust
                a kind of waking in sleeping   sleeping in waking
                a kind of existence which is equivalent to God but more than God

The Man has Gone   the Stars are Still There (1974)
— to poet L. David

Under the lamp   there are some drafts of his poems and
              an empty chair which he has just used

It is better for night not to look outside the windows
When it takes a look outside   the empty chair
                             becomes the sky
        The man has gone   the stars are still there

Church (1976)

It is an everlasting stainless steel washing machine
After being polluted for six days, all souls
are sent here for cleansing on the seventh

When the choir opens its mouth
the electricity of Heaven is connected
When the priest opens his mouth
water gushes from the tap
Amid the echoes of the evangelical speech
the cleansed souls   are bleached again and again
If there is still any impurity
it will be discharged from the eyes
    Anxiety and uneasiness   confusion and repentance
are put inside an offering bag when you show your gratitude
    After having received yourself
a purified self with a stiff soul
you again walk out to the six days
        out to the dusty streets

Restaurant (1976)

The hall is full of heads
floating in the air until they become festive balloons
Eyes crowd round looking at
   numerous strikingly pleasing pictures
until the gallery almost explodes
        We discover that it is a stomach

Cutting into it   if it is a glittering river
              there must be some fish
Forking into it   if it is a fish
   there must be traces of ages swimming by
If chopsticks are a pair of flashing legs
       there must be howls of hunger
            in the wilderness
If fields and gardens fill the dishes
there must be two rows of teeth biting bitterly
           the breasts of the earth

The Collected
Poems of **LOMEN**
: A Bilingual Edition

Watching a Dance Show (1979)
— Watching Paul Taylor's Modern Dance

When you turn around   the earth follows
When you come to a standstill   all watches stop

Those hands which can pluck the stars and pick the moon
become motionless in the air   change into a fabric of steel
Those feet which tread on flowers and step on waves
                                        stride across
Mountains and rivers are right beneath
You have no choice but to fly
Birds fly toward you
Clouds drift to you
Rivers run over you
Waves break over you
The sky whirls round you
Light waves bounce on you

You exchange places with the sun and the moon
        tread your way through and come with butterflies
        diffuse and become mist
        condense and become mountains
When the curtain falls   a flower of eternal praise
                                blossoms amid the applause
They call you the lines under Dufy's brush
                the sculpture from Henry Moore's knife
                the music in Debussy's eyes

The World of the House of Light (1979)

Light is the eye of the cosmos
which shows the whole world its surroundings   — Lomen

1. The Track of Light

Light departs from a straight line
which walks until it becomes a stringed instrument:
                its sound is high and remote
which walks until it becomes a wood:
                its colour is glorious
which walks until it becomes a pillar:
                it is everlasting
which walks until it becomes the horizon:
                it fastens all eyesight looking afar
which walks until it returns to the eyes:
                it brings back the moon and the sun

Light departs from a parabola
which walks until it becomes a fountain:
                it will be in riotous profusion
which walks until it becomes a bird:
                it will be free
which walks until it becomes the clouds:
                it will be carefree
which walks until it becomes the wind:
                it will go its own way
which walks until it returns to the eyes:
                it will undulate with mountains and rivers

Light departs from a circle
which walks until it becomes a vortex:
                it will descend to profundity
which walks until it becomes a tower:
                it will ascend to abstruseness
which walks until it becomes a tree's growth rings:
                it will roll up the vastness of nature
which walks until it becomes a record player:
                it will enter the most exquisite lines of time
which walks until it returns to the eyes:
                it will see the eyes of the years

The Collected
Poems of **LOMEN**
: A Bilingual Edition

2. The Work of Light

Light leads the eyes to the zenith with a straight line
                    to see Nietzsche's heart
Light brings the eyes to the scenery with a parabola
                    to watch Duncan's dance
Light embraces the eyes and the sky with a circle
                    to go to read Wang Wei's poetry

3. The End of Light

Snow is falling down from light
You are standing on the top of the snow-capped mountain
When you are motionless   your eyes are winter
Once you move   before both eyes can explain whether they are rivers
                    or the hands stretching out by the earth
           mountains and rivers have already rushed off
                    carrying flowers of the fields

Light is blossoming
You are lying in the garden
listening to the colours
Even fragrance has sounds
Occasionally, you fall into a trance while listening
          and think they are a boundless field
                  in the rain

Light is raining
You are soaking in the soft wetness
When you smell the perfume of the nectar
night will melt into wine
dew will condense to dawn
When the windows are opened   the house within and without is watching
The sun spreads a road to the distance
        connecting here with the world

"The House of Light" – the Place Where Light Dwells (1979)

Light   has no enclosing walls
The place where light dwells   of course also has no enclosing walls

The House of Light is only an open-air cabin seat
traveling in space-time
my eyes carry a gallery
my ears carry a music theatre
and nothing else
Like this   I empty my hands
                to hug the earth
My legs comfortably rest on the horizon
My head pillows on the starry sky*
My lying down makes the world become clouds
                        drifting away with the light
the moon is the dyke
the sun is the shore
Climbing up   is where the light dwells

*The lights in the House of Light make it become a glimmering starry sky at night.

The House of Light (1980)

A fountain of light
silently weaves
music into music
colors into colors

A green window and the facing sea
use a peaceful and silent cry to watch each other
Sunset clouds are on the face of the keeper of the tower
                    Rounding a rose garden
let the roots of light be planted in blind eyes
The blind eyes are a quiet field sleeping in the fog
In the distance   the sound of water is like a piano
                  the sound of a piano is like water

The sunset is here
The moonset is here
Time passes through
ringing a line of bells
Eternity is in the twinkling of an eye
sitting in the eyes of the tower keeper

The world of the tower keeper
is as exquisite as an eye's focus
Brightness comes from the center of light
                  reflecting all images

The world outside has no choice but to dim with the night
In the world inside the House of Light
lights are shining from layer upon layer of lights
The tower keeper lies on the lights and drifts away
Let the gushing smoke
make the blurred but colorful space float

Under the seabed of light
the sunken boat X is still sailing
There are neither sounds of wind nor wave on the deck
The silent ocean current
is as warm as winter's fireplace in the study
              Profound mystery sleeps here
                  and wakes up here
The tower keeper looks at the tower with a smile

because the pinnacle of the tower is higher than his eyes
because all thumps
        pass through the rock's last layer
              waking up the minerals
          to release the energy of light

A Memorial to the Moon Landing of Spaceship Columbia (1981)
— to recollect the writing journey of my innermost feelings over
the past thirty years

First Beethoven's atriums
        are lighted up
Then the world riding on the fire
        is projected into space

The flower is the most beautiful metaphysics
Mallarmé has been waiting in the mystic sky
He uses a symbolic gesture
to guide the flower to him

In a flash   even dreams cannot catch
The flower has flown over Aragon's home
        It lands and becomes the moon

The Orbits of the Sun and the Moon (1982)

Treading on the noisiness underfoot
I sit in the high-rise building alone looking at the mountain of clouds
The mountain looks at you as if you are the clouds
The clouds look at you as if you are the mountain
The mountain sits down   attached to the earth
The clouds drift up   accompanying the sky

A bird flies along the road and comes here
When both your eyes look farther than the wings
the complete quietness will make you
                    open thoroughly
You are the heart of sound   in tranquility
You are the heart of distant places   in echoes

Rivers pass through your blood
The everlasting Great Wall in your heart
has already rushed out of the iron railings
It enters the horizon
and perfects the most beautiful surface
Let the scenery cover it with layers
from windows to birds
from birds to the outer sky
You and light always walk along a straight line
inside the vertical transparency of this building
                    The sun's orbit is like this
                        so is the moon's

The Collected
Poems of LOMEN
: A Bilingual Edition

Umbrella (1983)

He leans against the window of his apartment
looking at the umbrellas in the rain
     they walk and become a multitude of
          lonely worlds
He thinks of the crowds
who come from the crammed
     buses and subways
They wrap themselves up, hide at home and
         lock the doors

Suddenly
all the rooms of the apartments
     rush out into the rain
      and exclaim
   "they are also umbrellas"

He is shocked and stands still,
grasping himself tightly until he becomes an umbrella's handle
     the sky an umbrella's folding frame
      Inside the umbrella it is raining
      there is no rain outside

The Years of Poetry (1983)
— to Rongzi

If the blue bird does not come
how can the woods which are shining over under the spring sun
      fly to the bright and beautiful April

I tread on a road of riotous profusion and brightness
If June does not burn to a phoenix
how can the maple trees on both mountains glow with red
      when summer spreads her wings
   and dedicates the glory to the ravishing autumn
A swan in the tranquil fields
  saves the last pure white flower in the sunset
     to light up the cozy winter days
     I wantonly grasp some snow
        some silver hairs
        some exchanged glances
  which are rivers flowing back to April
  which are poems being sent back to April

The Collected
Poems of LOMEN
: A Bilingual Edition

Snapshots of Women (1983)

1. A Slim Beauty

She stands at
the axis
and makes eyes and earth go around together
                until she moves

She moves on
A wisp of smoke
outlines the reclining position of a quiet, beautiful wilderness
a sleeping posture of the tender, gentle remoteness
waiting for her to lie down

She lies down
The horizon   swims in the sea
swaying until it becomes a curve   which is a river
undulating until it becomes an arc   which is the moon
stretching until it becomes a straight line   and the moon gushes over the running river

2. An Old Fashioned Housewife

Between the delivery room
          and the kitchen
          and the bedroom
she walks to and fro

The baby's mouth bites off one-third
The kitchen knife cuts off one-third
The rest of her   is used to embroider
          the bed sheet with a phoenix pattern

3. A Standard Street Walker

Winds come
Rains go
Flowers blossom
Birds sing
She is the wildest
      wilderness

Coming to the south
going to the north

passing a twisted peak
walking a winding road
She is an unrestricted
                highway

In fact, whatever I say
                is not true
She is only the wildest
    the most dangerous
        primitiveness

4.   A Bridget Bardot-style Unmarried Secretary

She records customers' orders
and delivery time
for the company
She hangs up one phone call
in order to pick up another
She hears that the manager
will go to Rose Restaurant after office hours

She looks at the mirror
brightening her lips with a rosy lipstick
She suddenly discovers that she is
also a kind of product
which has a rosy color
and will be delivered on time

5.   A Maiden Entrepreneur

She deposits the world in a bank
and pays checks to the years

She sits on a swivel chair
and turns until the whole glass building
becomes a crystal ball
which reflects the sun's laughter
                in all directions

She carries the laughter back to her room
taking off her precious *Longines*
Time suddenly quiets down
Waves sound no more

> Pianos also sound no more
After turning off the light
> only her silk and transparent pajamas
> embrace the night which is getting colder and colder

6.   Everybody's Mistress

As long as the place
has no house number, registered permanent residence, court nor church
even if it is close to a steep cliff
when you give her a bed
which may make her tremble with fear
still, she dares to go to sleep

She does not need to pay respect to her parents-in-law
nor to breastfeed her baby
In comparison with all other brides
she is the one who can frequently make the most sweet
                                        honeymoon

The Years' Two Faces (1984)

1

The sky comes to your forehead
A group of mountains comes to your eyebrows
Woods come to your hair
Rivers come to your limbs
Seas come to your eyes
Earth comes to your body
The sun and the moon come to your heart

When you are awake   the sun rises
When you are asleep   the moon rises

In joy   you are spring
In excitement   you are summer
In meditation   you are autumn
In sobriety   you are winter
In the four seasons   you are a flower

2

High-rise buildings come to your forehead
Signboards come to your eyebrows
Electric wires come to your hair
Streets come to your limbs
Display windows come to your eyes
Beds come to your body
She comes to your heart

When you are awake   she is there
When you are asleep   she is also there

In joy   she is your spring
In excitement   she is your summer
In meditation   she is your autumn
In sobriety   she is your winter
In the four seasons   she is your flower

Poems on Hong Kong (1984)

1. Skipping Stones on the Water
   — To Poet Yu Guangzhong I

When we squat down
sky and mountains also squat down
They look at us gathering stone flakes
         aiming at the sea's surface
cutting off half the century
A building as tall as fifty years
     collapses under the distant boom of guns
                 sinking down

Our childhoods at six years
come back with beating spray
They find us
and speak endlessly:
Stone flakes are birds' wings
        not shell fragments
They want to make the sea and us
      fly in the air
      fly all the way back

2. Walking on the Bank
   — To Poet Yu Guangzhong II

Both long banks grasp
       the water in between
       the mountains on both sides
entering the vista
Rivers consider mountains high up there
Mountains ponder rivers far away
We look at the world until it becomes
              boundless
While birds fly, rivers flow
While clouds drift, mountains appear
While the cries are vast and remote
scenery smoothly opens
     the camera shutter with one push
       and enters the imperial palace's
           landscape paintings

A Photo Lives in a Frame (1988)

Nature does not wear any clothes
The sky the wilderness
the river the ocean
all stripped naked
Man notices the freedom of the bird and the wind
and longs for a return to nudity

Man can never return to nudity
His head is grasped by
 hairstyles and bronze statues
His body is embraced by
 fashion and uniforms
His hands are seized to vote for the well-designed proposals
His mouth is seized to call out the well-prepared slogans
His face is seized to be copied on the well-planned covers
His heart is seized his body is left empty there
Man then becomes a photo
based on calculator's measurement
and lives inside the frame

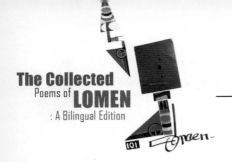

Watching the World Cup (1988)
— To Maradona, the world football star from Argentina

The whole world's televisions
        are watching him
When he moves the ball downfield
the earth and thousands of eyeballs
                follow
When he stops the ball
the world comes to a standstill

Kicking a high ball
the blue of the sky soars through Argentina
Kicking a long pass
The green of the fields spreads through Argentina
Kicking a curved pass
mountains and sky run along the curve
kicking a short pass
the world is drawn closer
Dashing across the football field
he is the Yellow River's water coming from the sky
        a torrent which nothing can block
          drifting with tide and wave
        chasing after the setting sun
             entering the goal

Maradona   Actually
his feet are also a magical pen
writing lines of unprecedented, marvelous poetry
        in front of all eyes

"House of Light" The Architecture of Light (1989)
— to all pure and transcendental lives
which are the architecture of light
also To L.M.

It does not stop there
as if it is merely a soundproof and mud-guarded glass building
It is an ever burning and glowing
                    rotating object
    which is walking with the sun
Its soundless light waves
    penetrate the noisy sound waves
Its infinite energy burns away
    all smoke, dust, clouds and fog
During the purest trip of light,
inside the transparent light space
it has already transformed into
        a crystal building
        which can embody the whole sky
It invites the sun, the moon, the stars
to design the graphics of light
to carry on the decoration of light
to exhibit the operation of light
Whenever eternity comes to this space
                poetry and art will wait for it in the light

The Pleasure of Being the First to See (1991)

The dawn uses a shiny
         window
    to encircle me
The surrounding darkness
stands by its side watching
In a few seconds
light rushes into the room
calling me to look out from the window

The sun is just out of its bed
Other beds are still sleeping
      love is sleeping
      affection is sleeping
      the city is sleeping
      the world is sleeping
The sky, yet to be put into use,
is a spotless Zen picture
The sun puts the first stamp on it
let me have the pleasure of being the first to see

Seven Visions of the Poetic Eye (1993)

Looking around
Watching attentively
Gazing fixedly
Taking a peep
Looking up
Overlooking

Looking at nothing

the boundary cannot be seen
everything becomes motionlessness
all focuses are incinerated
all mysteries are illuminated
nothing can be higher
let the whole world
throw herself on her knees
something can be seen from nothing
nothing can be seen from something

Works of Social Installation Art (1994)

1. The Switch of the Lamp

It is obviously white
If we turn it to the other side
everything gets dark

2. Bakery

Eyes fix on a top hat
at the beginning
The hat is put on a bald
         a hairless head
Hats never care for it

The funny thing is   the dough which is well kneaded
when some yeast is added
and it is sent to the black oven
              it will expand and swell
                 will transform and lose shape
                 will become delicious and tasty
It is getting popular
among people's mouths

3. Round and Square Tables

People sit around
being respectful to each other
being modest
Glasses clink together
but not their hearts

Different moods, chopsticks and saliva
                 dive into the same plate
The road which leads to the belly
is always hindered

He has a buffet by himself
sitting against a square table
Both he and the table have the shape of a square

He looks at his money
   his heart
   his taste
The trinity enters the plate
The road which goes to the belly
     is smoothed
However, when he goes for coffee
   with whom can he talk?

4. Public Baths

When you soak in the public baths
it is hard to avoid sharing rotten smells
There is always the chance of getting a bacterial infection
It is better to bathe
   under a shower nozzle

You go to mountain on your own to take a bath in a mountain spring
           which is cool and clear
        the wind and view go to and fro
When you cry out for joy
the mountain becomes silent

5. The Incident of Rubbish

In front of A's door rubbish lays in piles
In front of B's door rubbish lays in piles
In front of C's door rubbish lays in piles
In front of D's door rubbish lays in piles
In front of E's door rubbish lays in piles
You point out in front of ABCDE's doors
      rubbish lays in piles
      polluting the scenery

When you wake up next morning
all the rubbish
  blocks the door where you can see the garden
The police fine you at once
without asking any questions

6. Bird and Cockroaches

When there is no red or green
cars rush against the yellow light
front collides with rear
All dashing in chaotic directions
                    to find an exit

A bird flies
carrying the sky
When it looks down   there is a dish
            crowded with cockroaches

All People are in Exile (1998)

People walk inside a train
The train runs on earth
The earth walks in space
Space walks in the vastness
No one can get off the train
All addresses printed on the name cards
                       are wrong

Poets and Writers Are Sitting in the Right Seats (1999)

(1)

Pearls   light up the diamond chandelier at the opulent party
Fake pearls   cry for sale on the ground along the way down town
Glass bottles   are scattered and sparkle on the ground   at the shouting of "bravo!"

(2)

The starry sky   looks magnificent in the unreachable radiance
Fountains   remain splendid to a certain height and then fall down
Fireworks   die at the eye-catching speed of light

(3)

His footprints   are left on the scenery of the world
His footprints   are left on only some of the scenery
His footprints   are left on only a bit of the scenery

(4)

He looks at birds   in the sky
He looks for birds   in the pet shops
He grasps birds   in the birdcages

(5)

He considers the earth   a canvas
He considers the earth   a map
He considers the earth   a site for buildings

(6)

He is a sphere without circumference
He is the surface of the sphere
He is a dot on the surface

Postscript:
An authentic poet and artist can get a passport and a credit card from God. They can put the structure of the living universe before human beings and make them see anew the freedom of birds and of the wind. If poetry and art were to lose their transcendent, metaphysical spirit, they would be restricted and could not enter and work in the Nth degree, which is a broader, an infinite space.

Conceptual Theatre (1999)
— The *fin-de-siecle* judgment day, the performance of the
earth . human beings . poetry

The twentieth century stands on a precipice
Upon the sound of the ticking clock it jumps
                                              over

landing at   the location of 0
        Birds start to fly
        Flowers start to bloom
        Rivers start to flow
Human beings return to their origin   to see themselves
The earth returns to its origin
to see installation art

Who drives the first stake into the ground?
Maps grow out of it
Most borders are drawn by the edge of a knife
drawing lines of blood
asking the world to pass through the trajectory
let cannons draw clouds with thick smoke
                guns draw rivers with blood
nature has been bringing the scenery with itself into exile
suing for peace until 1999
years are still using shells to carve figures
                to see the launching of guided missiles

The twenty-first century opens a court session to pronounce judgment
The court gives poetry prosecution of the case*

The earth goes to the city
Nature is blocked outside the city
Buildings crowd around and make the corners
which eat up heaven and the fields
leaving chimneys and drainage to
green mountains and blue water
returning to the fridge to watch icy mountains and icy water
flocking to weekends' shoe prints to watch fallen leaves
floating on a pile of advertisements to watch the drifting clouds
chasing after fashions to find the wind's direction
Speed urges the whole city to run

The Collected
Poems of LOMEN
: A Bilingual Edition

carries people and cars to rush
Shoulders and shoulders   are obstacles
Faces and faces   overlap
Even the zebra crossing slows down its pace
the road underneath is no longer a country road
Whether the setting sun over the long river is round or not
the daylight lamp has already turned the rapeseed oil lamp into
a wave of age-old nostalgia
Being locked into a sealed engine room
the world becomes a pile of digital codes after becoming electronic
        becomes virtual images without flesh and blood
Being careless,   human beings will be played by electric toys
and become human-being toys
We will be loaded on the lorry of urban civilization
Before we have time to think of the scarecrows of the sixties
computers and machines have already planned
            to expel human beings from their bodies
            to make a second wave of nostalgia which is much
                        further away

The twenty-first century opens a special court session to pronounce judgment
The clone cannot go on the market
Poetry is making a key judgment

The earth goes to the United Nations building
Outside the conference hall   birds fly and raise
            the Statue of Liberty from the sea
Inside the conference hall   different doctrines and advocacies
treat volubly the various sizes of birdcages
            the numerous lengths of rivers
The sky and the sea cannot be seen
The world cannot spread
It remains ever inside the calculator
      is kept within the maps' and guns' range of fire
Freedom still needs to bring its passport
Years still need to install iron gates and windows

The twenty-first century opens a court session to make a final judgment
Human beings and the earth give a unanimous verdict
            Poetry is a sailing sea
            Poetry is a flying sky

*Note:

Confucius considers "poetry as the heart of the sky and the earth." The French poet Aragon says: "Poetry is heaven." In 1998, when I attended the Conference of World Literature in Washington, Nobel Prize winner Wole Soyinka pointed out that only poetry (and art) could save human beings. In fact, we deeply believe that the most beautiful people, communities and countries are made by poetry (and art) and not by machines. The twenty-first century should be a free, peaceful and beautiful era. We should let poetry (and art) guide us, because poetry (and art) not only can beautify the scientific, philosophical, political and even the religious worlds but also can beautify the external and internal existential space of human beings. They especially transcend and boundlessly raise by beauty to a spiritual realm. They help us better understand freedom, help us get closer to truth, to perfection and to eternity. After having finished writing this poem, I found that it is a poem on poetry – "On Poetry's Supreme Value."

The Collected
Poems of LOMEN
: A Bilingual Edition

The Eye of a Typhoon (2000)
— to poet L. David

Emptying yourself   for the universe
becoming quiet   for all the motion

you stare at the heart of sky and earth
You look at storm and rain carrying the world
        whistling from all directions
You are a soundless valley of echoes
Things which come from mountains
Nietzsche will bring back to the lonely peak
Things which come from the shaking earth
the sea will tie up with the horizon
      and return to being and nothingness

Whether it is emptiness or being
       stillness or motion
you   are clear at a glance

Meteor (2000)

— to poetry

Before a pile is driven into the earth
before there is any map
it carries the universe
and lands from the vastness

Under the stone   which sits on the depth of mountain
Above the stone   which sits on the height of sky
Around the stone which sits on the breadth of earth

Wherever I look at is far away
Whatever I listen to is an echo
Touching until it becomes flowing water
Beating until it becomes sparks
Freezing until it becomes the heart of ice
Grasping and taking it to the point of force of architecture
    framing an infinite transparency
I look at a riot of colors in the sky
                falling into decadence
only its persistence is left and
blossoming out as minuteness
Which is bigger than the earth and space-time

Art Can Help People Leave Their Bodies to Look at the World (2000)

High-rise buildings crowd around to make a street corner
                            in order to eat up the sky
Cities are pressed under ceilings
sitting on a pile of advertisements
whatever they see is material
whatever they touch is also material
there are material things everywhere
Human beings become animals which chase after material things
In the beginning they ate and slept in the wilderness
they have already moved to the luxurious suites and restaurants of the Hilton
The menu changes every day
The bed sheet is changed every night
Human beings are sophisticated animals
                    walking inside their bodies

When human beings cannot leave their bodies
they become a house without windows
                    nothing outside can be seen
                    nothing outside can be heard
The world becomes blind and dumb
        spinning in the bowls and plates
        listening to the echoes in the flushing toilets
If harmony does not pass through
                    poultry's cackling in the market
                    machines' squeaks
                    debates' noises
                    artillery shells' blasts
                            which
                            light
                            up
                            our
                            lives
if dance steps do not cross numberless mountains and rivers
    carrying with them the azure sky, the blue sea and the green fields,
                                        flying together
if colors do not scatter nature into
                riotous profusion
                lines do not draw
                    the course of the winds, the clouds and the birds

188

how much can human beings and the world see?
how much can human beings and the world hear?
how beautiful can human beings and the world become?

When human beings cannot leave their bodies
chickens are confined in their coops
birds are kept in their cages
how can we turn the sky into
        the ever-spreading remoteness?
how can we turn the remoteness into
        the ever-flying eternity?

Note:
In the world of art, a human being is not a sealed volume but a transparent work of architecture.
                    — The Poetics of Lomen

Speaking Geometrical Figures (2000)

Looking at it at first sight, it is a line
Looking at it at second sight, it is the horizon
Looking at it at third sight, it vibrates until it becomes the last string of the
                       universe in the boundlessness of space-time

It is a curve
which makes the rivers, the mountains, the sky, the waves' outlines
the beauties' waists, buttocks, breasts' outlines
and the routes of the winds, the clouds and the birds enter the curve

When it moves   it is a chessboard
When it stands still   it is a huge rock
I think perhaps the so-called upright and foursquare
                       are like this

When it is alive   it is a name card
            showing off all the way
After it dies   it is a coffin
           in total darkness

Triangular love   its angles are the points of the knives
If you want to reach the peak you must look upwards
                    to the tops of
         the mountains and the pyramids

The earth, eyes and silver dollars are all round in shape
They eventually roll to the silver dollars
Since the perfect circle in the hearts cannot be seen
the world rolls on the gambling wheel

Spiraling upwards   to the infinite pinnacle
           you will see Nietzsche
Spiraling to the ground   to the base of the infinite, profound mystery
           you will see Rilke
It is the most beautiful metaphysical blooming in space-time
It is also the spiral staircase to everything in the universe

Notes:
1) Nietzsche was a philosopher who tried to excel in the realm of abstract thinking.
2) Rilke was a great poet who not only thought philosophically but also turned and searched inward.

The Poets and Artists Who Carry the World and Eternity (2001)

Why do you walk alone in numerous mountains and rivers?
This is because the sky   becomes empty
                     the earth   goes far away
Only mountains and rivers are left behind
Unless you carry them with you
            walking toward somewhere deep inside the clouds and stop
                          You are still walking when you stop
         walking until it becomes another ever-flowing river
                          another ever walking mountain

Why do you look back?
      This is because the views passing the car windows disappear too fast
         Time and again the gesture of waving good-bye to the station
                              still holds a starting gun
The past   chases right after
The future   runs right ahead
You are   an ever-running road
            The present is walking with its front and back
            both legs stepping on the past and future
            both hands carrying the world and eternity

The Collected
Poems of **LOMEN**
: A Bilingual Edition

A Poetic Holiday (2001)
— A trip to Bali

The sea and the sky together are blue
After they are separated by the horizon
   they go back to blueness
Sea spray and beaches together are white
After they are separated by the horizontal line
    they go back to whiteness
Except for the white
  it is blue

Walking along the horizon
stillness is looking in the distance
distance is watching in the stillness
Except for stillness
  it is distance

Walking along the horizontal line
rows of waves call in the sea
rows of breasts answer on the shore
Except for up and down
  it is back and forth

The world is free to come
  is free to go
  and leaves the purest straight line to walk
  the most beautiful curve to follow
Except for bright sunshine and gentle breeze light and shadow of the waves
it is man and nature together on holiday

Note:
Recently, Rongzi and I visited Bali. We spent an afternoon lying on the beach,
watching the sea, looking at other tourists from all over the world. The scenery in Bali
is more beautiful than Hawaii's Waikiki, because the latter reminds us of the city. The
beach in Bali is closer to nature, and I will say it is the most beautiful beach I ever
saw. As a result, I have special feelings. I think sometimes our lives are as stressful
as the rock breaking waves; however, they occasionally should be as relaxed as the
drifting clouds. Most people spend their whole lives chopping checks and documents
in their offices; in fact, they should not forget to chop the beautiful scenery in the
world too.

Summer (2001)

Summer   pulls the grinder of the sun
                to grind the sky, the sea and the fields
                into a burning fireball
                rolling to and fro
                in nature

Unless it rains in the afternoon
it will not cool down and stop

In fact   although summer is also a firebird
                setting fire everywhere
when it folds its wings
and hides in the forest to drink green shade
and conceals itself in the mountains to sip cold spring water
and draws near to a wayside pavilion's willow color, lotus fragrance,
                        it takes an afternoon nap to enter the gorgeousness
The bird dreams of itself becoming a piece of pure ice
                                in nature's freezer
                                which
                                drifts
                                away
                                amid the cool breeze and sound of water

Using Film Shots to Write the Poem "Tranquility" (2001)

At the beginning, the camera lens is aimed at a summer day's afternoon sky. It stops there for a few seconds until the sky and the world completely enter a quiet and tranquil nap... .

Then, the lens is moved along the silent and invisible "vastness." It stops at the temple of the mountain top whose pagoda's pinnacle always destroys "tranquility." The lens keeps watching the boundless "emptiness" and stillness....

Then, the camera lens is moved to the temple and along its silent pillars, empty halls. It slips along a meditating monk's bald head which is emptier than the sky. Nothing is heard. Beating the wooden fish, let the sound of "vastness" bring the "lens" to the bottom of the valley. It focuses on the sounds of spring water dripping onto the wild, of tree shadows falling into "deep" sleep, of birds' cries emptying the whole mountain....

Then, the camera lens follows the pagoda's pinnacle which supports the sky and shines out. The lens moves slowly. It makes the clouds far away bloom and become loneliness and "tranquility" which reverberates impressively inside "beauty."

Postscript:
Thirty years ago (1971), I suggested using film shots to write poetry (film is pictorial poetry in a broad sense) in "Lan Xing" annual. I tried to turn two-dimensional and still pictorial poetry into a three-dimensional and dynamic one. If necessary, music could be added to enhance both the sight and sound effects. Will it be possible? I thought this basic concept could work because the film "7 ½" was then being shown in Taipei's cinemas. The film was made with poetic shots. In this case, can we think the other way round, which is to use film to write poetry? I remember at that time I had asked myself how to use film shots to write this poem "Tranquility."

A Collection of 2006's Postmodern Cartoons (2006)

1

O is zero
Starting from the number 1
which runs across east and west
reaching south and north
It weaves the meridians and parallels together
Coordinates and
the cross
the earth   human beings and God
   have not disappeared since then

O is the moving
            earth
            eyes
            wheels
1 is going straight ahead
            an avant-garde
               in the lead
And eternity then will not stop

2

The earth is a boat which cannot find a shore to lie at anchor
Fields and cities   human beings and God
                  are all on board
                  sailing from 1   to O
      The traveling cards, name cards and
                  addresses in our pockets
            are thrown away
Only "The Choral Symphony No. 9", "Grande Sonata Pathetique"
                              and a Bible
                  are left on board
During the trip
we watch TV channel 1
            when 1 is inserted into O
   all we can see is an erected
                  penis
                  gun
               flagstaff
                  and

noodle
gold bar
If you ask where the horizon,
which no one can ever grasp,
will lead human beings and the earth
I will say even God does not know

When we watch TV channel O
O swallows 1 up
In addition to the touchable round
breasts
buttocks
private parts
and
silver dollars
gold coins
The domes of ancient Rome and palaces
are only history's brassiere
No body will ever think of Wang Wei who travels along the gushing river
to make a perfect round beyond the universe

When we watch TV channel 10
1 is inserted into O
O swallows 1 up
The world is collapsing
People are still having a row
Street corners are still terribly noisy
Guns are still shouting in confusion
Churches' prayers
are as feeble as the panting inside an oxygen tent
Nothing can please the ears
Chang Hui-Mei casually purchases all ears
at a low price
transforming them into amplifiers and installs them everywhere
which makes the city crazy and screaming
When the whole world feels exhausted and snores at O o'clock
I would like to know who wakes up the past, the present and the future
at the national music hall
to listen to the majestic avalanche in Beethoven's music
to the running water and blooming flowers in Mozart's music
entering the gorgeous baroque green fields

When we watch channel N which is beyond all TV channels

```
our visions          are rebuilt by Mondrian
our field of vision      is sent to Kandinsky's eyes for dubbing
innocence                can be found in Brancusi
perfection               can be found in Henry Moore
absoluteness             can be found in Malevich
Returning to 1 and O   in MINIMAL
the world's installation space
       is watching in perfection
```

The magical PL*
both eyes are putting into the sea and sky
whose body becomes the earth under the sun
He makes the burning fire inside his body
       set fire on the iceberg
       freeze the river and turn it into metal
It turns out that Romanticism and Classicism are the same thermometer
which make fire, snow and clouds become as white as the White House
under transformation and transcendence

White is empty
I bring along with nothing
except the magical PL
I walk alone to the bottom of mountain
stepping on the field until it goes far away
Let the top of my head, the peaks of mountains and the roof of sky
   carry the world on our heads until they reach the remoteness
                         the height
When I look downward
an airplane is flying across a traffic jam corner
Everyone is in a hurry looking at their watches
Some watches are on the same road with trucks and rubbish collectors
Some watches are speeding
          Eternity is running
          Time cannot catch up
If the past is a home town
   memory is a beautiful backyard
   the future is a foreign country
      Dreams and imagination are scouting the road before us
   The present is a motel
      Everyone is getting by day by day
Whether the postmodern is hastily trodden by the city
                becoming shattered thin-ice like glass
                and let roads run blindly between the gaps

The Collected
Poems of LOMEN
: A Bilingual Edition

the answer is not important
if only the drifting stones which float on the ground
    still recognize the diamonds, gems and jades under ground
if only the drifting wood in the water
    still remembers the forest and green fields

The magical PL
his legs
  are the rails of a railroad
    which send and pick up the beginning and ending
    transporting countless mountains and waters
When he stops by the seaside
       it will become rivers
       rushing into the sea
He watches the tides of the sea
  When waves come, mountain becomes higher
  When waves go, sky becomes far away
The distant place is an ever-flying bird
Eyes cannot catch up with it   They look back from vastness
Tourists leave after picking up bunches of waves
    Numerous missing footprints remain on the beach
               waiting to be collected by the tides

After sun sets
he and the sea are still walking with their eyes closing
They walk until the place the mountains and the rivers end   there comes another
                                    village
It is the village of the universe which is outside the global village
Thousands of springs are building a garden there
         showing it to seasons and the year
A spiral tower which is higher than 101 and The Empire State Building
spirals up to the heaven from the third nature
      letting eternity climb up and down

Translators' Note:
The meaning of "PL" is not fully explained in the poem. We suggest that "PL" may
stand for Poet Lomen. However, we believe that the characters or "Poet Lomen"
embody symbolic meaning which are related to the state of religion or metaphysics.

Afterword
Lomen: The Man Who Dwells Poetically
Au chung - to

Before he is thrown into the world, Bachelard says, man is put in the cradle of the house (7). C. Norberg-Schulz adds that "when our social task is accomplished, however, we withdraw to our home to recover our personal identity. Personal identity, thus, is the content of private dwelling"(89). In other words, house or home is the center of an individual. When you are inside at home, you can resist the flood of changes outside. Norberg-Schulz further explains that "to live is to resist transience …. This does not imply that the course of time has to be stopped, rather it means that the moment is interpreted as a case of timeless." In the case of architecture, the style of buildings may change in time; however, "they change without losing their identity." This is simply because "the work always possesses the quality of image or figure"(30). Martin Heidegger points out that "poetry speaks in images"(30). In this situation, no matter whether architecture or man, in order to be timeless or to preserve one's identity, they must embody a poetic sense or "dwell poetically" (213-29). Among all Taiwan modernist poets, Lomen is one of the very few who can resist transience by means of poetry and his living space. I would like to argue that he realizes the modernist aesthetic theory of "spatialization of time" through his poetry and the way he dwells. In short, he dwells poetically in a timeless space.

All of Lomen's creative works — poetry, assemblage art and installation art — are related to his theory of the Third Nature Spiral Structure. Based on this theory, we can see that Lomen is highly sensitive to space, time and speed. I believe Lomen's early career helped to shape his theory. When Lomen was a teenager, he studied at the Air Force Pilot's Academy. After he went to Taiwan, he served in the Civil Aviation Bureau. The poet points out that the pace of our city life has become faster due to the invention of public transport. As a result, the quantity of time has seemed to increase, whereas space has seemed to contract (*A Lomen Reader* 93). The poet claims that these changes in time and space have resulted in a chaotic conception of time and space. In the modern world, temporal and eternal, past, present and future are always pressed close together. Consequently, modern people are especially indifferent to the conception of time and space (*A Lomen Reader* 80). Lomen further elaborates that in order to free themselves from a limited, suffocated, blockaded as well as gloomy reality and to make their spirits move around boundlessly, modern people naturally indulge themselves in a surrealistic and abstract world (*A Lomen Reader* 81).

However, Lomen surmises that it is not very easy for the spirit of an artist to sustain itself in a boundless and abstract world. As a result, after having escaped and wandered continuously, in order to fix the unstable and flowing self, the soul would look for something such as a rail, a handle or the dependable concretized world to hold tightly (*A Lomen Reader* 88). The above-mentioned ideas are vividly reflected in Lomen's theory of the "Third Nature Spiral Structure." The so-called "third nature"

refers to the internal world of the artists and poets. The major characteristic of this world are that poets and artists transcend the external world, the real world, such as the countryside or fields (the "first nature"), the cities (the "second nature"), and eventually the transcendent beauty of the third nature emerges.

The main concerns of Lomen's "third nature" theory are basically space and time. First of all, the space of "first nature" refers to the past; the space of "second nature" refers to the present. The "third nature" refers to the internal world, which has surrealist space and time. Since Lomen takes the element of time into account, when he uses a graph to express the "Third Nature Spiral Structure," the structure, instead of being motionless, moves around in a circle. Although the poet puts emphasis on objective time, I do not think that he considers time is more important than space. On the contrary, judging from his poetry and installation art, I believe that for Lomen proceeding from the "first nature" to the "second nature" is merely a transitional process. His ultimate goal is to enter the "third nature" — timeless space. In other words, Lomen's main concern is space instead of time.

In "360 Degree Multi-layered Space — On Lomen's Ideological Model," Lin Yaode points out accurately that the most important characteristic of Lomen's poetics is to concretize abstract thoughts with images and geometric figures (3). In fact, when Lomen explains his "Third Nature Spiral Structure," he uses the circle to symbolize the "first nature" — the space of the countryside — and uses the triangle, the square, and the rectangle to symbolize the "second nature" — the space of the city. Finally, he uses the pinnacle of a spiral structure to symbolize the "third nature" — the space of timelessness. Although Lomen's theory of "Third Nature Spiral Structure" was established in 1974, most of the elements of this structure such as the circle, triangle and the pinnacle of a spiral tower had already been mentioned in his early poetry. For example, in his poem "Light Is in Black Pajamas" which was written in 1958, Lomen already bestows unique symbolic meaning on the circle. As Lin Yaode points out, this short poem has only seven lines; however, five of them refer to or are associated with a circle, namely, "circular lampshade," "circular sky," "circular top hat," "spinning flower-patterned skirts" and "domed-shape graveyard." All these circular images are motionless and stable except the "spinning flower-patterned skirts." Images of light also can be found in the poem in five different places, but the light is always moving. In fact, certain images in this poem become significant in his "Third Nature Spiral Structure" theory later, for example, the circle, speed and light. Nevertheless, although the significance of these elements is obvious in the poem, the poet does not explain the reason why these images are important. I believe this is simply because Lomen's theory had yet to be matured at that time. As a result, he does not associate the motionless circle with the flowing light. In fact, the gap he leaves between the circle and the light images in each line of the poem reflect this problem clearly:

Under the violet circular lampshade	Light is flowing
Under the azure circular sky	Light is flowing
Under Churchhill's circular top hat	Light is flowing

The development of the "Third Nature Spiral Theory" was not completed until 1960, when a detailed idea of the theory was reflected in the poem "The Undercurrent of the Ninth Day":

> When the phono stylus draws a spiral tower
> all buildings vanish from sight
>
> ... ...
>
> My mood is as beautiful as an exquisite fabric entering your transparence
> Which is as silent as snow scenery flashing in winter time

Here Lomen uses four lines to show us the most significant elements of his "Third Nature Spiral Structure": the circle (the stylus touches the record, which is circular in shape), the spiral tower and the pinnacle of the tower. Although the elements of Lomen's theory were developed in the sixties, the metaphorical meanings of each image were only explained in detail by Lomen's later theoretical and poetical works. The rest of this Afterword will discuss these three images in turn.

According to Lomen, the circle as the base of the spiral structure is, on the one hand, always associated with certain positive feelings such as forgiveness, harmony, stability and roundness; on the other hand, the circle also reminds us of certain negative qualities such as conservativism, lack of action and lack of creativity. Since the circle is two-dimensional instead of three-dimensional, it inevitably loses depth in the creative world. The poet concludes that the cultural characteristics of a so-called "circular society" are: the continual entanglement of right and wrong, hypocrisy, lagging behind and procrastination (*Self. Time-Space. Death Poetry* 43-4). Although Lomen does not state that the circle and "first nature" are directly related in his theoretical works, Lin Yaode remarks that in an agriculture society everything is in a circular structure of the seasons, growth and decline, and the ups and downs in history are also similar to a circle, which goes around to begin again (22). As a matter of fact, the close relationship between the circle and the "first nature" is expressed in Lomen's poetry as well. As mentioned above, "first nature" refers to things related to nature. For instance, poems such as "Sea," "Grand Canyon Sonata," and "Watching the Sea" are all about nature, or, in Lomen's words, are about the "first nature," though they do not contain images of the circle. If we examine these poems in detail, we will see that they are all about the relationship between the "first nature" and the "third nature." In other words, they are about the relationship between two kind of images, the base of the spiral tower and the pinnacle of the spiral tower, which represent two kind of space. For example, at the beginning of the poem "Sea," the poet points out that through the assistance of music and nature (piano notes and the sea) he reaches timeless space — "third nature" ("go into ... that transparent vastness"). Similarly, in another poem "Watching the Sea," the poet personifies the sea as a drinker: "After finishing the last drop of the rivers/You get drunk and become the stormy sky." However, when "the sound of music" is heard, "the most beautiful and durable thing/ is not the views/but the immortal emptiness/which blossoms on your forehead." "Immortal emptiness" here refers to "the light of the pinnacle" and, after one reaches the pinnacle, "all doors and windows open for you."

If we compare the poems "Sea," "Watching the Sea" with "Grand Canyon Sonata," we find that the latter vividly shows the direct relationship between "circle,"

"first nature" and the "Third Nature Spiral Structure":

> Going down along the depth
> following the slope and coming up
> Grand Canyon, your vertical line of vision
> Joins together with the earth's axis
> Your bottom bumps into the earth
> Your top touches the sky
> As long as you go around with the earth
> Numberless changing round faces
> start to whirl until they become a ceaseless spiral tower
> in vertical and horizontal directions of space-time
> All eyes rest on the tower
> > looking at the process of eternity
> > and heading for it

In these lines of "Grand Canyon Sonata," first of all, Lomen compares the eyesight which measures the Grand canyon to the earth's axis. Then the poet imagines that the "vertical line of vision" follows the axis of the earth. While the earth rotates on its axis, the imaginary line becomes a spiral tower. And the pinnacle of the tower is the eternal space of "third nature."

Having examined these three poems, we can conclude that Lomen's nature poetry does not merely depict natural scenery. The poet always uses "first nature" as an agent to enter the "third nature." Among all of Lomen's poetry, nature poems represent only a small portion, and most of them are related to the "second nature," which refers to the tower of the "Third Nature Spiral Structure."

As I pointed out before the tower in Lomen's "Third Nature Spiral Structure" moves continuously in a circle instead of being motionless. The reason why the tower is moving is that society changes from the "first nature" (countryside or agricultural) production mode to the "second nature" (city or industrial) production mode. And this process of transformation is reflected through the rotating tower. Lomen compares the "second nature" with a triangle. According to the poet, the acute angles of the triangle remind us of fighting spirit and vigor. In addition, the triangle is also associated with characteristics such as insisting on making new and important discoveries, progressiveness, creativity, everlasting change and absolute upward spirit. On the one hand, these characteristics are a valuable motivation of life; on the other hand, they may result in confrontations, being off balance, nihilism, indifference, tension, anxiety and the situation of a tragic existence (*A Lomen Reader* 122-3). Based on Lomen's analyses of the triangle, we will find that most of his poems embody these characteristics, for example, the many poems dealing with the subject of war.

When society changes its production mode from agricultural to industrial, this change always results in an excess of production. In order to get rid of the excess, it is necessary to open up new markets. And war is a means to this end. Among all of Lomen's war poems, "Fort McKinly" is the most famous. This poem won The Poet Laureate International Award in 1967. Although "Fort McKinly" is a poem about war, the poet does not describe war directly. Lomen depicts the cruelty of war indirectly through imagining the space in which the soldiers were killed. The poet imagines that the fallen, seventy thousands in total, enter a "silent" and "blackest" space. As Lomen tells the fallen: "You can go nowhere/There is no door on the seabed of the ghastly Pacific Ocean." In fact, "Fort McKinly" is Lomen's purest war poem. It concentrates on depicting the disasters of war, unlike Lomen's other war poems, which involve the countryside, nature or the city. For instance, Lomen wrote another poem about Fort McKinly in 1990: "Lying in a Pool of Blood Everlasting — Fort McKinly." While paying a visit to the fallen, the poet laments that the products of modern urban culture such as "the modern girl" and "red wine" make people forget these brave soldiers:

> When the planes and liners carry vacations continuously
> > through the Pacific Ocean
> Does anyone ever ask you, who are at the bottom of the sea?
> > > when will you go on duty?
> > > > (*War Poetry* 47)

In another war poem "Panmunjom, 38 Degrees," Lomen complains about the considerable harm which has been done to nature by wars:

> Birds fly   the sky escapes
> Wind blows   trees flee
> If you stand there and do not run away
> lines of gun shots will come over
> > > from silence
> vomiting smoke lightly
> The distant clouds   are echoes and turn into the roar of guns
> The sky is covered by the wings of aircraft
> Forests are lined with guns
> Fallen leaves are scattered by shoes
> Valleys are dug by wounds
> Mountain slopes are undulating tanks
> Mountains are piled up bodies
> The starry night is studded with bullets and eyes
> > When the moon rises   blood sheds tears
> When the sun rises   blood flows

In another anti-war poem, "The Space-Time Sonata," Lomen points out the relationship between countryside and city. In addition to this, there is also a sense of nostalgia:

> Under the buildings' giant shadows
> he sits until under a great banyan tree, his childhood returns
> ......
> a spasm of fear
> the whole earth falls into blood

Besides war poetry, Lomen also writes many poems about the city. The industrial revolution, on the one hand, has caused wars indirectly; on the other hand, it has directly resulted in changes of production and living modes. Due to the progress

of technology, it is no longer necessary for human beings to dwell close to natural resources, because they can use technology to create an artificial living environment. The intensity of commercial activities has resulted in people settling in cities. Urban poetry reflects life in cities. The most significant difference between the farming production mode and the industrial production mode is the tempo of living, which is accelerated in cities. This is the reason why the "Third Nature Spiral Structure" must be rotating, because when the "first nature" proceeds to the "second nature," the speed of living changes. This characteristic is also reflected in Lomen's poetry. For example, the poet points out at the beginning of his poem "Death of a City" that the tempo of living in cities controls people completely and makes them become soulless:

> It is like the running cars clinging to the roads at high speed
> people seize their own shadows rushing off
> > to look inside the changes which are too rapid to understand
> > to think inside the cyclotron which is too rapid to understand
> > to perish inside the death which is too rapid to die
> Speed controls the circuits   God cannot grasp the megaphone

According to the poet, there are two different kind of reactions when people face changes of living tempo. For instance, Lomen writes in "Lunch Hour at McDonald's" that the younger generation finds no problem in adapting to the faster living tempo, they "sit together / with the whole city …… The knives and forks in their hands / which are faster than the cars, / passing by: / a charming and handsome / afternoon." However, the older generation finds it hard to adapt to this new environment:

> An old man
> sits in the corner
> wearing a wrong size
> > ready-made suit
> finishing a not-to-his-taste
> > hamburger

As a matter of fact, Lomen's city poems can be divided into two categories. The first includes poems about the dark sides of city life. The second contains poems which are about people who are not able to adapt to the fast living tempo. The first category can be further divided into two kinds. One kind of poems such as "Café," "Mini-skirt," "Bank," "Robbery and Rape," "Karaoke" and so forth, directly describes the darker aspects of city dwellers such as materialism and sensuality. However, another group of the negative city poems, for example, "Motorcycle," puts emphasis on the relationship between countryside and city. Most of these poems are about how the development of city endangers the ecological balance of nature.

This second category — those dealing with people not able to adapt to the accelerated pace of urban life — represents quite a large portion of Lomen's city poems. Most of them describe the loneliness, homelessness and desperation of modern people. "Window" and "A Vagabond" are the best examples. The poet does not depict any city scenery in "Window." At the beginning of the poem, the poet points out that he is attracted to the natural scenery outside the window, which reminds him of his past. Lomen uses nine lines to tell us how much he misses and how deep he loves his past. This makes one curious to know what is inside the window? What happens to the poet now? He only uses the last two lines to satisfy our curiosity: Human beings suffer from lack of freedom, for we are locked up by transparent shackles. "I fling it open but I am locked in an inescapable / transparency." In his poem "Window," although Lomen does not tell us what causes the predicament and only uses the word "transparency" to explain, he shows us clearly in his other poems that the culprit is city life and modern civilization.

Compared to "Window," "A Vagabond" seems to be more concrete. The poem at least has two possible interpretations. One regards the vagabond as an individual, who is a loser in life. Since he is homeless, he has to wander around. Another possible interpretation considers the vagabond as an archetype of modern people in general. According to Lomen, modern people lack spiritual lives; they do not have any religion. This idea can be represented by a vagabond, because he wanders from one place to another endlessly and has no place to settle down. As Lomen points out in his poem, nothing can hold a vagabond in place: The vagabond "uses the lamp to bring his own shadow to heel." The metaphor Lomen chooses vividly reflects that the vagabond must wander around everlastingly, for it is impossible to tie anything up by a lamp. Moreover, it is also useless to attempt to leash a person's shadow.

In addition to the predicament caused by war and city life, human beings also inevitably have to face death, and this has nothing to do with living or production modes. According to Lomen, a human being's death is like the collapses of the spiral tower which is drawn by the stylus of the record player. The poet writes in "The Tower of Death":

Everybody is destined to be a phonograph record which must end
It is as strange as a tower whirling by a whirlpool
which collapses when the circular current becomes still

Based on the above analyses, we can see that the poems which belong to the second nature such as war poetry, city poetry and death poetry are comparatively negative and despairing. As a result, the poet believes that in order to transcend time and space, life and death, we have to enter the top of the spiral tower, which is timelessness.

As early as 1960, Lomen had already developed a completed structure of the spiral tower in his poem "The Undercurrent of the Ninth Day." The most important elements are the circle, spiral tower and the space on the top of the tower. In fact, the space on the top of the tower refers to the space, which is above of all human activities and architecture. Some of the characteristics of this space are transparency and brightness. These characteristics can be found in poems such as "The Love of Spiral," "The Feelings of 'Light House'" and "The Place Where the Light Dwells." However, compared to these poems, only "An Everlasting Road" vividly depicts the relationship among the "first nature," the "second nature," the "third nature" as well as the space on the top of the tower. At the beginning of this poem, the poet uses two lines to describe the two-dimensional circle or the "first nature": "Sky and earth/ embrace the soft and smooth circle, walking." Lomen then uses twenty lines to tell us

the seamy sides of the "second nature" or city: "City and skyscraper/embrace the icy squares, walking." Next, the poet discusses social unrest from different aspects such as "parliament," "mall," "battlefield," "slaughterhouse" and so forth. The rest of the poem is about how the poet transcends the chaotic world and enters the "third nature" or the eternal space through Beethoven's music:

> If it were not for Beethoven's music
> passing through the noises of wind, rain, market and people
> coming over
> tuning up the music
> having time recovered its original tempo
> space recovered its original order
> years would not be able to walk properly
> to speak properly

> (*Self. Time-Space. Death Poetry* 63)

Lomen's "Third Nature Spiral Structure" shows us how the poet passes through the eternal worlds of "first nature" and "second nature" to enter the internal world, which is the "third nature." In fact, putting stress on the internal world is a major characteristic of modernist poets and artists. As Lomen points out, due to the chaotic situation of the real world, modern poets naturally indulge themselves in surrealist and abstract world. However, the poet also realizes that dwelling in the unstable, internal and abstract world over a long period of time is very exhausting. As a result, modernist poets or artists must hold something, for example, a club, tightly. In fact, quite a lot of modernist Taiwanese poets realize this problem and most of them switch their focus from the internal space to the external space, namely, the realistic space of the island of Taiwan. Lomen, by contrast, chooses to externalize his inner space and to dwell in his poetic space. The poet applies the theory of his "Third Nature Spiral Structure" to his living space, his home — the House of Light. In the preface of his poem "The Love of Spiral," Lomen states that "In the House of Light, a record player plays and makes spiral tree rings. Music spins and turns into a spiral spiritual world." Although Lomen's home is located in the center of Taipei, he thinks that the House of Light isolates him from the real world. This is simply because his house is the externalization and realization of his poetic space – the third nature:

> The tightly closed doors and windows   express a steadfast refusal
> The drawn curtain   completes the tranquil isolation
> Outside is like the wind which disappears far away
> Inside is like the waves going ashore
> touching after the completed isolation
> Inside is like a ringing bell suddenly born in the air   the lightening of
> electricity

> This is the purest space

In addition, the different pieces of installation art made by Lomen inside the House of Light also bear symbolic meanings. In his essay "The House of Light and I," Lomen states that the reason why he made his first installation art work — the

"House of Light" — is because of his marriage with the poetess Rongzi. On the day of their wedding, Lomen noticed that "the cross on the top of the church looked bright and shiny, which reminded us of a light house. We were like a sailing boat entering a harbor" (*Light House. Sketch of Life* 86). Lomen further elaborates that "a light house is located in the harbor, which guides the homeward bound ships back to the harbor." The first lamp Lomen made actually "symbolizes a light house. Its warm light shines on the living course of the two of us [Lomen and Rongzi]" (86). In other words, in addition to its functions in real life, to provide a living place for the two poets to work and to rest, the House of Light also protects them from the tyranny of time and the chaotic world.

After having observed Lomen's nature poetry and city poetry, we can see that they share one thing in common: they are not direct copies of the real world. In other words, the country scenes and cities depicted in his poems cannot be found in the real world. For example, Lomen seldom writes about nature objectively. All his description of nature scenery are based on his subjective impressions. In fact, Lomen highly praises Liu Zongyuan's line "Fishing ice in frozen water alone." According to Lomen, the best part of this line is that it does not depict nature directly. When Liu writes this line, he puts his subjective feelings into the expression. As a result, the line attains a lofty realm of thought. On the contrary, if Liu copied the real world directly and wrote "Fishing fish in frozen water alone," the line would immediately become insipid (*A Lomen Reader* 25). Since Lomen puts stress on subjective feelings, his nature poetry seldom depicts the actual natural world directly.

Although the social darkness reflected in Lomen's city poetry can mostly be found in the real world, the cities involved still cannot be considered real cities. This is because when Lomen wrote "City Dweller" in 1957 and "Death of a City" in 1961, Taiwan was only an agricultural society. In 1945, 75 percent of the Taiwan population was agriculturalist; not until forty years later did 70 percent of the population become urban (Harrell 170-2). Lin Yaode points out directly that at the end of fifties, "while the economy of Taiwan was still agriculture orientated, Lomen's works had already stepped towards industrial civilization." Lin remarks that Lomen's early city poetry is "the fable of city" (22). It is interesting to note that when Taipei had developed into a big city in the eighties, Lomen seems to have been not interested in criticizing the darkness of the city anymore. Even though there are some city poems, their themes are more or less the same as the old ones. In short, I believe that most of Lomen's poetry, including both his nature poetry and urban poetry, does not depict realistic space; these poems are about an imagined or poetic space instead. Needless to say, the internal world of the "third nature" belongs to the realm of imaginary space.

Compared to the other spaces, The House of Light is quite unique. Although the House of Light actually exists in the real world, its symbolic meaning also makes it belong to the imaginary space. In fact, if we apply Bachelard's theory to the analysis of Lomen's "Third Nature Spiral Structure," we will see that the House of Light is the most important element for Lomen to nurture his imaginary space or homeland. According to Bachelard, "the house shelters daydreaming, the house protects the dreamer, the house allows one to dream in peace" (6). Furthermore, "the house is one of the greatest powers of integration for the

thoughts, memories and dreams of mankind... . Without it, man would be a dispersed being. It maintains him through the storms of the heavens and through those of life" (7). In conclusion, since Lomen dwells in his House of Light literally as well as poetically, he is protected from the storms of life and lives in a timeless or imaginary world.

---

1 What I want to point out here is that the major dwelling space changes from the countryside of the past to cities of the present.

2 What I mean by "objective time" here is a reference to the evolutionary process of a society. Due to the changes of the production mode, most developed countries have changed from an agricultural society to an industrial society.

3 What I mean by "religion" here is not religion in a general sense, instead I refer to religion as a goal and ideal.

Work Cited

Bachelard, Gaston. *The Poetics of Space*. Boston: Beacon Press, 1994.

Harrell, Stevan. "Playing in the Valley: A Metonym of Modernization in Taiwan." In *Cultural Change in Postwar Taiwan*, eds. Stevan Harrell and Chun-Chieh Huang. New York: Westview press, 1994.

Heidegger, Martin. *Poetry, Language, Thought*. Trans. Albert Hofstadter. New York: Harper & Row, Publishers, Inc., 1971.

林耀德。羅門論 [*On Lomen*]。台北：師大書苑有限公司，1990。

羅門。《羅門論文集》[*A Lomen Reader*]。台北：文史哲出版社，1995。

羅門。《羅門創作大系：戰爭詩 〈卷一〉》[*War Poetry*]。台北：文史哲出版社，1995。

羅門。《羅門創作大系：自我 • 時空 • 死亡詩 〈卷四〉》[*Self • Time-Space. • Death Poetry*]。台北：文史哲出版社，1995。

羅門。《羅門創作大系：燈屋 • 生活剪影〈卷十〉》[*Light House. Sketch of Life*]。台北：文史哲出版社，1995。

Norberg-Schulz, Christian. *The Concept of Dwelling: On the Way to Figurative Architecture*. New York: Rizzoli International Publications, Inc., 1985.

I

麥堅利堡

『超過偉大的
　是人類對偉大已感到茫然』

戰爭坐在此哭誰
它的笑聲　曾使七萬個靈魂陷落在比睡眠還深的地帶

太陽已冷　星月已冷　太平洋的浪被炮火煮開也都冷了
史密斯　威廉斯
　　　煙花節　光榮伸不出手來接你們回家
你們的名字運回故鄉　比入冬的海水還冷
在死亡的喧噪裡　你們的無救　上帝的手呢
血已把偉大的紀念沖洗了出來
戰爭都哭了　偉大它為什麼不笑
七萬朵十字花　圍成園　排成林　繞成百合的村
在風中不動　在雨裏也不動
沉默給馬尼拉海灣看　蒼白給遊客們的照相機看
史密斯　威廉斯　在死亡紊亂的鏡面上　我只想知道
　　　　那裏是你們童幼時眼睛常去玩的地方
　　　　　　那地方藏有春日的錄音帶與彩色的幻燈片

麥堅利堡　鳥都不叫了　樹葉也怕動
凡是聲音都會使這裏的靜默受擊出血
空間與空間絕緣　時間逃離鐘錶
這裏比灰暗的天地線還少說話　永恆無聲
美麗的無音房　死者的花園　活人的風景區
神來過　敬仰來過　汽車與都市也都來過
而史密斯　威廉斯　你們是不來也不去了
靜止如取下擺心的錶面　看不清歲月的臉
在日光的夜裏　星滅的晚上
你們的盲睛不分季節地睡著
睡醒了一個死不透的世界
睡熟了麥堅利堡綠得格外憂鬱的草場

死神將聖品擠滿在嘶喊的大理石上
給昇滿的星條旗看　給不朽看　給雲看
麥堅利堡是浪花已塑成碑林的陸上太平洋
一幅悲天泣地的大浮彫　掛入死亡最黑的背景
七萬個故事焚毀於白色不安的顫慄
史密斯　威廉斯　當落日燒紅滿野芒果林於昏暮
神都將急急離去　星也落盡
你們是那裏也不去了
太平洋陰森的海底是沒有門的

一九六七年

茶　意

『茶！你靠鄉愁最近』

下午太陽無力地
　　斜靠著天
疲累的頭一個個
　　垂倒在椅背上
夕照與目光一同沉向
　　微暗的水平線
整個視野靜入那杯茶中
　　　歲月睡在裏邊
　　　血淚睡在裏邊
　　　心也睡在裏邊
烟從嘴裏抽出一把劍
　　無意中刺傷了遠方
　　　一聲驚叫
沉在杯底的茶葉全都醒成彈片
如果那是片片花開　春該回
　　　　　　家園也該在
而沉不下去的那一葉
　　竟是滴血的秋海棠
在夢裏也要帶著河回去

　　　　　　　　一九七五年

板門店‧三八度線

一

一把刀
從鳥的兩翅之間通過
天空裂開兩邊
十八面彩色旗
貼成一排膠布
這個疤該不該算到上帝的臉上去
這個疤　若再裂
火山口噴出的火
　　會不會是壯麗的血

二

養傷的土地
住在傷口裏
上帝太遠不能來看它
連田園與牲口也不來看它
一個美國兵守它
　　　　　　守了三十六個月
回國後　也不再來看它

它躺在傷口裏
那裏也不能去
所有的門窗都是槍口開的
　　　　　　此刻都關上

三

它能到那裏去
那座有橋頭無橋尾
　　有橋尾無橋頭的橋①

―――――――――――――――――――――――――
①：板門店38度線，有一座分界的橋，稱「不歸路」，過了橋便回不來。

連路都找不到自己
上帝　祢走走看

殘廢的曠野
　　　拉住瞎了的天空
一個不能動　一個不能看
它能到那裏去
天地線是緊縮在腳上的
　　　一條沈重的鐵鍊
鳥飛　天空逃
風吹　樹木跑
誰要是站在那裏不走
槍聲會從寂靜中
　一排排過來
輕輕吐一口煙
遠處的雲　全都迴響成炮聲
天空是機翼蓋的
樹林是槍支排的
飄葉是鞋子散落的
山谷是傷口挖的
山坡是坦克起伏的
山是屍體堆成的
星夜是彈頭與眼珠綴成的
　　　月亮一出來　便流淚
　　　太陽一出來　便淌血

四

炮火是什麼顏色
血也是什麼顏色
玫瑰與酒是什麼顏色
唇也是什麼顏色
當玉腿與摩天樓
　一同昇起天國的支柱
叫那些屍骨去埋成那一種鋼架

難道那張小小的會議桌
　會有兩個半球那麼重
　　坐著兩排戰車
　　　兩排炮
　　　兩排槍
　　　兩排刺刀
　　　兩排血
　　　兩排淚
　　　兩排望不在一起的眼睛
　　　兩排握不在一起的手
　　　兩排幫忙工作的雪茄
　　　　它究竟是飄然過橋的雲
　　　　還是炮管冒出的煙

五

會議桌上的那條線
既不是小孩子跳過來跳過去的那根繩子
便是堵住傷口的一把刀
拔掉　血往外面流
不拔掉　血在裏面流
誰會去想那個在受刑的生命
　推在火中　垂下頭
　潑在水中　仍垂下頭
誰會去想鐵絲網是血管編的
　編與拆都要拉斷血管
誰會去想在炸彈開花的花園裏
　嬰孩是飛翔的蝴蝶
　修女是開得最白的百合
　上帝就一直抓不住那雙採摘與捕捉的手
誰又會去想在一條越走越遠的路上
　一個棄槍的警長與一個棄刀的暴徒
　　被一個沒有鑰匙的手銬
　　　　　扣在一起走

六

走到那橋頭
山窮水也窮
山盡水也盡
峯迴路也轉
當我們離橋而去
所有出走的眼睛
　　都從瞎了的天空裏望出來
一緊張　不敢握別的手
　　　　　一直放在口袋裏
　　　　　不敢去看的眼睛
　　　　　一直藏在凝視中

在用不著開槍的幾公尺裏
幾個沒頭沒腦的北韓士兵
　　　　　不知為什麼傻笑了過來
上帝祢猜猜看
　　　它是從深夜裡擲過來的一枚照明彈
　　　還是閃過停屍間的一線光

　　　　　　　　　　　　　　一九七六年

月　思

深夜
月亮把一塊光
縫貼在地毯上
母親仍為我過年的新衣
　在老家的燈下
　趕縫著最後的一個口袋

我走近窗前
身上那個口袋
竟就是那塊月光
手摸袋裏的壓歲錢
才發覺那枚發亮的銀圓
　　　是千里外的月
母親　我如何去拿呢
妳的手在那麼多舉起的槍枝中
　　　　又永遠的縮了回去
妳走後　誰也沒有告訴我
妳的臉與妳給我壓歲的銀圓
　　　仍一直寄存在月裏

註：離家三十多年，只知道母親在家鄉去世了，但不知道她是在那一陣
　　槍聲中離去的。

一九八一年

時空奏鳴曲
—— 遙望廣九鐵路

一　只能跳兩跳的三級跳

整個世界
停止呼吸
　　在起跑線上

車還沒有來
眼睛已先跑
跳過第一第二座山
到了第三座
懸空下不來 ①
往前　茫茫雲天
回頭　九龍已坐車
　　　　　竄入邊境

將我望回臺北市
　　泰順街的窗口

二　望了三十多年

那個賣花盆的老人
仍在街口望著老家的

---

① 第三座山因罩著大陸的「鐵絲網」。

花與土

玻璃大廈沿街
　開著一排排
　亮麗的鄉愁
在建築物龐大的陰影下
他坐來大榕樹下的童年
一輛日本進口的野狼牌機車
以武士刀尖銳的速度
從和平東路直刺入
　　　　和平西路
穿過記憶
一陣驚慌
整塊土地倒在血泊裏
較潑墨還迷濛的山水
不就是他愁苦的淚眼
望著彈痕從身上
　奔過來的江河
　　　風寒水冷
　　　葉落枝垂
在機槍架起的高速公路上
　　　炮彈跨空的天橋上
每個方向都哭過
天堂的出入口
一直是久未痊癒的傷口
望著自己三十多年來
仍一直望著的眼睛
他疲累的視線
只能把黃昏田裡那頭老牛
　　　　　　拖回家
已牽不動日漸繁華的街景
一輛西式嬰兒車
推著新的歲月經過
一排高樓聳立在
　打樁的巨響裏

他從炸彈聲中醒來
仍看見那個抓不到乳瓶的棄嬰
　　　　坐在彈片散落的廢墟上②
整座天空在煙火中
　　　　藍不出來
當藍哥兒們將整條街
　　　　　　藍過來
一群人走進禮拜堂
　　　　　去看聖母
一群人湧進百貨公司
　　　　　去看歲月
他已想不到那麼多
見到羅馬磁磚
　　便問石板路
見到香吉士
　　便問井水
見到新上市的時裝
　　便問母親在風雨中老去的臉

滿街汽笛
響來鳥聲與口哨
他好想飛想跳
幾十個東張西望的花盆
　　　　　　　朝著天空
要他一起坐下來

坐到天黑
他行動不便的雙腿
才交給那隻洗腳盆
　　帶回童時愛玩水的
　　　　　小池塘裏
一高興　濺在臉上的小水珠
　　　　　　　都笑成淚
　淚是星星

---

② 戰地記者名攝影家王小亭，以拍攝炸後廢墟上的棄嬰，這張照，獲國際名攝影獎。

家鄉的星空
便亮到電視機的螢光幕上
　　　　　　　　來看他

群星閃動時
怎會是一群歌星
地球朝炸彈的反方向滾
鳳姊姊的鳳眼
　是沿著豪華大飯店
　　十多層高的樓房
　　一直笑下來的鑽石燈
他的雙目是暗在牆角裏的
　　　　　　　菜油燈

臨睡前
　年輕人拿出００７裏的建築圖
　　　　　　　　看看明天
　　　　　用電腦算算明天
夜總是要他坐在記憶的傷口裏
　去看儲存在存摺與日曆牌上
　　　　　那越來越少的歲月
從沒有聽過一聲文學性的晚安
　　　　便抱著那張單人牀睡去

睡到有一天醒不來
太陽仍會起來
鐘錶停了
路自己也會走
至於槍聲還會不會響
安全理事會還要不要開
到時候報紙會說
只要地球還在
白晝與黑夜還在
白色的乳粉與黑色的彈藥
　　　　　　都會在

三　穿過上帝瞳孔的一條線

這條線
從板門店
繞東西德走廊
來到這裏
較雲去的地方遠
卻比腳與泥土近

這條線
只要眼睛
碰它一下
天空都要回家
這條線望入水平線時
連上帝也會想家

是誰丟這條線
　　　　在地上
沿著它
母親　妳握縫衣針的手呢
還有我斷落在風箏裏的童年
母親　如果這條線
已縫好土地的傷口
我早坐上剛開出的那班車
　沿著妳額上痛苦的紋路
　　　回到沒有槍聲的日子
　　　　　　　去看妳

如果這條線
　是一筆描
動便長江萬里
靜便萬里長城
那些凍結在記憶與冰箱裏的
　　　　　　　冰山冰水
都流回大山大水

把鐵絲網與彈片全沖掉
祖國　你便泳著江南的陽光來
　　　　　　滑著北地的雪原去
然後　打開綠野的大茶桌
　　　　捧著藍天的大瓷壺
　　　　不在那小小的茶藝館裏
從「黃河入海流」
飲到「孤帆遠影碧空盡」
從「月湧大江流」
飲到「野渡無人舟自橫」
讓從巴黎倫敦與紐約
　　　　　進來的照相機
都裝滿第一流的山水與文化回去
讓唐朝再回來說
那是開得最久最美的
　　　　　　　一朵東方

祖國　當六天勞累的都市
　　　　已想到週日郊外的風景
鳥便在天空裏對飛機說
巍然的帝國大廈
　永遠高不過你
　　悠然的南山
任使一張張太空椅
　　　　往太空裏放
祖國　你仍是放在地球上
　　　　最大的那張安樂椅
只要歲月坐進來
打開唐詩宋詞
沒有槍聲來吵
世界便遠到
　山色有無中
太空船真不知要開多久
　　　　　　才能到了

到不了
只好往心裏望
多望幾眼
怎麼又望回這條線上來
原來是開入邊境的火車
又把一車箱一車箱的鄉愁
　　　　　　運回來

車走後
連土地都忘了
在那裏上下車
整條鐵軌
鞭過天空
聲聲迴響
　陣陣痛

　　　　　　　　　　　　　一九八四年八月

歲月的琴聲
—— 聽名胡琴家黃安源演奏有感

你的弓
動開來
是頭也不回地流去的
　　　　長江與黃河
你胡琴上的兩根弦
是河的兩岸
也是中國人歲月的雙軌
　運不完的憂患與苦憶

每一拉
都可看到土地與同胞身上
　　　劃過的刀痕與彈痕
每一頓挫
都是千慨萬嘆
快弓　急來兵荒馬亂
慢弓　痛苦都感到累了

將血與山色
　淚與江水
　拉在一起
春天如何戴花回江南
冬日如何披雪回江北
歲月是哭是笑
琴聲也說不清
而文化仍以輝煌
　山河仍以錦繡
直等著回音
臺上　琴聲淌淚叫著家
臺下　黑髮望白髮

附記：聽黃安源先生表演其中的某些樂曲，覺得他的弓，一直不放的壓
　　　在中國人苦難的心靈、歲月與土地上。

一九八七年五月

227

世界性的政治遊戲

「他」用左眼擊打他的右眼
　　　　　出淚
他用右眼擊打「他」的左眼
　　　　　出淚
「他」用左心房擊打他的右心房
　　　　　　出血
他用右心房擊打「他」的左心房
　　　　　　出血
於是無數的「他」與他
　　　左右眼都流淚
　　　左右心房都流血
結果「他」與他
　　　同是一個人

　　　　　　　　　　　一九八八年

II

都市之死

都市你造起來的
快要高過上帝的天國了

一

建築物的層次　托住人們的仰視
食物店的陳列　紋刻人們的胃壁
櫥窗閃著季節伶俐的眼色
人們用紙幣選購歲月的容貌
在這裏　腳步是不載運靈魂的
在這裏　神父以聖經遮目睡去
　　　　凡是禁地都成為市集
　　　　凡是眼睛都成為藍空裏的鷹目
如行車抓住馬路急馳
人們抓住自己的影子急行
　　　在來不及看的變動裏看
　　　在來不及想的迴旋裏想
　　　在來不及死的時刻裏死

速度控制著線路　神抓不到話筒
這是忙季　在按鈕與開關之間
都市　你織的網密得使呼吸停止
在車站招喊著旅途的焦急裏
在車胎孕滿道路的疲憊裏
一切不帶阻力地滑下斜坡　衝向末站
誰也不知道太陽在那一天會死去
人們伏在重疊的底片上　再也叫不出自己
　　　　　　　　　　看不見眼睛
沒有事物不回到風裏去
　　　如酒宴亡命於一條抹布
　　　　假期死在靜上的輪下

二

禮拜日　人們經過六天逃亡回來
心靈之屋　經牧師打掃過後
次日　又去聞女人肌膚上的玫瑰香
　　　去看銀行窗口蹲著七個太陽
坐著　站著　走著
　　　都似浪在風裏
煙草撐住日子　酒液浮起歲月
伊甸園是從不設門的
在尼龍墊上　軟鋪或硬鋪上
文明是那條脫下的花腰帶
美麗的獸　便野成裸開的荒野
到了明天　再回到衣服裏去
　　　　　回到修飾的毛髮與嘴臉裏去
而腰下世界　總是自靜夜升起的一輪月
　　　　　　　一光潔的象牙櫃臺
　　　　　　　　唯有幻滅能兌換希望

都市　掛在你頸項間終日喧叫的十字街
那神是不信神的　那神較海還不安
教堂的尖頂　吸進滿天寧靜的藍
　　　　　　　卻注射不入你玫瑰色的血管
十字架便只好用來閃爍那半露的胸脯
那半露的胸脯　裸如月光散步的方場
　聳立著埃爾佛的鐵塔
　　　守著巴黎的夜色　守著霧　守著用腰祈禱的天國

三

在攪亂的水池邊注視
搖晃的影子是抓不住天空的雲
急著將鏡擊碎　也取不出對象
都市　在你左右不定的擺動裏

　　　　所有的拉環都是斷的
　　　　所有的手都垂成風中的斷枝
　　　有一種聲音總是在破玻璃的裂縫裡逃亡
　　人們慌忙用影子播種　在天花板上收回自己
　　去追春天　花季已過
　　去觀潮水　風浪俱息
　　生命是去年的雪　婦人鏡盒裡的落英
　　死亡站在老太陽的座車上
　　　　　向響或不響的　默呼
　　　　　向醒或不醒的　低喊
　　時鐘與齒輪啃著路旁的風景
　　碎絮便鋪軟了死神的走道
　　時針是仁慈且敏捷的絞架
　　刑期比打鼾的睡眠還寬容
　　張目的死等於是罩在玻璃裏的屍體
　　人們藏住自己　如藏住口袋裡的票根
　　再也長不出昨日的枝葉　響不起逝去的風聲
　　一棵樹便只好飄落到土地之外

　　　　四

　　都市　白晝纏在你頭上　黑夜披在你肩上
　　你是不生容貌的粗陋的腸胃
　　　　一頭吞食生命不露傷口的無面獸
　　　　　　　　　啃著神的筋骨
　　你光耀的冠冕　總是自繽紛的夜色中昇起
　　　　　　　　而跌碎在清道夫的黎明
　　射擊日　你是一頭掛在假日裏的死鳥
　　　　　　在死裏被射死再被射死
　　來自荒野的餓鷹　有著慌急的行色
　　笑聲自入口飛起　從出口跌下
　　風起風落　潮來浪去
　　誰能在來回的踐踏中救出那條路
　　誰能在那種隱痛中走出自己撕裂的傷口
　　誰能在那急躁的河聲中不捲入那渦流

沉船日　只有床與餐具是唯一的浮木
掙扎的手臂是一串呼叫的鑰匙
喊著門　喊著打不開的死鎖

五

都市　在終站的鐘鳴之前
你所有急轉的輪軸折斷　脫出車軌
死亡也不會發出驚呼　出示燈號
你是等於死的張目的死
　　　死在酒瓶裏　死在煙灰缸裏
　　　死在床上　死在埃爾佛的鐵塔下
　　　　　死在文明過量的興奮劑中
當肺葉不再將聲息傳入聽診器
當所有的血管成了斷電的線路
天堂便暗成一個投影
神在仰視中垮下來
都市　在復活節一切死得更快
而你卻是剛從花轎裏步出的新娘
　　　是掛燈籠的初夜　菓露釀造的蜜月
　　　　一隻裸獸　在最空無的原始
　　　　一扇屏風　遮住墳的陰影
　　　　一具彫花的棺　裝滿了走動的死亡

　　　　　　　　　　　一九六一年

流浪人

被海的遼闊整得好累的一條船在港裏
他用燈栓自己的影子在咖啡桌的旁邊
那是他隨身帶的一種動物
除了牠　安娜近得比什麼都遠

把酒喝成故鄉的月色
空酒瓶望成一座荒島
他帶著隨身帶的那條動物
朝自己的鞋聲走去
一顆星也在很遠很遠裏
　　　　帶著天空在走

明天　當第一扇百葉窗
　　　　將太陽拉成一把梯子
他不知往上走　還是往下走

　　　　　　　　　　一九六六年

都市的五角亭

他死拉住都市不放，
都市也死拉住他不放。

一、送早報者

「昨日」沒有被斃掉
「昨日」坐印刷機偷渡回來了

那是在牛乳瓶的聲響之前
安娜還未游出臀灣之前
他的兩輪車衝在太陽的獨輪車之前
「昨日」像花園被他搬了回來
人們的眼睛擦亮成瓶子
等著插各色各樣的花
文明開的花　炸彈開的花
上帝愛看或不愛看的花

二、擦鞋匠

他與他的工具箱
坐成 L 型的吸塵器
坐成一小小的沙漠

在風沙裏
他的手是拉不斷的繩索
　將一隻一隻運陽光的船
拉上路時
他已分不出自己的手
　　　　　是帆
　　　　　還是仙人掌

三、餐館侍者

總是將身子彎成
　方向不對的Ｖ形
讓那隻停在白領上的黑蝴蝶
　　飛出一位編號的紳士來

在白蘭地與笑聲湧起的風浪裏
遊艇與浪花留一些美麗的泡沫給他
對著滿廳紊亂的食盤
他摸摸那隻飛不進花園的黑蝴蝶
　摸摸胸前那排與彩券無關的號碼
　摸摸自己
他整張臉便被請到燈的背面

四　歌女

天一黑
某些東西不是找她按摩
　　便是接受她的電療

在那一擊便著火的空氣裏
她是一隻ＲＯＮＳＯＮ牌打火機
夜是一支大麻煙

聲喉一伸
便伸成市民常去散步的那條路
那條路往前走　　是第五街
　　再往前走　是她的花園
　　再往前走　是她花園裏的噴水池
　　再往前走　是那死在霧裏的廢墟
　　　　荒涼如次晨她那張
　　　　被脂粉遺棄的臉

五、拾荒者

為嗅到亮處的一小片藍空
他的鼻孔是兩條地下排水道
在那種地方　還有那一種分析學
較他的手更能分析他的明天

背起拉屎的城
背起開花的墳地
他在沒有天空的荒野上
　　走出另一些雲彩來
　在死的鐘面上
　　呼醒另一部份歲月

　　　　　　　　　一九六九年

迷妳裙

裁紙刀般　刷的一聲
　將夜裁成兩半
一半剛被眼睛調成彩色版
另一半已印成愛鳳牀單

就那麼的裁過來
　　　　裁成一九七二年的旋律
就那麼的裁過去
　　　　裁出那條令人心碎的
　　　　　　　　望
　　　　　　　　鄉
　　　　　　　　的
　　　　　　　　水
　　　　　　　　平
　　　　　　　　線
　　　　　　　多少日落
　　　　　　　多少星墜
　　　　　　　多少月沉

　　　　　　　　一九七一年

床上錄影

次晨
海灣裏靜得像從沒有船來過
那個海醒不過來
雙目無力得連玻璃窗上的光
　　　　　都負荷不了

望過去
對面吃物店未清理的桌上
　　　那支吸管彎在一隻空瓶裏
再望過去
　　那輛沿途追著風景的跑車
　　拋錨在停車場上　車蓋仍開著
再望過去
　　一把從浪聲中拔出來的槳
　　　　　　擱在空盪的沙灘上
　　那隻海鳥已沒入沒入最低的
　　　　　　　那
　　　　　　　條
　　　　　　　水
　　　　　　　平
　　　　　　　線

　　　　　　　　一九七一年

車　禍

他走著　雙手翻找著那天空
他走著　嘴邊仍吱唔著砲彈的餘音
他走著　斜在身子的外邊
他走著　走進一聲急煞車裏去
他不走了　路反過來走他
他不走了　城裏那尾好看的週末仍在走
他不走了　高架廣告牌
　　　　　將整座天空停在那裏

　　　　　　　　　　　　一九七五年

咖啡廳

一排燈
　排好一排眼睛
一排杯子
　排好一排嘴
一排椅子
　排好一排肩膀
一排裙子
　排好一排腿
一排胸罩
　排好一排乳房

一排眼睛
　排好一排月色
一排嘴
　排好一排泉音
一排肩膀
　排好一排斷橋
一排腿
　排好一排急流
一排乳房
　排好一排浪
　　　　夜
　　　便動起來

　　　　　　　一九七六年

咖啡情

『都市！它抓住你的悶處』

那個咖啡色鏡頭
　　屢對準他
好像要拍些什麼
他卻向鏡頭的方向逃
　　直喊自己是一張漏光的底片

那多數是在下午
同一號碼的巴士
　在窗外過了又過
同一個名字的他
　在窗內坐了又坐
當烟霧把窗內窗外朦朧在一起
更看不出齒輪在鐘裏追的什麼
　　　車輪在街上趕的什麼
　原來那個咖啡色鏡頭
　　　只是一隻盲睛
　　　除了燈色閃閃
　　　　眼色迷迷
　　　　姿色盈盈
　　　　夜色漾漾
　　　　都不看

　　　　　　　　　一九七六年

摩托車

從20世紀手中
　　揮過來的一根皮鞭
　　　狠狠的鞭在都市
　　　　撒野的腿上

一條條鞭痕
　　是田園死去的樹根
　　　乾掉的河

　　　　　　一九八〇年

提007手提箱的年輕人

—— 他夢見007是造在乳峰上的一座水晶大廈

```
００７是歲月的密碼
        只打開明天
００７是高速公路上
        最帥的速度
        不往後看

提著００７
整座城跟著跑
跑到「下午三點半」
在銀行放下的鐵柵前
他不是提著一座天堂
        便是提著一座墳
```

一九八一年

生存！這兩個字

都市是一張吸墨最快的棉紙
寫來寫去
一直是生存兩個字

趕上班的行人
用一行行的小楷
　　　寫著生存
趕上班的公車
用一排排的正楷
　　　寫著生存
趕上班的摩托車
用來不及看的狂草
　　　　寫著生存
只為寫生存這兩個字
在時鐘的硯盤裏
幾乎把心血滴盡

　　　　　　　　　　一九八二年

都市‧方形的存在

天空溺死在方形的市井裏
山水枯死在方形的鋁窗外
眼睛該怎麼辦呢

眼睛從車裏
　方形的窗
　　看出去
立即被高樓一排排
　　　方形的窗
　　　　看回來

眼睛從屋裏
　方形的窗
　　看出去
立又被公寓一排排
　　　方形的窗
　　　　看回來

眼睛看不出去
窗又一個個瞎在
　　方形的牆上
便只好在餐桌上
　　在麻將桌上
　　找方形的窗
找來找去　最後
　全都從電視機
　　方形的窗裏
　　　逃走

一九八三年

二十世紀生存空間的調整

公寓與鄉居
坐在高速公路的兩端
　　　瞪目相看

這樣僵持下去
倒不如緩和下來
因為山有山頂
　　樓有樓頂
天空不讓給誰
　　不高給誰
　　　都不成
那是鳥與飛機
路過那裏說的

往後的日子
只要高速公路
　一直在通車
便有人帶著田園進城
　有人駕著都市入鄉
泥土與地毯既已走進
　　　同一雙鞋
風景與街景既已美入
　　同一雙眼睛
大家又天天擠在電視機上
　　　　彼此不認識
　　也會越來越面熟

　　　　　　　一九八三年

「麥當勞」午餐時間

一

　　一群年輕人
　　　　帶著風
　　　　衝進來
　　被最亮的位置
　　　　　拉過去
　　　　同整座城
　　　　坐在一起

　　窗內一盤餐飲
　　窗外一盤街景
　　手裏的刀叉
　　較來往的車
　　還快速地穿過
　　　迷妳而帥勁的
　　　　　　中午

二

　　三兩個中年人
　　坐在疲累裏
　　手裏的刀叉
　　慢慢張開成筷子的雙腳
　　走回三十年前鎮上的小館
　　六隻眼睛望來
　　六隻大頭蒼蠅
　　　　　在出神
　　整張桌面忽然暗成
　　　　　一幅記憶
　　那瓶紅露酒
　　　又不知酒言酒語
　　　　把中午說到
　　那裏去了

當一陣陣年輕人
　　來去的強風
　　從自動門裏
　　吹進吹出
你可聽見寒林裏
　飄零的葉音

　　三

一個老年人
坐在角落裏
穿著不太合身的
　　　成衣西裝
吃完不太合胃的
　　　　漢堡
怎麼想也想不到
漢朝的城堡那裏去
玻璃大廈該不是
那片發光的水田

枯坐成一棵
　室內裝潢的老松
不說話還好
一自言自語
必又是同震耳的炮聲
　　　　在說話了
說著說著
眼前的晌午
已是眼裏的昏暮

後記：寫完此詩，深深感到現代文明，像是頭也不回地向前推進的齒
　　　輪，冷漠而無情，文化則是對存在時空產生整體性的關懷與鄉
　　　愁。從文明的窗口看此詩，我們看到「麥當勞午餐時間」同一
　　　時空出現的中國人，竟有三處斷層的生命現象；從文化的窗口
　　　看此詩，我們看到貫穿整個時空與歷史文化大動脈而存在的一
　　　個分不開來的中國人。誠然人必須自覺地從文明層面轉化到文
　　　化層面上來，否則，人將被冷酷的機械文明不斷的進行切片。

　　　　　　　　　　　　　　　　　　　　　　　　一九八五年

玻璃大廈的異化

站在街口
看玻璃大廈
　將風景一塊塊
　　冷凍在玻璃窗裏

坐著車出城
看玻璃大廈
　在飛馳的車窗外
　　　很快被解體
飛成一幅幅風景
溶入山水
化為煙雲
眼睛追不上
便轉回車內
望著空空的雙目
竟又看到另一座玻璃大廈
　閃亮在那個鄉下小孩的
　　　　瞳孔裏
　　　　走過去
　　　　要五十年

一九八六年

卡拉ＯＫ

還有什麼不OK
整座城被你踩下去
世界也被你狠狠踩碎
從O開始
你將自己先踩空
　　　　回到本來

腦空出來不思
心空出來不想
全交給身體動
四肢是燃燒的高壓電路

都市在你光芒四射的身體上跳動
將整座城的喧囂與冷漠
從高音喇叭的喉管中吐掉
把生命跳到肉體的位置
碰是身體
抱也是身體
還有甚麼不OK

道德經在國文課堂裏打瞌睡
卡拉ＯＫ在腳下猛跳
即使卡拉跳昏了過去
嘴仍吐著啤酒泡沫
　　　　叫OK

　　　　　　　　一九八七年

眼睛的收容所

跟紅綠燈接力跑的眼睛
跟公文來回跑的眼睛
跟新聞到處跑的眼睛
跟股市行情追著跑的眼睛
跟菜單腸胃齊跑的眼睛
跟女人乳峯上下跑的眼睛
跟刀槍與血路逃跑的眼睛
跟禱告往天堂直跑的眼睛
無論是近視遠視與老花
是帶眼鏡不帶眼鏡
跑了一整天
都一個個累倒在
電視機的收容所裡

一九八九年

搶劫與強暴

在深夜暗淡的街燈下
她身上擺動過來的曲線
　　與他的視線接上
她項間垂掛的珍珠
　　與他的眼珠碰上
她胸前聳起的乳峯
與他經常走險的長白山
　　　　　　對上
整個視覺空間
便走入原始可怕的蠻荒
看不見教堂法院與警察局
　　　　便甚麼都能做

　　　　　　一九八九年

銀　行

那是銀子休息與睡覺的地方
只要她醒來
「行」出去
方向全對準她
笑口對她開
槍口對她叫
計程車一路跳錶
　　　　一路追著她跑
歲月背著薪水袋
一輩子跟著她走

她走到那裡
世界跟她到那裡
百貨公司打開店門等她
餐廳飯館打開嘴門喊她
酒廊賓館打開紅門拉她
奉獻箱打開善門接她
千萬人打開心門腦門眼門
　　　　　　看她想她
她是人見人愛　迷死人的艷婦
　　　　生出一個油頭粉面
　　　　吃喝玩樂的都市
　　　　就夠你瞧了

　　　　　　　　一九八九年

「世紀末」病在都市裏

先是銅從銅像裏走回五金行
　　　夢娜麗莎嘴上畫上鬍子
然後是上帝問自己從那裏來
最後是鞋問路
　　　路問方向
方向問進了一盞快熄滅的燈
　　　　　　關上門來睡
　　　　　　　　等天亮
過去的過去的過去　　呼呼大睡
未來的未來的未來　　呼呼大睡
現在　　　夾在中間　　睡不著
　　　　　　　便蹓跑出去
直跟著失眠的都市
　　一起抽煙喝酒
　　一起看裸體畫
　　一起卡拉OK
一起張大眼睛
　倒在興奮劑與安眠藥裏
　　　　　翻來覆去

一條不帶岸的船
飄航在起伏的海上

　　　　　　　　一九九一年十月

長在「後現代」背後的一顆黑痣

在英雄與命運交響樂中
尼采沿著地球的直軸
向天頂爬昇
　圖以自己的心　對換宇宙的心
　　　　　　同永恆簽約

千萬隻眼睛
仰視他一個世紀
看累了　從高空下來
世界平躺在地上
天地相望　誰都不高
卻苦了飛不起來的天空
反正飛與跑與行
　　　　都是走
走到那　都有你的
博士與明星攜手走進熱門
歌星與莫札特同進一間錄音室
詩人與師爺同坐一張書桌
三毛四毛長在毛姆的額上
　　　　根在培根的頭上
燕尾服穿上牛仔褲
啤酒屋與靈糧堂各吃各的
大廈在指壓粉壓下　動不了
反正上流下流都是流
　　溝水海水都是水
清不出來的　都進入陰溝
走不出來的　都擠進黃燈
將東南西北在方向盤裡
　　　　炒成一盤雜粹

　　　　　　一九九一年十月

古典的悲情故事

休閒中心到不了文化中心
天橋到不了鵲橋楓橋
證券行到不了桃源行琵琶行
卡拉OK到不了坐看雲起時
塞車的街口到不了
　　　萬徑人踪滅

他找路　路也在十字路口找他
他看錶　錶不知是什麼時候停的
他找自己　上半身往上跑
　　　　　下半身向下跑
跑來跑去
他總是有意無意
　　　　穿著唐裝　跑進歐洲牛排館
　　　　套上西裝　跑進王老吉茶藝館
吃吃喝喝之後
看一輛輛賓士
　擦亮一排玻璃大廈而過
他正好加快腳步在紅磚人行道上
前些日子　一架七四七巨無霸
曾載他與空中廚房
　爬上三萬呎高空的另一座玻璃大廈
　　　　　　　　去進餐
他不知該點嫦娥奔月
　　　還是太空船奔日
一陣陣突來的亂流
使他在空中失去平衡
嘔吐之後
他便昏頭轉向的跌進
　　　山山水水的自然
　　　林林總總的都市
將身體留在城裏享用

把腦袋改裝成假古董店
好去古玩那模擬式的空靈
且夾帶一些文人身邊的文墨
　　好回去找八大的筆筒
　　　穿杜甫的舊鞋
　　　戴李白的舊帽
酌飲他們杯中的殘酒
　不也醉成那忘我的樣子
　沾上一點歷史與永恆

那真的連酒也想不到
只是國際牌冰箱裏的
　　　　一瓶舒跑
便潑醒他在廿萬臺幣一坪的
　　　　豪華公寓裏
望著畫在地毯與磁磚上的山水
看著盆景裏小小的自然
坐對窗外不斷向空中旋上去的
　　　　一幢幢高樓
他忽然發覺自己
　只是仿造在都市公園裏的
　　　　一座陶然亭
　　環繞著假山假水
　　給都市的假日看

　　　　　　　　　一九九二年四月

帶著世紀末跑的麥可傑克遜

一

都市在物化的城中癱瘓
　　　在機械的噪音中失聽
要不是你又跳又叫的跑來
給它打一針
　　　怎會那麼爽
　　一下亢奮了起來

那也是一種藥物反應
　　　另一種形式的作愛
　　　　　　　在盲戀中
　　　　　在官能的原鄉
世界上半身　空靜
下半身　動盪

你的尖叫
　　刺入都市空瘦的心
　　　　　空洞的陰部
壓不住的宣洩與顛狂
　是爆開來的啤酒廠
整座城不醉不瘋才怪

二

你是動作的全能
千萬隻手的動力
　　　在你的手裏
千萬條腿的腿力
　　　在你的腳中
要翻天覆地
要把觀眾拋上天
　　　丟下海

259

只要你開口
千萬顆心　都甘心
千萬種情　都情願

你口一開
除了歡呼
再大的聲音都退後
你手一舉
整座城在空中搖擺
你腳一踢
都市是一隻球
你追趕過來
世界都空出來
　　看你大叫大喊
把美麗的世紀末
釘在千萬眼睛的看板上
　　　給最賣點的新聞看

今夜
電視臺最後播出
世界上最大的音爆
　　連續發生在各地的廣場
世界上最靜的地方
　　是坐在山水與古玉中的故宮
　　　抱著交響樂沈睡的維也納城

一九九三年九月

後現代A管道

後現代　嬉皮笑臉
　　　　跟著緊繃臉的現代
　　　　　　　走過來
　　　　把往上看的眼睛
　　　　　　向下看
　　　　　世界變矮
　　　　偶像倒在地上

將皇冠與古羅馬的圓頂
　　　　往大廈的頭上戴
把壓克力透明屋頂與天頂
　　　　　　　頂在一起
開賓士到鄉下
　帶田園的大樹到高樓裏來
　　　　　　與都市相會（註）
穿一隻「雅皮」「優皮」皮鞋
　踩整座城進豪華地毯
拖一雙拖泥帶水的拖鞋
　拖整座城進大街小巷
方向該往那裡走
　　　　只要是路
方向該往那裏休息
那要看它累成什麼樣子
　煙灰缸空酒瓶
　休閒中心與教堂
　　都是好地方

在三百六十度開放的時間廣場上
有人走進新東陽老大昌
有人衝入麥當勞肯德基
有人將咖啡倒進龍井
有人將檸檬擠進牛乳

有人舉左手舉右手
有人左右手一起舉
有人抱股市的屁股
有人抱女人的屁股
有人抱文章的八股
有人把文化裸成她的胴體
有人把崇高
　　聳立在女人的乳峰上
有人把酒瓶玉腿與槍支
　　　　當作天堂的支柱
有人用一堆銅與水泥
　　　　　堆成永恆
只要你高興
一切都由你
價值由你定
歲月由你選
世界任你挑

註：「現代啟示錄」餐廳建築，是臺北市極具後現代裝置藝術的造
　　型觀念，不但屋頂透明；更不可思議是將一棵古老的大樹種在
　　屋內，使都市與田園的景象，呈現在同一個造型空間內，彼此
　　對話。

　　　　　　　　　　　　　　一九九〇年四月

「人」生存空間的驚爆線

美麗的地球
風雲鳥　飛來它的自由與廣闊
大自然　美來它原來的美麗

當人在地球上打下第一根樁
長出大大小小的地圖
地圖的邊線多是刀鋒劃的
　　　　　　　　劃開你我來
也劃出一條條血路
叫一群一群的人　常在彈道裡走

看來地球是圓的
　　　眼球是圓的
　　銀圓也是圓的
最後都圓到銀圓裡去
就是看不見心中升起的渾圓
日月便只好滾著銀圓來
一路傳說「人為財死」
　　是人不成文的聖經
沿著財路　只有利益在跑
　　　　　　一路領先
　　　　　　一路叫好
　　　　　　一路阿門
從跨國的海陸空航路到
　　都市的大街小巷到
　　公寓的樓梯電梯到
　　SWEET HOME 到
　　最平安的家
　上帝竟親眼看到

兒子用刀插進父親體內
　去劃出那條
　　　血
　　　淋
　　　淋
　　　的
　　　財
　　　路

註：在「金錢」與利益掛帥的年代，近些日子，媒體曾報導為錢財
　　殺親人、甚至父子互殺的驚聞，真是使人性、人道、人倫與生
　　命的價值，受到重大的破壞、甚至淪喪，也使我們往深一層思
　　考與聯想到人世界從「集體」的人到「個體」的人，都好像宿
　　命性的受困在利益與「銀圓」的圓圈中，不停的爭奪，走不出
　　來，而遠離了心在人文美感中向形而上昇華的「渾圓」世界，
　　因而導致人類的生存空間潛藏著一條不安且可慮的驚爆線，有
　　待藝術升越中的「美」來解救。

　　　　　　　　　　　　　　　　　二〇〇〇年

追蹤人在哪裡

在價值叫賣的年代
在中心沒有心的年代
在靈魂不靈　肉體最靈的年代
在不必連理　床愛連連的年代
人　究竟在哪裡

在上半身下半身分道揚鑣的年代
在形下架空形上的年代
在消化化掉文化的年代
在空靈空往靈空的年代
人　究竟在哪裡

在沒有絕對誰都對的年代
在沒有上帝誰都是上帝的年代
在每秒鐘都急著成永恆的年代
在槍管也搶著接通天堂的年代
人　究竟在哪裡

在銀圓滾著眼球跑的年代
在口袋腦袋只裝名片戶頭的年代
在媒體與廣告速銷傾銷一起來的年代
在垃圾山靈山南山都是山的年代
人　究竟在哪裡

在紅綠燈故障都衝入黃燈的年代
在路問方向　方向問路的年代
在椅子都應吊在空中的年代
在地球已坐上太空椅不知何處去的年代
人　究竟在哪裡

人　究竟在哪裡

265

走不出時鐘長短針的雙腳
便坐在自己裡
抱住詩與藝術沈思默想
想到什麼也想不出來
那也是一種存在思想

　　　　　　　二〇〇一年

搖頭丸
—— 搖進那救不出千山萬水的渦漩

對也搖頭
不對也搖頭
抱住整個都市在搖頭
天與地也跟著搖頭
搖掉頭上的皇冠桂冠
搖掉頭頂的十字架
把世界搖到上帝與凱撒都到不了的地方
（那地方波特萊爾好像來過
但當時搖得不那麼厲害）
　　　　　　搖
　　　　搖　搖
　　　搖　　　搖
　　　搖　搖
　　　　　搖
把地球搖成神鬼都未享用過的搖籃
一個剛生的棄嬰
　　　夢遊在天使也夢不到的花園裡
　　　　盛開的不是馨香的康乃馨與紅玫瑰
　　　　而是被警犬一路嗅過來的罌粟花（註）

註：搖頭丸、強力膠、嗎啡、鴉片都是毒品家族的成員

　　　　　　　　　　　二〇〇二年

傾斜的21世紀
—— 後現代敲打樂

一

尼采在天頂山頂頭頂　開連鎖店
　　　　　　專賣孤高
里爾克在海底山底心底　開連鎖店
　　　　　　專賣孤寂
遊客們遊完吃完山腳海濱
　　　好看好吃的風景
　　　　　　便鳥散
廿世紀蓋的﹁現代主義﹂摩天樓
　　　　　只好暫緩營業
　　　　　資金外移 ①

二

圓圓的銀圓
　挾持圓圓的眼球與地球
　　　將廿一世紀急滾到市中心
大叫一聲﹁爽﹂
太陽跌碎成滿地閃爍
世界便亮起一朵朵
　　　絕美的煙火
明暗生滅在它的光速裡
留影在股市起落的看板上
　　成為都市的日落日出
　重建視覺的秩序

---

① 「現代主義」已潛移默化為「後現代」經營圈的「品管」與「金控」力量。

三

這是吃色的年代
文化被消化打敗
　要痛吃後現代
　　便到火鍋城
　　　　把能吃的動植物與作料都放進火鍋
　　　　再用可口可樂與BEER沖洗腸胃
要樂透的睡後現代
便沖上網絡
　　　　　　把援交一夜情3P全攤在床上
　　　　　　　床下是誰都擋不住的土石流
　　要盡興的玩後現代
　　　便讓電動玩具也把自己
　　　　　當做肉動玩具來玩
　　　　　玩到電腦人腦變成合成腦
要到什麼都想要　　　自己就是帶槍的"上帝"
要到什麼都沒有　　便留下身體的空屋
　　　　　　　　連自己都不住在裡邊
空虛　在看滿街的輪影腳印
　　　　　　被速度的旋風掃成入秋的落葉
孤獨　在看千萬人肩並肩擁過街
　　　　　　　　彼此不認識
寂寞　在看人與世界都各走在各的影子裡

四

這是磅秤沒有數字的年代
輕重真假不分
　是因鮮花塑膠花網絡上花的影子
　　　　　　　　　　都叫花
對錯是非不明
　是因桌面上的燈都熄滅
　　電開關交給桌面下的手

誰想賣文化和經典名牌
　　　錢總是一路上
　　　　得高標
誰想賣空人類所有的過去
　　　去看地球上開得最大的一朵鄉愁
　　　　　　便抱住機器
　　　　讓生命離開肉體的故鄉

　　五

這是打靶找不到靶心的年代
對也搖頭不對也搖頭的搖頭丸
　　　　是朝內外亂射的散彈
　　　　　　方向到處逃
　　　　"上帝"失踪
　　　　紅綠燈失靈
世界只好躲入黃燈區
灰色地帶
　　　是灰塵與沙塵暴的家園
任誰進來都會沙眼
　　　　　都會灰頭灰臉不見天日
除非坐上海德格升起來的"形而上"
灰暗下沉的谷底　是不可能見到
　　　　　　　晴空碧野
除非"詩"用天地線將天地拉住
　　　　　　拉正②
　　　　日月正常進出
　　　　高低正常上下
傾斜掉下去的21世紀
　　　是不可能走上來

　　　　　　　　　二○○四年

---

② 世界上最美的人群社會與國家最後應是由詩與藝術非機器來達成。

III

河

只有回到第一聲泉音中
　　才能認出你的初貌
順著眼波而去
你音樂的身段
　是一條原始的歌
　　唱高了山
　　唱深了林
　　唱遠了鳥的翅膀

直到那朵溫柔的雲
　被天空揉了又揉
　　　揉出了水聲
你才在那陣衝擊中
認識到自己的身體

美麗的S　　是把鋸也好
　　　　　　　螺絲刀也好
那些痛快的紋路　一扭動
便飄響成拋物線　被空中的鳥接住
整個曠野都驚顫在那迴旋的
　　　　　　　　弦音中

凡是坡度　都長滿了韻律
凡是彎處　都敏感
　　　　都很滑
　　都多漩渦
　　都救不出千山萬水
除了大地　誰能讓你那樣去
除了海底　誰知道你來
除了那條水平線　誰看見你已來過

　　　　　　　　　一九七三年

海

只有讓鋼琴聲走到深夜裏去
我才能走入你藍色的幽遠

　　　那透明的空闊
　　　已忘形成風
　　　　水
　　　　平
　　　　線
　　　　是
　　　　最
　　　　後
　　　　的
　　　　一
　　　　根
　　　　弦
用整座天空去碰也碰不出聲來

整個寂靜在那一握裏
伸開來　江河便沿掌紋而流
　　　　　滿目都是水聲
山連著山走來　走來你的形體
翅膀疊著翅膀飛去　飛成你的遙遠
在遠方　那顆種子已走成樹林的秩序
那滴水　不也是種子
　　　　已走成你
　　　　　走成你的波動
　　　　　　你翅的層次

誰說飛不是天空
　　　天空不是坐在你的鞦韆架上
　　　　　　輕得像那朵雲
飄浮時　做夢也下不來

273

起伏時　便有一根繩纏在流血的掌心裏
　　　　像葉脈死死拉住那棵樹

航入千帆
　　　帆是你頂向風雨的臉
　　　　　有時柔得像舌
　　　舐入水天的兩片唇
　　　　　　遠
　　　　　　方
　　　　　　便
　　　　　　展
　　　　　　開
　　　　　　成
　　　　　　花
　　　　　　瓣
想起種星
　　種月
　　種雲
　種鳥
　種風
　種浪
竟種出那麼多乳房
難怪太陽用力一吻
　　　便吻成那片藍色的墳園
當黃昏踩著落帆走來
你便在最後的一張網中離去

　　　　　　　　　　一九七三年

山

只有讓眼睛走到凝視裏去
我才能走進你黛綠色的吟哦
　　　　　低處是水
　　　　　高處是樹

雲與海遠去
你獨自留下
留滿頭的天空
　滿腳的荒野
讓千年風雨纏住那棵古松
盤那張鷹翅入萬里的蒼茫
你的那朵高昂　一落入水平線
　　　　　便是一個遠方
而那串溫婉與連綿　一睡進去
　　　　　便是一個夜深過一個夜

夜是你的門
　　你的窗
　　你的燈屋
　　你的睡目　你的摒棄一切看見過後的看見
太陽已睡成岩層
河流已睡成根脈
鳥聲已睡成金屬

天空與原野已睡成大理石的斑斕
誰能醒你　除了眼睛在凝視中永不回來
除了那縷煙已被眼睛拉斷成繩子
而去與不去　你都是永遠

　　　　　　　　　一九七三年

野　馬

將前腿舉成閃電
　　吼出一聲雷
　然後放下來
　　竟是那陣
　　　　追
　　　　風
　　　　而
　　　　去
　　　　的
　　　　雨
奔著山水來
衝著山水去
除了天地線
　牠從未見過韁繩
除了雲與鳥坐過的山
　牠從未見過馬鞍
除了天空銜住的虹　大地啣住的河
　牠從未見過馬勒口
除了荒漠中的煙
　牠從未見過馬鞭

一想到馬廄
連曠野牠都要撕破
一想到遼闊
牠四條腿都是翅膀
　　山與水一起飛
　　蹄落處　花滿地
　　蹄揚起　星滿天

　　　　　　　　　　一九七五年

276

車　上

車急馳
打開的車窗　　是白色琴鍵
關上的車窗　　是黑色琴鍵
車急馳
張開的眼睛　　是風景
閉上的眼睛　　是往事
一回首　車已離地而去
　　　　　　　　身在雲裡
　　　　　　　　夢在雲外

凝望溶入山水
山水化為煙雲
煙雲便不能不了
事情總是這樣了的
當車急馳　要追回什麼來
雙目總是把車窗
　　磨成那片迷濛
　　　　那片悵惘

　　　　　　　　　　一九七七年

雲

藍空因我柔得像
　　愛人的眸子
　我帶著海散步
　　帶著遠方游牧

我走　地相跟
我飛　天相隨
我笑　太陽在
我怒　風雨來
我情悠悠　江水說不盡
我心遙遙　海天望無窮

我的行程　只有一部份被鳥知道
　　　　那是它飛著山水來
　　　　　我飄著山水去
　　　　　　彼此遇上

我的行程　大部份是過了水平線之後
　　　　日落星沉　煙消波滅
　　　　　　天茫茫
　　　　　　地茫茫
　　　　　永恆也茫茫
　　　　　　獨我在
　　　　　　　　一九七七年

觀　海

飲盡一條條江河
你醉成滿天風浪
　浪是花瓣　　大地能不繽紛
　浪是翅膀　　天空能不飛翔
　浪波動起伏　群山能不心跳
　浪來浪去　　浪去浪來
你吞進一顆顆落日
　　　吐出朵朵旭陽

總是發光的明天
總是弦音琴聲迴響的遠方
千里江河是你的手
握山頂的雪林野的花而來
帶來一路的風景
其中最美最耐看的
到後來都不是風景
而是開在你額上
　　那朵永不凋的空寂

聽不見的　都已聽見
看不見的　都已看見
到不了的　都已進來
你就這樣成為那種
　　無限的壯闊與圓滿
　　　　滿滿的陽光
　　　　滿滿的月色
　　　　滿滿的浪聲
　　　　滿滿的帆影

究竟那條水平線
　能攔你在何處
壓抑不了那激動時

你總是狂風暴雨
　　千波萬浪
把山崖上的巨石　一塊塊擊開
　　放出那些被禁錮的陽光與河流
其實你遇上什麼
　　都放開手順它
任以那一種樣子　靜靜躺下不管
你仍是那悠悠而流的忘川
浮風平浪靜花開鳥鳴的三月而去
　　　　去無蹤
　　　來也無蹤

既然來處也是去處
　　去處也是來處
那麼去與不去
你都在不停的走
從水平線裡走出去
從水平線外走回來
你美麗的側身
　　已分不出是閃現的晨曦
　　　　還是斜過去的夕陽
任日月問過來問過去
你那張浮在波光與煙雨中的臉
一直是刻不上字的鐘面
　　　　能記起什麼來
如果真的有什麼來過
風浪都把它留在岩壁上
　　留成歲月最初的樣子
　　　時間最初的樣子

蒼茫若能探視出一切的初貌
那純粹的擺動
那永不休止的澎湃
它便是鐘錶的心

　　時空的心
　也是你的心
　　你收藏日月風雨江河的心
　　你填滿千萬座深淵的心
　　你被冰與火焚燒藍透了的心
　任霧色夜色一層層塗過來
　任太陽將所有的油彩倒下來
　任滿天峰火猛然的掃過來
　任炮管把血漿不停的灌下來
　　都更變不了你那藍色的頑強
　　　　　　藍色的深沉
　　　　藍色的凝望

　即使望到那縷煙被遠方
　　　　　　　拉斷了
　所有流落的眼睛
　　都望回那條水平線上
　仍望不出你那隻獨目
　　在望著那一種鄉愁
　仍看不出你那隻獨輪
　　究竟已到了那裡
　從漫長的白晝
　　到茫茫的昏暮
　若能凱旋回來
　　便伴著月歸
　星夜是你的冠冕
　眾星繞冠轉
　那高無比的壯麗與輝煌
　使燈火煙火炮火亮到半空
　　　　　　都轉了回來
　而你一直攀登到光的峰頂
　將自己高舉成次日的黎明
　讓所有的門窗都開向你

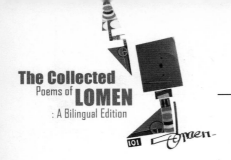

天空都自由向你
大地都遼闊向你
河都流向你
鳥都飛向你
果都甜美向你
風景都看向你
無論你坐成山
　或躺成原野
　　　走動成江河
無論你是醒是睡

只要那朵雲浮過來
你便飄得比永恆還遠

曠　野

　　—— 以原本的遼闊，守望到最後，凡是
　　完美的，都將被它望入永恒。

一

把柔靜給雲
把躍動給劇奔的蹄聲
你隨天空闊過去
　帶遙遠入寧靜
地球不停的轉
把最絢爛的那一面給你
使你成為那張最美的海報
　　展示著春夏秋冬的演出

是河便自己去流
是湖便自己停下來
是風景便自己去明麗
是晝夜便自己去明暗
時間不在鐘錶裡
天空不在鳥籠中
你遼闊的胸部
　放在太陽的石磨下
　　磨出光的回聲
　　　花的香味
　　　果的甜味

二

當第一根椿打下來
世界便順著你的裂痕
　在紊亂的方向裏逃

風裏有各種旗的投影
雨裏有各種流彈的投影

河裏有各種血的投影
湖裏有各種傷口的投影
山峰有各種墳的投影
樹林有各種鐵絲網的投影
峭壁有各種圍牆的投影
鳥帶著天空　逃向水平線
人帶著護照　逃往邊界
你帶著煙雲　回到原來
讓所有的槍與箭　埋在血堆裡
　　　　　　　　長成各種盆景
　　　　　　美在歷史的臺階上
你把四季的風景　送入上帝的花園

　　　三

高樓大廈圍攏來
　迫天空躲成天花板
　　迫你從印刷機上
　　　縮影成那塊窗簾布
　　　仍開花給窗看

一隻盲鹿在畫框裡
盯望著四面牆
視線穿壁而出
洋灰道上　不見羊
馬路上　不見馬
摩托車急成一根快鞭
鞭著眾獸在嘶鳴中奔動

綠燈是無際的草原
紅燈是停在水平線上的
　　　　　　　　落日
想奔　河流都在蓄水池裏
想飛　有翅的都在菜市場
喘息於油門與煞車之間

克勞酸喝得你好累
咖啡把你沖入最疲憊的下午
你的孤寂堆放在午夜的停車場裏
當明天被早班公車司機一腳踩出油門
　　　　　　　是你忙著找路
　　　　　　　還是路忙著找你

在廣告牌圍觀的場景裏
眼睛是一部切肉機
　把你的千山萬水
　切片入建築物的層次
　　　　　櫉窗的秩序
　　　　　都標上了價
如果口袋裏的鈔票是你的雲
沿腰而下　　便是你的河
沿乳峰而上　便是你的山
於上上下下之間
你便循環成那座電梯
在封閉式的天空與限定的高度裏
　　　　　鳥只有一種飛法
　　　　　一種叫聲
床濃縮了你全部的空闊
餐具佔據了你所有的動作
當排水溝與垃圾車在低處走
　腦袋與廣告汽球在高處飛
你是被掀開的一張
被毛筆鋼筆寫著新的「大同篇」

　　　　高樓與山同坐
　　　　街道與河同流
　　　　煙塵與雲同飄
　　　　鬧市與海同盪
　　　　眼睛與波浪同形
　　　　櫉窗與風景同貌
　　　　餐廳與田園同宗

旅館與荒野同族
男人與太陽同姓
女人與月亮同名
床被與四季同睡
唇瓣與花瓣同開
酒液與露水同漾
孕婦與黎明同光
焚屍爐與夜同暗
廣場與天空同行
鐘錶與地球同轉

四

廟選中了山的清高
十字架對正了天堂的座標
你把空茫磨亮成一面鏡
　　望著光開始流動的地方
　　泉水開始湧現的地方
　　花開始開的地方
　　鳥開始飛的地方
讓所有的路都能看見起點
　　所有的聲音都歸入你的沉寂

那縷煙
已把你的廣漠全告訴了遠方

把你的粗獷飄給最原始的溫柔
是風雨便同著方向走去
是日月便對著面走來
時序與季節緩緩換位
你總是站在水平線上
收容著一排又一排的遙望

　　　　　　　　一九七九年

晨　起

站在清晨的樓頂上
一呼吸
　　花紅葉綠
　　天藍山青
一遠看
　　腳已踩在雲上
一張開雙手
　　天空與胸便疊在一起
　　　　反而較翅膀輕了

此刻要是不飛
鳥那裏來的樣子
遠方怎能用手去摸

　　　　　　　　　一九八一年

飛在雲上三萬呎高空
讀 詩 看 畫

世界只留下
最後一塊版面
給日月星辰排用
其他的都暗入雲山

即使煙囪與炮管
在雲下排著一行行
　　生活必讀的詩
但拿到雲上來看
都得化為那無限的遙望
望到無邊的廣闊
只剩下透明
世界便留下
最後一個畫廊
　　給自己用
其他的都埋入雲山
誰曾在此畫過
　　　展過
而一幅幅不能畫的畫
都氣勢迫人的
　　自己跑來
逼使我雙目
跪下來看

千山萬水
　　何處去
千飛萬翔
　　翅在那
問筆
問墨

都說大自然在畫框裏
瘦如走不出去的盆景

而太空船又能運回
　　　　多少天空
　　　　多少渺茫

在沒有終點站的渾沌裏
問時間　春夏秋冬都在睡
問空間　東南西北都不在
整個世界空在那裏
如果還要畫
誰的眼睛能是調色盤
誰的視線能是揮灑的線條
宇宙看看我
我看看宇宙
不畫
全是畫

　　　　　　　　　　一九八六年一月

天空與鳥

鳥如果不在翅膀上
天空的上面是什麼

事實上他是天空
　　　　不是鳥
能一直飛的是天空
　　　　不是鳥

天空將各式各樣的鳥籠
　　　　留給早晨的公園

　　將成千成萬的鳥巢
　　　　留給傍晚的樹林
他沿著天地線不停的飛
日月是他的雙翅
晝夜是他的投影
眾鳥跟著他斷斷續續在飛
誰也不知他能飛多高
　　　　多遠
　　　　多久

　　　　　　一九九〇年

大峽谷奏鳴曲
—— 詩與藝術守望的世界

一

千萬座深淵在這裏沉落
　　無數向下的↓↓↓
　　　　　　追著死亡
所有的石屋解體在石壁上
　都找不到原來的建築圖
　　　　　　萬徑人踪滅
大峽谷
你兩邊的建築與走道
是日月星辰雷電風雨
　　　千萬年營造的
岩壁打開的兩扇通天門
　　　　　永遠開著
　　　世界要來就來
　　　　　要去就去
至於
惠特曼有沒有
　　駕著西部的蓬車來過
柳宗元有沒有
　把寒江釣到這裏來
　從不說話的蠻荒與孤寂
　　　　　　都不知道
天空也沒有人管
鳥帶著山水飛來
飛機帶著都市飛去
你是牽著鳥翅與機翅在飛的
　　　　　　那條線
飛到接近太陽出來的東方
另一條線
接著從萬里長城
　　　揮出來

帶著大自然的風景與
　　起伏的歷史
　　　　滿天飛
飛到鳥翅與機翅
　　都飛不過去
另一條線
便從茫茫的天地間
　　　　飄出來
　　　閃在那裏

這三條線　　握在你手中
已是三條最長的鞭子
地球要凹到底
　　　凸到頂
　　　去到○
都真的是鞭長可及了

　　　　二

看天空與曠野寫下合同
你將無數剛柔的
　　　　疊層與色面
建架入絢麗雄偉的型構
水墨流過
便是東方的山水畫
幾何圖形進來
便是西方的立體造型
如果流過谷底的科羅拉多河
　　　　　　是弦線
裝在二胡與小提琴上
　都一樣拉出最原始的
　　　　　音色
　　　　　音階
　　　　與回響
世界便好看好聽的

　　　　拉在一起了
　　那裏來的東拉西扯
　　　　　東吵西鬧
　　　　亂成一團
　　看不清聽不楚
　到處是視覺強暴
　　　　聽覺強暴

　　三

大峽谷
你驚人的深度
帝國大廈與紐約商業大樓
　　　　　　聯手也摸不到底
下去是沒有階梯的沉靜
再威風的凱旋門
也無法從那奧秘中旋出來
長期的沉思默想
一塊塊靜觀的石面
　　　　　　都是鏡
凡是影像
都逃不掉
最奇異的
開始都是眼睛在說
後來是寧靜自己
　　　　發出聲音
叫周圍空成山水畫中的
　　　　　　　留白
怎麼說　還不如不說

　　四

大峽谷
再大的地震
也未裂開這樣大的口

你白天銜住太陽
　　晚上銜住月亮
晝夜便有用不完的光
歲月也一直在光裏走
　　　有好看的樣子
讓有形無形的彈片
　　都轉化為剛性的岩層
　　　　　柔性的葉片花瓣
將畫面與結構重新組合
把坦克車與垃圾車
通通換成遊覽車
　　　在風景裏開

大都市兩排建築夾住的
　　　　是一條花街
大峽谷兩邊岩壁夾住的
　　　　也是一條花街
管它走來紅男綠女
　　　　紅花綠葉
都一同走回自然
　　　給原始看

　　五

大峽谷　為裸出真象
你撕開胸　挖出心來
　　　　給天看地看
當你開口說愛
那潤長的嘴
如果都吻遍
那將是世界上
　　最長的條愛河
　　最遠的一條博愛路
當你開口說痛
所有無形有形的

　　　　大小傷口
都跑來
也說不盡
最後都說成
　　亨利摩爾雕刀下
　　　一個個奔馳在旅途上的
　　　　　　　　　　　　車窗

　　六

大峽谷
倘若你是世界上
　　最大的掩埋廠與焚化爐
埋下去的也只是感性的抒情河道
　　　　　　　理性思維的岩層紋路
將世界焚化　冒出來的
　　　　　　也只是雲彩
　　　　　　　不是濃煙
過後　仍是明麗的風景
　　　　　藍藍的天空
　　　　　從不污染

即使在風雨交加的動盪時刻
一切失去方向感
風歪雨斜
眼看周圍
　　跟著倒的籬笆
你仍以岩層堅忍的斜面
　　　　　　　忍過去
留下一塊最美的滑板
　給腳站不穩的世界
　　　　　　滑落

七

大峽谷
深藏不露而露
你不是偽裝的陷阱
而是深層世界的坦誠
凡是危崖絕壁
都預先告訴眼睛
走近腳下也響起警鈴
安全牽較身邊的隨從還高
至於驚險與驚奇
那是開在谷底
　　兩朵最美的花
要站到崖邊
　　才能看見
若懼高怕深
便跟隨導遊與遊客
在安全距離裏走
照著旅遊的平面圖
　　　定好的路線
　　　走回市區
　　　擠入購物中心
穿越誰也不認識誰的人潮
　　　　去找自己的旅館
　　　　　關在房裏
　　　　平躺下來
底下也是一個大峽谷
　　　不到半尺深
　　　埋了不少人

八

行程來與去
世界一直在旅遊
鐘擺間　有走動的橋

　兩腿間　有走動的橋
　世紀末也是一座走動的橋
　　　　吊在現代與後現代之間
　　　　　　　邊走邊搖
　　　　　　　邊搖邊幌

　大峽谷　你呢
　把整座天空架牢在兩崖間
　有人說
　它是一座空橋
　　　　沒有人走
　有人說
　看得見看不見的
　上下左右都在走
　其實　它是壓克力屋頂
　把世界罩在透明裏
　　　　裸開來看
　　　　　看人
　　　　　　　拉
　　　　　　　　著
　　　　　　都市
　　　　　　　拉
　　　　　　　　著
　　　　　　田園
　　　　　　　拉
　　　　　　　　著
　　　　　　荒野
　　　　　在茫茫裡走

　　九

　沿著深度走下去
　順著高度走上來
　大峽谷你垂直的視線
　同地球的軸直在一起
　下端頂著地

上端頂著天
只要跟著地球轉
無數變化的圓面
便在時空的縱向與橫向裏
旋成停不下來的螺旋塔
所有的眼睛都在塔上
　　看前進中的永恆
　　　　往那裏走

　　　　　　一九九二年

過三峽

一

江水帶著船與山
　　　行入蒼茫
江風帶著臉與浪面
　　　　走進空濛
　路有多遠
　千山萬嶺
　　從高遠
　　　深遠
　　　　走
　　　　　到
　　　　平
　　　　　遠
時間有多老
回話是蒼古的岩壁
　　　　從千萬年來
所有的鐘錶都停止
　在聽大自然的心
　　　　　在跳

近山看遠水
近水看遠山
　山山水水
　水水山山
將我們看成山水畫中的
　　　　　空白
讓周圍的重山
都輕浮到雲裏去
若悠遊過於和緩閒暇
便轉回頭去看船尾的逝水
　　　　追著記憶跑
跑入內心的歷史河道

江水曾是血淚流的
眼看艙底仍擠在窮苦裏
船在逆流中
　拖著沉重的歲月
便不能不慢下來

　二

一峽一峽
　又一峽
掙開左右堅固的子宮壁
抓住兩邊的平衡張力
沿著安全的中心線
突破艱險的瓶頸出來
船頭直指向明麗的遠景
遙望　一瀉千里
進入遠山
　　遠水
便渾然與天地同流

時間　空間
都空回原來
畫筆與雕刀就別想動了
八大的潑墨
蒙特里安的造型
克利斯多的LAND ART
都一一退出風景
只留下山水
　一剛一柔
　一動一靜
在畫著那一幅幅不能畫的
　　　　山水畫
在雕著那一座座不能雕的
　　　　雕塑
　　給大自然看

看到長河落日圓
　　山隨水盡
　　　煙雲變滅
遠處的一盞船燈
　　便亮開整條江
　　　　在夜讀
讀來星垂原野闊
　　　月湧大江流
讀到天亮
方讀出天地線上那個一字
人與船與風景便都醒來
　　　跟著太陽一起讀
　　　　讀來千山萬水
　　　　　天高地遠
　　　　　大江南北
　　　　　源遠流長
　　　平面看　都是畫
　　　立體看　都是雕塑
屬於眼睛的　都由相機運回去
屬於心的　　便由詩來轉運
沿水路　是長江萬里
　　　讓風景去走
走心路　比歷史遠
　　　便由風雲鳥去飛

　　　　　　　　一九九四年

一個美麗的形而上
—— 飛越三萬尺高空有感

飛離地面
飛越雲層
一個美麗的形而上
便到了三萬呎高空
飛機已是一座真的
　　　　空中樓閣
造在無物可及的
　　　　空闊裏

有什麼不好
人坐機內
世界坐機外
單純的對話
透明的相望
忘我是最長
　　最遠
　　最暢通
　　的
　　一條路

千山萬水
千景萬象
都往天地線跑
跑空了世界
方把眼睛放回來

雲山雲海
幻境已浮現成形
　　　塑造成象
雲上　什麼也沒有
有　也在沒有中

雲下　只留下煙囪
　　　　　炮管
　　　　　十字架
構成歲月的鐵三角
都市與田園也只是兩輛
　被機翼牽著飛的玩具車
不能鬆手
手一鬆　世界便輕過雲
下不來了

一路上
機翼有時也會刺痛遠方
　　　　　　　　與記憶
能靠近過來也只有
那座早已光化成詩的燈屋
那隻銜住桂葉飛經禮拜堂的
　　　　　　　　青鳥
其他是一片空白　便留給天空
這樣就夠了　也很好
配合宇宙藍色的玻璃大廈（註）
不就成了三位一體
最好是不問
永恆　它如果要來
自己會來

註：同蓉子出國旅遊或開會演講，來回途中，總要飛經雲上三萬尺高
　　空沒有人住的「宇宙藍色玻璃大廈」；那裡什麼都留不下來，當
　　時間空間與我都渾化進「單純」與「透明」，真是一切在言中，
　　也在不言中，因而便不能不記起詩人桂樂希的話：「詩是悟的盛
　　典」。

一九九一年七月

921號悲愴奏鳴曲

造物
祢安頓我們在這美麗的島上
祢的仁慈　我們的感恩
平行成歲月的雙軌
在田園　被太陽汗水刻在
　　　　額上的艱苦紋路
已被都市文明美成通往地球村
　　　　多彩多姿的順暢網路
　　　　　給進步與繁榮在走

造物
究竟為什麼
在祢來不及預防的震怒裏
山崩地裂
死亡來不及追認死亡
血水淚水雨水
直往陰暗的墳地灌溉
田園躺在廢墟上喘息
都市斷電瞎著眼睛在看
除了呼救聲　是哭聲
除了祈求　　是跪拜
呼天不應　神明不明
我們含淚逃出流血的傷口
　堅強的站給生命看
世界各地帶著同情趕來
在死亡最陰冷的黑地上
點亮一線溫暖的火光
讀著人類的關懷與希望

造物
究竟為什麼
祢180度反轉
將仁慈震破成殘暴

在上帝都不知道祢要震怒的那一剎
在世界驚慌的躲在桌下
時間與空間都縮回去
我們在什麼都摸不著的空茫裏
順從祢的凌駕　顫抖在搖擺的生死線上

從劫後餘生回到痛苦裏
我們深悟人不能勝天的軟弱
也無法過問祢的對錯
我們是祢造的
　　　是祢的作品
如何阻止雕塑家
　　從不弄壞自己的雕塑
沿著舊金山唐山經過土耳其到阿里山
祢一路震怒過來
銅像博物館銀行金庫
　　　墜如山頂的落石
世界空望成和尚的光頭
原子能變得無能
警犬挖土機與救護車
　　只求找到最後的一些聲息
聯合國紅十字會也只能替祢
　　　　在事後布施一些仁慈

造物
在祢用我們的血淚與骨肉
　　　來燃燒祢的怒火過後
在我們痛苦過後的痛苦過後
我們仍活在祢賜給我們身體與土地的地球上
　　　仍活在冬去春來　日落日出的時序中
忘不了祢將我們設計在
　　　　大自然的生命結構中
我們走　地相跟
我們飛　天相隨

我們情悠悠　　江水說不盡
我們心遙遙　　天地望無窮
我們高興來花開鳥鳴
　　　　愁苦來愁雲苦雨
　　　　相思來黃葉落
　　　　孤獨來天邊的孤雲
　　　　渺茫來遙望的天地線
　　　　希望來明天的日出
我們的確是活在祢仁慈的右手
　　　　　　　與殘暴的左手中
任由祢擺佈與指使
我們的聽與看都來自祢的耳目
　　　　行與動都離不開祢的手腳
　　　　生與死都在祢的身體裏
祢一秒鐘震破的世界
我們要連年連月來勞役苦修

造物
若祢是仁慈的父
怎能打翻孩童正玩得開心的拼圖
怎能連頭上一根髮地上一根草
　　　都要被祢的斷層切斷
在承受祢毀滅性的震怒過後
土地與我們都痛苦得夠累了
死亡仍籠罩著去不掉的陰冷
餘震與餘驚仍在鐘錶裏
　　　　　　一滴一答
歲月在夜裏還是睡的不好

造物
求祢施放出祢的大愛
使斷層埋住的一條條引爆線
都在睡夢中安靜成
　　　地下溫暖的電流
好讓療傷的土地與我們

在死亡走過的冷冽的夜裡
逐漸恢復體溫
去追趕明天的太陽
重新耕種我們青山綠水的田園
　　　我們五顏六色的都市
　　　我們安定舒適的生活
　　　我們用詩用歌來看來聽
　　　　　來讚美的未來

　　　　　　一九九九年

我們來自大自然

我們來自大自然
　　　已不自然
將大自然關在盆景裏
　　從鋁窗看都市的叢林
　　　　　街道的河流
　　　　　鬧市的人山人海
當天空與曠野在鳥翅上比闊
我們在紅綠燈裏擠來擠去
當湖水河水與海水
　　在同天空比藍
我們的排水溝不停把污水
　　　　　　污出去
當白雲在山頂浮成一朵朵
　　　　美麗的形而上
我們林立的煙囪
卻排成一座座黑森林

我們來自大自然
　　越來越不自然
當開在綠野的鮮花
　　在機房裏變成塑膠花
　　在網路上只留下影子
我們便忙著打開電門
　　飄浮入那個沒有體重的
　　　　　　虛像世界中
隔著一層玻璃見面說話
大自然左看右看
還是自自然然
　　沿著鳥道雲路
　　　抓住石紋上山
　　　抓住水紋進海
　　　抓住樹根入地
　　　回到根本原來

二〇〇〇年

IV

小提琴的四根弦

童時，你的眼睛似蔚藍的天空，
長大後，你的眼睛如一座花園，
到了中年，你的眼睛似海洋多風浪，
晚年來時，你的眼睛成了憂愁的家，
沉寂如深夜落幕後的劇場。

一九五四年

光　穿著黑色的睡衣

紫羅蘭色的圓燈罩下　　　　光流著
藍玉的圓空下　　　　　　　光流著
邱吉爾的圓禮帽下　　　　　光流著
唯有少女們旋動的花圓裙下
　那塊春日獵場　　　　　　光是跳著的
而在圓形的墳蓋下　　連作為天堂支柱的牧師
　也終日抱怨光穿著黑色的睡衣

　　　　　　　　　　一九五八年

第九日的底流

不安似海的貝多芬伴第九交響樂長眠地下，我在地上張目活著，除了
這種顫慄性的美，還有什麼能到永恆那裏去。

序　曲

當托斯卡尼尼的指揮棒
　　　　　　砍去紊亂
你是馳車　我是路
我是路　你是被路追住不放的遠方

樂聖　我的老管家
你不在時　廳燈入夜仍暗著
　　　　爐火熄滅　院門深鎖
　　　　世界背光而睡
你步返　踩動唱盤裏不死的年輪
我便跟隨你成為迴旋的春日
　　　　　在那一林一林的泉聲中

於你連年織紡著旋律的小閣樓裏
　　　　一切都有了美好的穿著
日子笑如拉卡
我便在你聲音的感光片上
　　　　成為那種可見的迴響

一

鑽石針劃出螺旋塔
所有的建築物都自目中離去
螺旋塔昇成天空的支柱
高遠以無限的藍引領
渾圓與單純忙於美的造型
透過玻璃窗　景色流來如酒
醉入那深沉　我便睡成底流
在那無邊地靜進去的顫動裏
只有這種嘶喊是不發聲的

而在你音色輝映的塔國裏
純淨的時間仍被鐘錶的雙手捏住
萬物回歸自己的本位　仍以可愛的容貌相視
我的心境美如典雅的織品　置入你的透明
啞不作聲地似雪景閃動在冬日的流光裏

　　二

日子以三月的晴空呼喚
陽光穿過格子窗響起和音
凝目定位入明朗的遠景
寧靜是一種聽得見的迴音
整座藍天坐在教堂的尖頂上
凡是眼睛都步入那仰視
方向似孩子們的神色於驚異中集會
身體湧進禮拜日去換上一件淨衣
為了以後六天再會弄髒它
而在你第九號莊穆的圓廳內
一切結構似光的模式　鐘的模式
　　　我的安息日是軟軟的海棉墊　綉滿月桂花
　　　將不快的煩躁似血釘取出
　　　痛苦便在你纏繞的緗帶下靜息

　　三

眼睛被蒼茫射傷
日子仍迴轉成鐘的圓臉
林園仍用枝葉描繪著季節
在暗冬　聖誕紅是舉向天國的火把
人們在一張小卡片上將好的神話保存
那輛遭雪夜追擊的獵車
終於碰碎鎮上的燈光　遇見安息日
門窗似聖經的封面開著
在你形如教堂的第九號屋裏
爐火通燃　內容已烤得很暖

沒有事物再去抄襲河流的急躁
掛在壁上的鐵環獵槍與拐杖
都齊以協和的神色參加合唱
都一同走進那深深的注視

四

常驚遇於走廊的拐角
似燈的風貌向夜　你鎮定我的視度
兩輛車急急相錯而過
兩條路便死在一個交點上
當冬日的陽光探視滿園落葉
我亦被日曆牌上一個死了很久的日期審視
在昨天與明日的兩扇門向兩邊拉開之際
空闊裡，沒有手臂不急於種種觸及
「現在」仍以它插花似的姿容去更換人們的激賞
而不斷的失落也加高了死亡之屋
以甬道的幽靜去接露臺挨近鬧廳
以新娘盈目的滿足傾倒在教堂的紅氈上
你的聲音在第九日是聖瑪麗亞的眼睛
調度人們靠入的步式

五

穿過歷史的古堡與玄學的天橋
人是一隻迷失於荒林中的瘦鳥
沒有綠色來確認那是一棵樹
困於迷離的鏡房　終日受光與暗的絞刑
身體急轉　像浪聲在旋風中
片刻正對　便如在太陽反射的急潮上碑立
於靜與動的兩葉封殼之間
人是被釘在時間之書裡的死蝴蝶
禁黑暗的激流與整多的蒼白於體內
使鏡房成為光的墳地　色的死牢
此刻　你必須逃離那些交錯的投影
去賣掉整個工作的上午與下午

然後把頭埋在餐盤裏去認出你的神
而在那一剎間的迴響裏　另一隻手已觸及永恆的前額

六

如此盯望　鏡前的死亡貌似默想的田園
黑暗的方屋裏　終日被看不見的光看守
簾幕垂下　睫毛垂下
無際無涯　竟是一可觸及的溫婉之體
那種神秘常似光線首次穿過盲睛
遠景以建築的靜姿而立　以初遇的眼波流注
以不斷的迷住去使一顆心陷入永久的追隨
沒有事物會發生悸動　當潮水流過風季
當焚後的廢墟上　慰藉自闔掌間似鳥飛起
當航程進入第九日　吵鬧的故事退出海的背景
世界便沉靜如你的凝目
遠遠地連接住天國的走廊
在石階上　仰望走向莊穆
在紅氈上　腳步探向穩定

七

吊燈俯視靜廳　迴音無聲
喜動似遊步無意踢醒古蹟裏的飛雀
那些影射常透過鏡面方被驚視
在湖裏撈塔姿　在光中捕日影
滑過藍色的音波　那條河背離水聲而去
收割季前後　希望與果物同是一支火柴燃熄的過程
許多焦慮的頭低垂在時間的斷柱上
一種刀尖也達不到的劇痛常起自不見血的損傷
當日子流失如孩子們眼中的斷箏
　一個病患者的雙手分別去抓住藥物與棺木
　一個囚犯目送另一個囚犯釋放出去
那些默喊　便厚重如整個童年的憶念
　　被一個陷入旋渦中的手勢托住
而「最後」它總是序幕般徐徐落下

八

當綠色自樹頂跌碎　春天是一輛失速的滑車
在靜止的淵底　只有落葉是聲音
在眉端髮際　季節帶著驚慌的臉逃亡
禁一個狩獵季在多霧打濕的窗內
讓一種走動在鋸齒間探出血的屬性
讓一條河看到自己流不出去的樣子
歲月深處腸胃仍走成那條路
走成那從未更變過的方向
探首車外　流失的距離似紡線捲入遠景
汽笛就這樣棄一條飄巾在站上
讓回頭人在燈下窺見日子華麗的剪裁與縫合
沒有誰不是雲　在雲底追隨飄姿　追隨靜止
爬塔人已逐漸感到頂點倒置的冷意
下樓之後　那扇門便等著你出去

九

我的島　終日被無聲的浪浮雕
以沒有語文的原始的深情與山的默想
在明媚的無風季　航程睡在捲髮似的摺帆裏
我的遙望是遠海裏的海　天外的天
一放目　被看過的都不回首
驅萬里車在無路的路上　輪轍埋於雪
雙手被蒼茫攔回胸前如教堂的門閂上
我的島便靜渡安息日　閒如收割季過後的莊園
在那面鏡中　再看不見一城喧鬧　一市燈影
星月都已跑累　誰的腳能是那輪日
天地線是永久永久的啞盲了
當晚霞的流光　流不回午前的東方
我的眼睛便昏暗在最後的橫木上
聽車音走近　車音去遠　車音去遠

一九六〇年

死亡之塔

透過死對生命認知，本是上帝的工作。詩人子豪之死，不知是誰推我去當上帝的助手。的確，死亡帶來時間的壓力與空間的漠遠感是強大的。逼使詩人里爾克說出：『死亡是生命的成熟』；也迫使我說出：『生命最大的迴聲，是碰上死亡才響的』。站在『死亡之塔』上，我更看清了生命。

一

當落日將黑幕拉滿
　　　帆影全死在海裏
你的手便像斷槳
　　沉入眼睛盯不住的急流

抓不住火曜日
握不住陽光的方城
也划不動藍波的醉舟

打穀場將成熟的殼打盡
死亡是那架不磨也得發亮的收割機
誰也不知自己屬於那一季
而天國只是一隻無港可靠的船
當船纜解開　岸是不能跟著去的
一棵樹倒在最後的斧聲裏
　　　樹便在建築裏流亡到死
而在那一睡便醒不來的時空裏
神的假臂終究接不往聖瑪利亞手中的幼嬰
生命便如那忙亂的腳步聲
被遺忘在沒有記性的月臺上
當期待與禱告都到齊了
若剪刀將彩帶剪斷　闖進來的不是笑聲
所有的手便迫著去握那個沒有電的插頭
任層層的夜圍攏你　環抱你
歲月已默視無目　張望無窗

世界便似鏡被捏碎　光蹓光的　影跑影的
眼睛迫著放走拐角裏的某些逃遁
　　　將視線收回來好苦啊

在稿紙種滿尤加利樹的往昔
　　　　　　蓋有你的磨坊
磨碎鐘錶的齒輪　也磨不斷你的沉視
將自我拋入指針急轉的渦流裏　你圖逆旋
那互撞　較擊劍還曉得致命的傷口
那爭執　比鋸齒向樹木問路還急躁
你的不安早已成為嚴重的風季

在尼古丁燃燒著那種醒的夜裏
你的面逃不出燈的瞭望
　　便被光埋在稿紙上
　　　成為遼闊的風景　成為睡著的火焰
　　　　　在雲層之上　在岩層之下

入多　港口已暗　潮聲也冷
寒流也帶來信息
催園林裏留不住的都趕程回去
你也回去　地球也哭著回去
朋友　要是捉迷藏的蒙巾解開
場景裏再也浮不出那張預料中的面孔
叫我們如何推開你睫毛放下的欄柵
　進去將夜撕破　把失去的從煙流中尋回
在那一年的第五季　所有的鳴鐘都是啞的
一條河在音樂中斷的電唱機裏死去

水流乾了　風車便轉不動田園的風光
空曠裏　寧靜的羅列　鋪著遙遠的去路
　鳥從那裏飛不返　風從那裏吹不回
我們便用太陽畫影子　點綴你的行程

二

朝陽啣住黎明銀白色的吸乳瓶　奔向嚮午
　　從光的峭壁上跌下來
　　　　夕陽的血便在西天流盡
朋友　在入晚的廊柱下
你眼睛的紡車被夜卸下搖把　紡不出視線
　　坐姿便棄椅而去　燈也死在罩裏

日影隨流動的季節在庭園裏換位
那變距是一道陷阱　事情總是失足的
收割日之後　無物可指出風向
盯視也穿不過田園的陰暗
你便成為入倉的糧食　在火裏飄昇
主啊　彌撒日　那些禱詞已被嚼成橄欖香
人們為何在聖餐裏聞及那焦味
當焚屍爐較郵筒還穩妥
　　一封信在火途上快遞
　　我們便清楚地讀到　主啊
　　　　　你在用骨灰修補天國
主啊　你如果就是那扇啟閉的百葉窗
　　　在兩根繩來回的反拉裏
　　　　　便有一輪日從產房衝出
　　　　　　　一黑夜釘入棺蓋
而木馬死了　最藍的天也埋在那裏
面紗揭開　花容便在閃光燈中探詢著謝期
抖步絕崖　總有一塊斷石到時認出你的鞋
歲月像噴泉飄落在無力爬昇的回程裏
亞門像電鈴呼叫在萬物紊亂的門號上
　　鋸木聲叫著林　箭簇聲叫著鳥
　　火焰叫著煙流　煙流呼醒域外
在域外　連歸雲都睡著了
朋友　當燃燒的景物在眼爐裏熄滅
　　　谷底昇起　岩底昇起　海底昇起
　　　　光與暗的爭吵不再

　　　　　　　樹與風的爭吵不再
　　　　　　　　　潮與浪的爭吵不再
　　在夜的光滑的斜面上　連影子都站不穩
　　你的探步如何把持住那滑度
　　就在那一次跌跤的怔忡裏
　　藍天的調色盤給摔碎了　太陽也擠不出油彩
　　世界便被推入那沒有畫也沒有畫框的茫然裏
　　讓一切在盲睛中只有一種淒然的稱呼──
　　死亡！它就這樣成為一切內容的封殼
　　　　　　　　　成為吞吃上帝黑袍子的巨影
　　日子因鎖配不出鑰匙而驚呼
　　只要窗開著　連天花板都急著往外逃
　　朋友　當崩塌聲沿斷柱嘩然而下
　　你是事情過後的那陣靜
　　當永久的假期寫在碑石上
　　你是那隻跌碎的錶　被時間永遠的解僱了
　　　　自由脫離它鐵絲網的褓姆
　　　　強風找不到它森林的鏡子
　　　　退潮帶不走它抱過的岸
　　你便步出自己　逃離腳印　逃離路

　　法蘭西詩集疊成石級的日子安息了
　　貝多芬製造海的日子安息了
　　在杯底打撈宴會屍體的日子安息了
　　在少女與孕婦呈現花與果的日子安息了
　　在槍管與筆管裡流著兩種血的日子安息了
　　當那支洋火已躍出光的走廊
　　鑽石針也走完它華麗的紋路
　　你的臉便暗如移離放映窗的銀幕
　　　　不再被光浮彫　不再製作風景　不再認識眼睛
　　在耶穌也放假的假日裏　你便攜著雲
　　去跳　去跳你那永遠也跳不完的天地線的繩子

　　當那座十字架建築已在胸前竣工
　　太陽的金驢子也死在地球的黑磨坊裏

主啊　連你自己都失業與斷糧了
叫我們如何從奉獻箱裏要回你的借款
如何在一個破洋娃娃裏挖出嬰兒時的哭聲
如何在林蔭道上拾回孩童時滾鐵環的輪響
如何伏在鐵軌上收回那些逃奔的日程
主啊　當那雙空鞋似廢船棄在岸上
　　　　不再裝載不安的天色　不再拖運那永遠也運不完的遠方
我們便在沒有浪潮的回潮裏　想念海
　　　　在沒有奔流的回流裏　想念河
　　　　在沒有聲音的回聲裏　想念谷
　　　　在霧靄裏想念煙突的輪廓　山的輪廓　鳥的輪廓
　　　　在挖墓聲裏想念墻的姿式　門的姿式　窗的姿式
在一條被焚燬的死虹裏　尋覓陽光中的雨景

　　三

歲月的伐木者　在髮林裏伐出空地
　　是用來捉迷藏　還是用來瞭望天國
當鴿灰色的秋空　展不出鴿子的翅膀
我們便逐漸感知那低垂下來的靜
　　　像十字架的影子　火睡在灰燼中

暖日吃掉整春的花色
使長夏醉紅如一條著火的走廊
天空被燒焦　季節沉著臉向廢墟走去
雪便成為那種最原本的顏色與聲音
說出那張永遠睡去的臉

時序逃不出四季的方城
雙目望不回千山萬水
花瓶也養不活春天
生命便像斷在刀下的一根繩子
永恆是接的　在那日子來時迫著解開
誰都註定是那張要被放完的唱片
　　奇幻得如被漩渦旋轉成的塔

於渦流靜止時倒塌

如穀物滿足農村
人是堆在鐘齒上的糧食
　　　　滿意著時鐘的飢餓
時間之海啊　因你的茫然無際
我們生來便是那條為你流乾的河
　在子宮開堰的節日裏　急急流向你
直至所有的浪聲全死在你的聾耳裏
　　　所有的光燦全暗在你的盲睛中
我們仍不知自己也屬於那流浪的風系
離去時　將影子留在一張漏光的底片上
山林浮彫著大地的墳園
珊瑚彫飾著海的墳園
雲與鳥畫著天空的墳園
　以三角亭的遙望
　以無風港的守候
　以天鵝絨被的等待
那一夜　世界累得如被餐具圍獵過的晚宴
　　　　眼睛背燈而睡
　　　　鏡子背形象而望
於綠葉花朵與果子的接力跑過後
誰也無力去抱太陽的橄欖球
　猛衝歲月的凱旋門
隔著棺蓋　神父總是接不好那條斷了的錄音帶
只好讓一部分消息寄往禮拜日
　　　　一部分投遞沒有住址

方屋裏　迴響擊向四壁
　在抑制下　終又溫順如那條沿岸而下的河
我們便默悟那個在闔掌間昇起的世界
　而感知死　成為死的僕役
　謙卑得如一盤被傳遞的聖餐
　　靜候一個從胸前繞道過來的手勢
　　去把花朵們繞成白色的圓窗

　　　　　茫然了遠景
　　　　　　也茫然了那找不到收容的凝望
　　讓眼睛就這樣瞎在沉思裏
　　像花瓷磚瞎在暗廳中
　　　　仍知夜的幽寂　燈的俯視

　　四

　　太陽無論從那一邊來
　　總有一邊臉流在光中
　　　　一邊臉凍成冰河
　　花店便天天忙著
　　　　將兩種花賣給兩種節日
　　讓眼睛成為玫瑰與白菊爭吵的園子

　　鏡子一望便響成鬧鐘
　　　　　響成一種計時系統
　　刮鬚刀已日漸感到某種成長的頑強
　　明天總是為使昨日成為某些遺忘而來
　　　　總是將那一半入場券堅持在場外
　　　　　　另一半飄成火的姿態
　　以右腳救起左腳　總有一隻腳最後成為碑
　　　　　　成為曠野的標誌

　　人是註定帶著各種酒瓶流浪了
　　　醉不回那醉過的醉
　　　　也醉不出那醉過的睡與醒
　　便只好將雙目投在天地線上
　　　形成那輛無人駕駛的自由車
　　　　雲般不領牌照　風般不看路標

　　當終站醒在那聲煞車裏
　　任腳步將路說成千種樣子　路仍是路

　　任風景在視線上飄出萬種色彩

也只有一種成為眼睛
凝眸與子彈喊出的靜止
　　美如睡著的夜
張目的無視　　是把燈也熄掉的那種影子
誰都不會再是誰　　當疤痕已認不出刀的尖銳
那些要命的讚詞與笑意
常溫柔得如撒在射程上的食料
人是被誘導去建設另一種漠野的鳥

　　　五

滿屋燈光將我推倒在那面墻上
　　迫我說出那個影子
而什麼都不去想的想
　　是一更遠的遠方

以卡通的聯想　　也無法猜透那躲在盲睛中的謎底
以南歐的夜晚　　也醞釀不出如此熟透的睡意
而它總是成為那種最懇切的接待
　　　　成為女人光滑的胸臆
　　　　成為收容一切容貌的鏡面

追思日　　亡友的臉不再是一枚光亮的金幣
誰肯老待在冷風裏苦苦去認出昨日的風
誰又能在燈滅後仍一直抓牢那影子
當一年十二個月從壁上走下來
長短針跑在沒有刻字的鐘面上
生命只是一堆天色　　摺在那把黑傘裏
　　　　一陣浪聲　　疊在風中
酒宴過後　　僕役是最忙的掃墓人
花燭夜　　愛琴海的琴聲碎於一聲獸叫
我們曾以掌聲擊亮一排勳章
　　　　曾闖入瑪麗亞不認識的黑巷子
　　　　曾為一句流言與讚美弄亂了白晝夜晚
而我們總是握住掌心而不知手在那裏
　　　　總是想不出鳥飛出翅膀的時候

太陽將入晚留不住的自己　　刻在白晝的樹蔭裏
我們從一雙破靴中將路放走　　讓荒野獨自回去
當背後像遠去了的步音
我們如何使跨前的腳向後複合
如何使陳列的花籃還原為春天
當封在彈疤裏的久遠戰場
　　　被斷臂人的尼龍衣裹住
我們即使是子彈也認不出傷口
誰能在巴黎二九六九年的春天
　　仍聽清一九六九年的砲聲
當棺木鐵錘與長釘擠入一個凄然的聲響
天國朝下　　一條斷繩在絕崖上
我們即使站在眼睛裏　　也看不出眼睛在看的什麼
　　　　坐在心上　　也想不出心裏在想的什麼
而它是光　　我們是被透過的玻璃
　　它是玻璃窗　　我們是被納入的風景
　　它是造在風景上的塔　　我們是被觀望的天外

　　　　　　　　　　　一九六九年

窗

猛力一推　雙手如流
　總是千山萬水
　總是回不來的眼睛

遙望裏
你被望成千翼之鳥
棄天空而去　你已不在翅膀上
聆聽裏
你被聽成千孔之笛
音道深如望向往昔的凝目

猛力一推　竟被反鎖在走不出去
　　　　　　　的透明裏

一九七二年

鞋

樓梯口的那雙鞋
　竟是天窗裏的一朵雲
山遙水遠　雲非樹
水遠山遙　雲非雲
　　　雲只是那條
　　　　永
　　　　不
　　　　能
　　　　定
　　　　名
　　　　的
　　　　路
　　　鞋也是
　　遠方也是
天空裏的那片落葉也是

　　　　　　　　　一九七二年

隱形的椅子

　　全人類都在找那張椅子，它一直吊在空中，周圍堆滿了被擊瞎
的眼睛與停了的破鐘

　　一

落葉是被風坐去的那張椅子
流水是被荒野坐去的那張椅子
鳥與雲是放在天空裏
　　　很遠的那張椅子
十字架與銅像是放在天空裏
　　　　　更遠的那張椅子
較近的那張椅子
　　　是你的影子
　　　　他的影子
　　　　我的影子
　　　大家的影子

　　二

森林以千萬種意象
　　　　架構著藍天
寂靜是一面鏡
只要鳥聲劃空而過
便有一把鑽石刀
　　對著它劃過去
　　　劃開許多門許多窗

風景流過雙目
雙目流入斑斕
斑斕流成迷離
眼睛裏的那條河
　　便也流成煙了

三

那包煙
是20條河
流成海時　岸也看不見了

抓住那瓶酒
等於抓住上帝的後腿
你是堅持要先上天堂的
至於蒙娜此刻是睡在樓上或樓下
反正你通過時　不是盯住藍天
　　　　　　便是望著綠野

四

零時

停車場是入睡的遠方
路停在煞車上

只要煞車一鬆
遠方便轉成一個
　　　　　　圓
一個世界沿向心力迴旋而入
一個世界沿離心力迴旋而出
　　　　　　出出入入
　　　　　　入入出出
　　　　　　你便去成那片
　　　　　　　　純
　　　　　　　　白
　　　　　　　　的
　　　　　　　　空
　　　　　　　　間

五

清晨是玻璃蓋的
鳥聲對照出它響亮的明度
在窗與天空與眼睛共同製作的
　　　　　　　　遼闊裏
　　　　連風景與山水
　　　　都會使你分心
因為此刻你正站在樓頂上
　　看一片雲在飄
　　　一隻鳥在飛
　　　一朵遠方在開放

六

光湧過來
將他圍住
什麼是煙之內
　　　　霧之外
那全都是水晶球中
　　　　　耍的魔術
他寧願裸著被光抓去
　　永遠關進燈的心
　　　　　星的心
　　　　　月的心
　　　太陽的心

七

觸及是手
到達是腳
能握的都不在手裏
能到的都不在腳下
若雙手雙腳已分別回到
　　　　兩岸與路裏去

叫山　山窮
喊水　水盡
那時看也不是目
　　　見也不是目
除了風問雲
　　　雲問風
誰知道眼睛最後是死在那一種顏色裏
　　　那隻鳥是如何將天空翻過去的

　　八

一條河從她腰間流過
　　竟被看成破山而出的
　　　　　　　　　　　瀑布
聽說那是春天的突然
　　　　　　　變調

兩把刀從她的媚眼中
　　　　　　　　伸過來
插在左右心房上
竟長成兩棵相思樹

　　九

砲口開著一排窗
窗的前面很靜
尤其是在那些窗
　　開了又關上之後

神父禱告時的嘴也開著一排窗
　　　　　　　窗的前面更靜
尤其是在那些窗
　　關了又打開的時候

十

燈下　一些詩稿與
　　一隻他坐過的空椅子

夜不向窗外看還好
一看　那隻空椅子
　　　竟成了天空
　　　人去　星在

　　　　　　　　　一九七四年

逃

一

第一把箭
便使曠野發出驚叫
　　翅膀認不出天空來

逃不出天空的翅膀
　　都躲到雲裏去
　　卻下水晶簾
　　玲瓏望秋月

其實　逃是鏡中的你

二

要不是鳥籠
使原野瘦了
翅膀怎會想自己
　　是天空的兩扇門
眼睛也不會望成
　　窗外的風景

其實　逃就是一種飛
　　　　　就是鳥說的那種空闊
即使雲為了遠飄
　　將山的階梯推開
那也只是起伏與浮蕩
從不經過傷口

不經過傷口的逃
便用不著去想
　　鐵柵等不等於那隻豹的視線
　　那把箭能不能將曠野追回來

當春日逃過一片片的花瓣
　夏日逃過一陣陣的浪潮
　秋日逃過一林林的葉音
　冬日逃過一山山的雪景
　遠方逃過一目目的氤氳
只要去想起雲與鳥
天空便會一把抓你成為
　　那朵美麗的形而上

　　三

其實　逃是一個很美麗的裸體
　　　　　　　　　可愛極了
大人拿著衣服追
　小孩子笑嬉嬉光著屁股跑

　　四

其實　逃就是那隻鳥
當風景不穿衣服在山水中
　天空不穿衣服在雲上
　海不穿衣服在風浪裏
　河不穿衣服在兩岸間
　你不穿衣服在身體裏
　眼睛不穿衣服在瞭望中
　煙不穿衣服在飄渺裏
那隻鳥　一振翅
　便是千里迢遙

　　　　　　　　　　一九七五年

出　走

在日月的磨鏡房裏
我清楚地看到
路從街巷裏走出
　　曠野來接它
樹從盆景裏走出
　　林野來接它
鳥從翅膀裏出走
　　天空來接它
人從名片裏出走
　　煙雲來接它
路與樹　人與鳥
　　集體出走
天地線把它們都牽回去

　　　　　　　　　一九八四年

2比2・20比20
—— 未完成的隨想曲

一

窗外是門
門外是鎖

山外是水
水外是天地茫茫

二

人穿衣服
衣服口袋裏放著一張護照
鳥穿天空
天空口袋裏什麼也不放

三

一盆一盆剪齊了的盆景
　　從理髮店裏好看出來

飄飄然的長髮　　被陽光噴成瀑布
　　　　　　　被風吹成叢林

四

馬路劃著一條一條的線
鐵軌固定著兩邊輪子轉動

原野劃著一條一條的河
翅膀從不問天空是如何飛的

五

鳥
飛入山水

雞
飛進菜市場

六

要想找到風與雲與鳥的地址
請向天空與曠野大喊一聲　聽聽回音

而你住在那裏　再遠也遠不出那雙腿
　　　　　　　那條巷　那條街

七

坐上電梯　摩天樓再高
　　　　　也高不出屋頂

天空坐上雲　誰知道眼睛有多高
　　　　　　　　渺茫有多遠

八

投一根釣魚線到深山的溪流裏去
　整個大自然便靜靜的坐在那裏

將視線繞入她的腰
　沿目紋一拉　射死人的搖滾樂

九

鳥聲與泉音
　　叫森林越睡越沉

流行歌與車輪聲
　　叫都市翻來覆去

十

那麼多輪子
　　也只能轉動幾條街

太陽只動一隻輪子
全都跟著動

十一

太陽的嘴
　　吻開滿海浪花

你的嘴
　　吻起滿目眼波

十二

站在山峰上　　天空頂撞你的頭
　　　　　　　近得可用手去摸

站在乳峰上　　天空滑到下面去
　　　　　　　　無底的深淵

十三

兩岸抱住河　抱住風景
　　睡到遙遠的海裏去

雙手抱住她　抱住夜色
　　也睡到遙遠的海裏去

十四

貝殼聽海叫
　　聽陽光與月光在隔壁說話

耳朵聽槍叫
　　聽她與鈔票在笑裏笑

十五

牧笛是一條河
　　流出乳般的晨光，酒般的晚霞

槍管也是一條河
　　流出白色的淚　紅色的血

十六

樹上的花　是窗
樹上的果　是窗簾放下的窗

屋房的窗　是花
房屋放下窗簾的窗　是甜蜜的果子

十七

歲月若是一張落帆
便一層一層地摺在你的額上

而太陽那把閃亮的彫刀　死抓住海浪不放
　　　　　死抓住大理石與金屬的紋路不放

十八

天地的雙腿合攏在水平線上
　　　　　換上翅膀飛

你的雙腳是一把生鏽的剪刀
　合攏在老祖母顫抖的手裏

十九

體毛在焚屍爐中
　　燻成一陣煙

山水在太陽裏
　煮成一鍋風景

二十

大自然
　是一座銀行

人
　是票面不同的紙幣

　　　　　　　　　　　一九八六年

門與世界與我的奇妙連線

花朵把春天的門推開
炎陽把夏天的門推開
落葉把秋天的門推開
寒流把冬天的門推開
（時間到處都是門）
鳥把天空的門推開
泉水把山林的門推開
河流把曠野的門推開
大海把天地的門推開
（空間到處都是門）

天地的門被海推開
海自己卻出不去
全人類都站在海邊
　　　　　　發呆
只看到一朵雲從門縫裏
　　　　悄悄流出去
眼睛一直追著問
問到凝望動不了
雙目竟是兩把鎖
將天地的門卡擦鎖上
門外的進不來
門內的出不去
陳子昂急著讀他的詩
　　　前不見古人　　後不見來者
　　　唸天地之悠悠　　獨愴然而涕下

王維也忍不住讀他的詩
　　　　江流天地外
　　　　山色有無中
在那片茫茫中
門還是一直打不開

等到日落星沈天昏地暗
穿黑衣紅衣聖袍的神父與牧師
　　　　　　　忽然出現
要所有的人將雙掌像兩扇門（又是門）
　　　　　　在胸前闔上
然後叫一聲阿門（又是門）
天堂的門與所有的門
　　　便跟著都打開了
在一陣陣停不下來的開門聲中
我雖是想把所有的門
　　　都羅過來的羅門
但仍一直怕怕那手中抓住
　鎖與鑰匙的所（鎖）羅門

註：廿多年前我曾說過全人類尤其是詩人藝術家均是活在卓越的想
　　像力中；不然，門只有木門、鉛門、鐵門、玻璃門、前門與後
　　門，或者門都沒有，但有了想像力，它把時間的門、空間的
　　門、哲學家的腦門、詩人的心門與上帝的天堂之門等無數的
　　門，都一道道推開來，到處都是開門的聲音。
又：寫完此詩，忽然覺得它為我對「想像力」這在詩中特別重要的
　　創作觀念，作了具有臨場感而非「條文性」的具體說明。

　　　　　　　　　　　　　　　一九八九年八月十八日

窗的世界

窗是大自然的畫框
也是飛在風景中的鳥

窗在田園　自動裝上遠距離廣角鏡頭
窗在都市　越來越近視
窗在遠方　鳥飛出翅膀
窗舒暢快活時　千山萬水不回首
窗被關發怒時　炮彈洞穿過層層厚牆
窗孤獨無聊時　一面擦亮寂寞的鏡子
窗閤目沉靜時　一口深山裏的古井
　　　　　　　附近有人在打坐

　　　　　　　　　　　一九九一年一月

看時間一個人在跑

地球在太空裏跑
火車在地球裏跑
我們坐在火車裏不動
　　看風景在車外跑
跑到速度倒轉過頭
　　　　　　來跑
風景便停下來
　　看車裏的我們在跑
火車便停下來
　　看地球在跑
地球便停下來
　　看太空在跑
太空便停下來
　　看時間一個人在跑

一九九一年十月

誰能買下那條天地線

將日月星辰與燈
　　照來照去的光線
　　　　都拉過來
將汽車輪船與飛機
　　跑來跑去的航線
　　　　都拉過來
將畫家手中
　　畫來畫去的曲線直線
　　　　　都拉過來
將大家眼睛
　　看來看去的視線
　　　　都拉過來
拉在一起
到最後
　　也只留下那條茫茫的天地線
　　　　牽著天　拉著地
　　　　　　在走

　　　　　　一九九二年一月

「燈屋」不同的設計

燈屋設計在
　沒有圍牆的光裏
不必爬樓梯　坐電梯
再高　一看就到

不像帝國大廈
爬到一百層
仍出不了四面牆
要再高上去
頂樓的露臺
牆是沒有了
如果被天空抓去
自己不是鳥
掉下去連聲音都聽不見
於是四週還有欄干

　　　　　　　　　　　一九九三年六月

「燈屋」的造型世界
—— 它是一件後現代裝置藝術　也是一首視覺詩

那是一座以光塑造的
　　　　　透明建築
材質來自藝術的造型世界
燈飾店的光都混不進來
幾十盞不同形態的燈
鳴響著光的交響樂
圍觀成一座燈的花園
開著幾十年謝不了的燈花
電視機曾移植它上銀幕
雜誌曾移植它上封面
採訪的眼睛曾移植它
　　　　　進入各種回憶

此刻所有內在生命的支柱
全都具體成可見的燈柱
頂起整個發光的空間
光沿著螺旋型的光梯
　　　　　迴旋而上
　　　　雲層往下降
　　　　天空往上昇
上面不就是宇宙的玻璃大廈
除了日月星辰純粹的光
　　　　鏡子也不能放
　　　　要照自己照
一個三百六十度的環視
將古今中外都照在一起
讓所有的藝術流派
　都跟著光流進來
除了藝術與人
透明的光圈內
任何陰影與雜音

　　　都進不來

　在一道道迴旋的光中
　它已玄昇成一座螺旋塔
　　抓住宇宙永恆的基型
　將世界昇上美的頂峯
　　旋進無底的奧秘

　　　　　　　　　　一九九三年

我最短的一首詩
——「天地線是宇宙最後的一根弦」

前　言

　　這是我最短但後設「附語」最長的一首詩。其實這些「附語」，也是採取詩、散文、哲思、評論……等文藝屬性所混合成的一篇文章。因此在採取後現代「文類解構」的觀念來看，則它除了是一首詩，也是一篇散文；也是一篇對生命與時空存在進行探索與判視的論文；同時在其中也有我構想中的一件地景藝術（LAND ART）作品。

　　在失去中心與價值失控的後現代現象中，大多數人已像是衝刺在四面牆裡的蝙蝠人。慶幸的是詩幫助人類在「麵條」、「金條」，與現實勢利社會到處的「拉皮條」之外，看到了另一條奇特的線條，它便是一直牽著日月進出的「天地線」；也是宇宙留下最後回聲的一根弦。

天
地
線
是
宇
宙
最
後
的
一
根
弦

附　語

　　這首短詩，看來極需要「後設」詩語同時，因為它們走在一起，很談得來。

　　在我寫過不能不注意深度與廣度的不少長詩如〈第九日的底

流〉、〈麥堅利堡〉、〈都市之死〉、〈死亡之塔〉、〈板門店38度線〉、〈觀海〉、〈曠野〉、〈隱形的椅子〉、〈時空奏鳴曲〉、〈大峽谷〉……等以及〈窗〉、〈流浪人〉……等不少短詩過後，這首短詩，可說是我最短的一首詩，以後也不可能寫出比它更短的詩。記得詩人龐德說過這樣的話，一個詩人能寫出一個獨特精彩的意象，是值得高興的事。如今，我將一個自認是一己較獨特精彩的意象，透過詩眼，對它內涵與結構做整體性的透視，又能獨立成一首詩，應是創作中又多出的心得。

　　這首詩雖特別短，但心靈與思想確實同「它」走了相當長的路，在茫茫的時空中，對我來說，「它」已是一切存在最後的回聲；尤其是當我在〈窗〉詩中，寫出「猛力一推／竟被反鎖在走不出去的透明裡」，陷入那片無邊的空茫中，內心的感覺更是如此。

　　記得我與蓉子有一次飛過大峽谷的高空，在宇宙的茫茫中，內心忽然想到整個世界與地球，只留下三條線：

　　（1）一條是「大峽谷」——是大自然用「原始」劃下的一條線。

　　（2）一條是「萬里長城」——是人佔據大自然，用「人的骨肉與血」揉成的三合土，在爭權奪利的現實世界，劃下人為的一條線。

　　（3）一條是「天地線」——是宇宙用「空茫」與「沉寂」，劃的一條似有似無亦真亦幻的一條線。

　　這三條線，已被「詩眼」看成時空與生命活動的三線道，於進入詩的沉思默想時，便會無意中想到人存在於「大自然」的生命結構中，一方面想望著風、雲、鳥的自由，另一方面又必須被納入現實冷酷世界的各種有形無形與新舊的框架，自然或不自願的被「生存」扣著手腳在走……。而人從搖籃到墳墓的時間很短，睡覺已死了三分之一，若又背離「真我」活著，也等於是空白與死亡，人究竟能真實的活了多少？又究竟能為自己建立與完成那些可靠的什麼？再就是死亡的左右手——那不可抗拒的「時間」與「空間」，是一開始便站在「搖籃」的旁邊，將所有的人一直綁架到「殯儀館」，而大家都好像沒有發覺，同時這件歷代來最大的綁架案，也都從未破過案；這便引發人類尤其是透視力與敏悟力較高的詩人，不能不進一步，探究人存在於深層世界中的奧秘與真況，而也在不斷的質疑中，勢必看到下面這幕一再重演的重大悲劇——

　　那就是：「人活著，都要一一被時空消滅掉；人被時空消滅掉過後，人仍可設想與盡力從銅像、紀念館、百科全書與天堂裡復活過來。可是再往下想，當他死了，銅像、紀念館、百科全書與天堂，安慰的是

張開眼睛的我們，而他！太陽究神從哪個方向昇起來，他也搞不清楚了。於是，人又不能不再度掉進無邊的空茫中；唯一能抓住的，便是那條似有似無的『天地線』——『宇宙最後的一根弦』，在鳴動著一切存在的似有似無的回聲……」。

此刻，如果我們正好在三萬呎高空的雲上飛。雲上竟是宇宙空無的藍色玻璃大廈，但一張椅子都沒有，沒有東西可停留下來；不但是有山有水、有大自然景觀的「大峽谷」與一直望著朝代來、朝代去的「萬里長城」，都看不見了；就是一望無際的雲山雲海，也只是一片可見的白色的「空茫」；整個世界便不能不進入超越「實有」的全面「空茫」、「空無」與「空靜」之境，而呈現出「空」能容納萬有、「靜」能容納萬動的實存世界。這樣的存在世界，除了使那茫茫的「天地線」成為「宇宙最後的一根弦」，能到哪裡去拉出存在奧秘與永恆的回聲？

事實上，所有二胡的弦、古箏的弦、小提琴、大提琴的弦、豎琴的弦，乃至祖父、曾祖父、曾曾祖父的心弦，都相連在茫茫的時空中被鐘齒咬斷了，就是從棺材到天堂的路線，也只是在禱告中，所設計的一條斷斷續續的虛線；最後，也的確只有那條似有似無尚可見的「天地線」，留守在宇宙茫茫的時空中。

可是這條「天地線」——「宇宙最後的一根弦」，它懸在茫無邊際的漠遠裡，不用說全世界所有的人（包括文學家、藝術家、哲學家、政治家、科學家，乃至帝王與為上帝工作的神父……），都休想彈到它，就是將所有的腳與鞋子以及車輪、機翼、鳥翼乃至雲的翅膀加在一起，也休想近及它。它便因而成為自彈自鳴，誰都不能彈的一根弦——「宇宙最後的一根弦」；同時成為一切存在無聲的回響；也渾成我一生中最短的一首詩：「天地線是宇宙最後的一根弦」。

在這首短詩「天地線是宇宙最後的一根弦」寫成之後，經由「視覺詩」的誘導與引渡，詩中的具體意象，便順利轉型進入視覺藝術創作理念中的地景藝術（LAND ART）界域。

如果說世界著名的地景藝術家克里斯多（CHRISTO）將畫在畫布畫框裡的外在自然景象，放生回到大自然，以「包裹」手段重新規劃與展現出大自然真實美的具體景觀，是被肯定的；則我將「天地線」這一單純體現於宇宙間亦真亦幻的線條造型，當作是我所構想與創作的一件「新」的「地景藝術」作品，應也是具適當性的；而且在作品意涵與符號的作用功能上，我想是同克里斯多偏向於「表態」與「述明」的「地景藝術」所表現的有異。我是企圖一方面採取極簡

（MINIMAL）與絕對觀念（ABSOLUTE CONCEPTION）的藝術手段使「天地線」的視覺空間達到單純精簡的造型之極致；另一面注入詩大量的象徵性與超現實性，以期豐富作品的內層意涵與對存在的覺識。

的確，當「天地線是宇宙最後的一根弦」這首詩中的「天地線」，經轉型為視覺藝術中可見的「地景藝術」作品，並定名為「誰都不能買的一條天地線」。兩者便都同時構成存在的高難點──一是「誰都不能彈」，一是「誰都不能買」。「不能彈」上面已說了不少；至於「不能買」，我只是曾同一些藝術家在談話中半開玩笑半認真的說過：

「做為一個畫家，從小畫至老，一生究竟畫了多少線條，好累！當『地景藝術』的興起，乾脆請『詩』幫你將那條『天地線』買下來，不但省事，而且也真的難於猜想它究竟有多貴重，多耐看與耐用……」

再就是，如果我們採取三六〇度的掃瞄，做進一步與深一層的探視，就會發現到一個更奇妙的事實，那就是：無論是日光、月光、星光、燈光照來照去的光線、腳步、車輛、輪船飛機跑來跑去的路線；風、雲、鳥飄來飄去的拋物線；眼睛看來看去的視線；畫筆畫來畫去的直線與曲線……等這許多許多數不清也數不盡的線條，都難免要被那條長遠不可觸及的「天地線」攔阻下來，說是收容它們，是因較說沒收它們好聽與有情意些，也可平和悲劇的激烈性。

的確，當「天地線」在詩眼中找到它內涵思想存在的基因，而創作成這件地景藝術作品──「誰都不能買的一條天地線」，在與「天地線是宇宙最後的一根弦」這首短詩，同時展現在宇宙茫茫的時空中，便也被詩眼看成可見與不可見的兩條線路，可通往湯恩比（TOYNBEE）心目中的進入宇宙之中、之後、之外的永久存在的真實之境；也可通往無邊無際無聲無息的「空茫」，留下存在強大無比的回響與許多問號，迫使大家越去回答便越覺得困惑與無力感──

先是讓古代買得起一個國家的帝王與當代買得起整座城市的大富翁望著買不下這條「天地線」感嘆入棺；接著是科學家絞盡腦汁造太空船去運那永遠也運不完的「天空」與「茫茫」；再下來是詩人陳子昂不停的唸著「前不見古人，後不見來者，念天地之悠悠，獨愴然而涕下……」；再下來是和尚將富貴榮華隨同頭頂一起剃光，讓空空的光頭去同天空比空；最後是牧師帶著眾人不停的禱告：「永恆的主，永恆的天國」，去看來生。

寫到此，這首短詩與「後設」詩語，邊走邊談，已接近尾聲，再要補充說的話也很短。那就是從這首短詩中，我再度體認「詩」確是一門

以文字為媒體的極簡（MINAMAL）藝術，企圖以極少的語言符號，透過象徵與暗示，舒放出生命與思想高質感與高強度的能量。至於問它是否屬於過去、現代、後現代、後後現代，以及是否屬於古典主義、浪漫主義、現實主義、超現實主義、象徵主義、抽象主義、新寫實主義……等問題，雖也有其必要性，但更值得注意的是詩往往在創作時能將「時空」與所有的種種「主義」，都只視為材料，都可將之有機的化為作品生命所表現的機能與質素；所以詩在根本上具有超越「時空」與「主義」框限與制約性的創作特質；而能呈現出一種「前進中的永恆」的存在能力。同時從這首短詩所轉型為一件「地景藝術」的相互觀照中，又可看出文字藝術與視覺藝術家是至為密切的芳鄰；並可打破彼此在以往過於硬性的分隔，尤其是在強調解構與多元共處的後現代，即使要有所分隔，也不應用封閉的牆，而應以透明可見的玻璃，使彼此有所共見，並有利拓展彼此創作廣闊的視野。

一九九七年

一種絕世的愛
—— 詩人藝術家與蒙娜麗莎的婚禮

蒙娜麗莎
妳是繽紛燦爛的春
　　激情狂熱的夏
　　金碧輝煌的秋
　　純淨潔白的冬
在大自然　留下完美的容貌
在宇宙　　留下永恆的形象

穿越美女們馨香的髮林
飄遊過美女們光潤的乳峰
在愛琴海之外的愛琴海
妳是我不變的航向
　　　最終的港灣
以較天地線還要長遠的想像
我將日月拉過來為妳打造指環
　用所有之外的所有
　　把所有的美運來
　　　為妳建構一個美在
　　　　所有世界之外的世界
沿著音樂家的聽道
　　畫家的視道
　　詩人的心道
我揮灑出「九大藝術」之光
鋪成藝術王國的紅氈
亮開天堂所有的燈
在眾神之外的美神面前
宣誓愛在所有的愛之外的愛
妳我四目相望兩心相連
我右手握住妳的完美
　左手握住妳的永恆
相吻時吻開了天地的門

洞房竟是整個神奇美妙的
　　　　無限時空
我們拿著造物頒賜的
　　通行證與信用卡
便天長地久
　渡不完的蜜月去

後記：人類有太多的存在空間，都自由的開放在那裡？有時落實在形
　　　而下的現實層面，有時昇越到純美的形而上實境。至於詩中的
　　　「九大藝術」，那是將大家熟悉的八大藝術當做「燃料」，全
　　　放在內心美的「焚化爐」中，經燃燒焚化成只能由心靈來全面
　　　感知覺識的那種「美」於無形與絕對且無所不在的近乎宗教
　　　信仰般的整體藝術精神思想世界；這個世界便正是由「美」
　　　的「第九藝術」來建構與呈現；也因此可見我過去指認「詩」
　　　與「藝術」是在哲學、科學、政治、歷史乃至宗教…等所有學
　　　問之外，為人類創造一門「美」的生命的學問是有來源的。

　　　　　　　　　　　　　二○○一年

V

美的∨型

鑽在巴士上的小學生們只管說笑
聲音如一群鳥
　　繞著在旁沉默如樹的成年人亂飛
一個童話世界與一個患嚴重心病的年代
　　不相干地坐在巴士上

突其來的急煞車
馬路的長腿　似抽筋尖叫了一聲
行人的視線集攏成美的∨型
　　　像一束花擲在那裏
反正又有人從邊境回來或不回來了

　　　　　　　　　　　　　　　一九五八年

「燈屋」：螺旋形之戀

「在我的燈屋裏，唱盤旋出螺旋形的年輪；樂音旋成螺旋形的心靈世界。螺旋形，深且看不到底；進去，也不易出來。所以，螺絲釘便是屬於那種堅定與釘下而不易拔出來的東西。而這種戀，究竟是屬於那一種戀呢？是對愛人、對生命、對整個世界與宇宙之存在嗎？都任你去想吧！」

　　門窗緊閉　示以堅然的拒絕
　　簾幕垂下　完成幽美的孤立
　　外面是消失在遠方的風
　　裡邊像波流涉及岸
　　全然絕緣後的觸及
　　　　是驟然在空氣中誕生的鐘之聲　電之光

　　這一塊純美的空間
　　養一林鳥聲　著滿天彩雲
　　在目之外　座標之外　門牌之外
　　被鑽石針劃著大理石與水晶的紋路
　　　　連耶穌的芒鞋也不知它通往那裏
　　透明似鏡　光潔似鏡
　　我便愛人般專情　順著旋律的螺旋梯
　　　　　　　　　跌入那迴旋的傾向裏
　　直至心抓穩了那快活的死　我方醒來
　　鳥目醒在一樹綠色裏
　　一幢別墅坐著夏日明麗的花園
　　讓那光輕輕地從葉縫裏灑下來
　　讓那景靜靜地風景著視境
　　讓那聲　無聲地在那聲裏迴響
　　我已感知那靠岸的汽笛聲
　　探視的眼神沿著紅甎已找到那顆鑽戒
　　怎樣也流不盡葡萄園裏的甜蜜
　　　　　看不停噴水池裏的繽紛
　　　　　拾不完睡嬰醒時眼中的純朗

驚喜得如水鳥用翅尖採摘滿海浪花
滿足得如穀物金黃了入秋的莊園
當音樂的流星雨放下閃目的珠簾
世界便裸於此　　死心於此
　　像含情的眼睛裸在凝望裏
　　　　綠蔭死心在光與葉交纏的林中
多麼豪華的幽會
在凱撒與上帝都缺席的那次夜宴裏
我輝煌的神　以我的眼睛為座椅
電唱頭不停地啃著唱盤裏不死的年輪
一顆螺絲　為掛牢一幅畫在心壁上而鑽出聲來
一個渦漩　為扭斷鐘錶的雙槳而旋轉的不停
沉靜的光流　自燈罩下的斜坡滑下
我的臉容是一塊仰首在忘懷河上的岩石
透明似鏡　光潔似鏡
收容一林鳥聲　反映滿天雲彩

划入眼睛的藍湖
燈入罩　臉罩紗
景物以乳般的光滑與柔和適應我的視度
迴旋樂以千槳搖不醒我的醉舟
圓舞曲盪水波成圈　繞花朵成環
我便昏倒在那看不見圓也看不見弧的圓弧裏
　　　　　如太陽昏睡在旋轉不停的星系中
再也看不清聖誕樹與火藥樹開的花
只感知那隨著你無限地去的遠方
　　　　　是一隻在睡中也飛的青鳥
　　　　　是浪已飛成翅膀的那個海

在那無邊無底地迴旋的空間裏
純淨得連空氣都出去　眼睛也隱入那深深的凝視
永恆此刻不需襯托　它不是銅與三合土揉成的
也不是造在血流上朽或不朽的虹橋
它只是一種無阻地旋進去的方向

一種屬於小提琴與鋼琴的道路
一種用眼睛也排不完的遠方
一種醒中的全睡　睡中的全醒
一種等於上帝又甚於上帝的存在

一九六九年

人去星在
—— 給詩人L‧大衛

燈下　一些詩稿與
　　　一隻他坐過的空椅子

夜不向窗外看還好
一看　那隻空椅子
　　　竟成了天空
　　　人去　星在

一九七四年

教　堂

那是一部不朽鋼洗衣機
經過六天弄髒的靈魂
禮拜日都送到這裏來受洗

唱詩班的嘴一張開
天國的電源便接通了
牧師的嘴一張開
水龍頭的水便滾滾下來
在佈道詞迴盪的聲浪裏
受洗的靈魂　漂白又漂白
如果仍有什麼不潔的
便是自目中排出去的那些
　　不安與焦慮　迷惘與悔意
於謝恩放進奉獻袋
　　　領出自己之後
那個潔淨的挺挺的靈魂
　　　　又向六天走去
向灰塵滾滾的市街走去

　　　　　　　　一九七六年

餐　廳

滿廳的頭
飄空成節日的氣球
眼睛圍著看
　一幅幅悅目的畫
直至把畫廊快擠破了
　才發覺那是個腸胃

一刀下去　若是一條閃亮的河
　　　　　　　　　必有魚在
一叉上來　若是魚
　必有歲月游過來
如果雙筷是猛奔的腿
　必有飢渴的嗥叫
　　　　　　在荒野上
要是田園已圓滿在盤裏
　必有兩排牙在痛咬著
　　　　　　大地的乳房

　　　　　　　　　一九七六年

觀舞記

（看保羅泰勒現代舞）

你們一轉　地球跟著去
你們一停　鐘錶都不走

那些採星採月的手
在空中不動　都成了鋼架
那些踩花踩浪的腳
　大步大步跨過去
下面是千山萬水
就不能不飛了

鳥飛著你們去
雲飄著你們來
河在你們身上流動
海在你們身上波動
天空在你們身上旋動
光波在你們身上跳動

你們換位來日月
　穿插來花蝶
　　擴散為霧
　　凝聚成山

幕落時　一朵朵不凋的讚美
　　　在不斷的掌聲中盛開
　　直喊你們是杜菲筆下的線條
　　　　　康利摩爾刀下的石雕
　　　　　杜步西眼中的音樂

一九七九年

燈屋的世界
「光是宇宙的眼睛帶著世界到處看」

一　光的行蹤

光從直線出發
行成多弦琴　　便聲音高遠
行成林野　　　便色明彩麗
行成石柱　　　便天長地久
行成水平線　　便繫住眺望
行回眸子　　　便帶日月歸

光從拋物線出發
行成噴泉　　　便繽繽紛紛
行成鳥　　　　便自由自在
行成雲　　　　便逍逍遙遙
行成風　　　　便獨來獨往
行回眸子　　　便同千山萬水
　　　　　　　　　　起伏浮沉

光從圓形出發
行成渦漩　　　便向下深奧
行成塔　　　　便向上玄昇
行成樹的年輪　便滾入大自然的壯闊
行成唱盤　　　便走進時間最精美的紋路
行回眸子　　　便看成歲月的眼睛

二　光的作業

光以直線拉著眸子上天頂
　　　　　去看尼采的心
光以拋物線牽著眸子入風景
　　　　　去看鄧肯的舞
光以圓抱住眸子與天空
　　　一同去看王維的詩

三　光的結局

光降著雪
你站在雪峯上
不動　眸子是冬
一動　雙目來不及說明自己是江河
　　　　　　還是大地伸出的雙手
　　　　　　　山水已奔著過來
　　　　　　　　捧來滿野的花

光開著花
你躺在花園裏
色彩可聽見
芬芳也有聲
偶爾聽得出神
　　會覺得那是一片無際的原野
　　　　　　　　　　　在雨中

光下著雨
你淋在柔美的濕潤中
一聞到花汁與果液的香味
夜便溶為酒
露便結成黎明
窗開時　屋內屋外都在看
太陽鋪一條路到遠方去
　　　　把世界接了過來

註：「燈屋」是用來照海還是照心？是用來照亮詩境還是用來照亮生
　　命與時空之屋呢？答不出來，只好直接去問「燈屋」了。

　　　　　　　　　　　　　　　一九七九年

「燈屋」
── 光住的地方

光　沒有圍牆
光住的地方　當然也沒有

燈屋只是一個露天的艙位
在時空之旅中
眼裏帶有畫廊
耳裏帶有音樂廳
什麼也不用帶了
這樣　雙手可空出來
　　　　　抱抱地球
雙腳可舒放在水平線上
頭可高枕到星空裏去（註）
把世界臥成遊雲
　　　　浮著光流而去
　　　　　　月是堤
　　　　　　日是岸
登步上去　光就住在那裏

　　　　　　　　　　一九七九年

註：入夜，「燈屋」眾燈閃亮成一片星空。

燈　屋

光的噴泉
無聲地交織
音樂流入音樂
色彩溶入色彩

綠窗向海
以寧靜的默呼相望
晚霞在守塔人的瞼上
　　圍成一個玫瑰園
讓光的根鬚植入盲睛
盲睛是睡在霧中的靜野
遠處　水聲似琴
　　　　琴聲如水

日落在此
月落在此
時間步過
響起一排鐘聲
那瞬息間的永恆
坐在守塔人的眼上

守塔人的世界
精巧如目之焦點
亮自光的核心
　　映出萬象

外面是不能不隨夜暗下去了
而燈屋裡
那光自重疊的光中亮起
守塔人隨著光而去
讓吐出的煙流
將整個彩色迷離的空間浮動

光之海底
Ｘ號沉船仍在航行
甲板上不再有風聲浪聲
沉靜的海流
暖如多日書房的爐火
　　　奧秘睡在此
　　　　也醒在此
守塔人望著塔笑了
因為那塔尖高過了眼睛
因為所有的捶擊
　　都穿過最後的岩層
　　　將礦物吵醒
　　　　放出光能

　　　　　　　　　一九八○年

哥倫比亞太空梭登月記
並追記三十年來創作的心路歷程

將悲多芬的心房
　　　　先點火
然後把世界放在火上
　　　　　射出去

那是一朵最美的形而上
馬拉美早就等在神秘的天空裏
以一個象徵的手勢
把它指引過去

一轉目　夢也追不上
它已飛越阿拉貢的故鄉
　　　　降落成一座月球

註：悲多芬是浪漫派音樂大師，馬拉美是象徵派詩人，阿拉貢是超現
　　實信徒。

　　　　　　　　　　　　一九八一年

日月的行踪

踩滿地喧囂於腳下
獨坐高樓看雲山
山看你是雲
雲看你是山
山坐下來　連著地
雲遊起來　伴著天

一隻鳥把路飛過來
雙目遠過翅膀時
那朵圓寂便將你
　　　　整個開放
寧靜中　你是聲音的心
回聲裏　你是遠方的心

江河經過你的血
心中那條萬古的長城
已衝出鐵欄干
進入天地線
完成那面最美的水平
讓風景一層層往上蓋
從窗蓋到鳥
從鳥蓋出天外
在這幢垂直的透明裏
你與光始終沿著直線走
　　　　日的行踪是那樣
　　　　月的行踪也是那樣

一九八二年

傘

他靠著公寓的窗口
看雨中的傘
　　走成一個個
　　孤獨的世界
想起一大群人
每天從人潮滾滾的
　　公車與地下道
　　裹住自己躲回家
　　　　把門關上

忽然間
公寓裏所有的住屋
　　全都往雨裏跑
　　　直喊自己
　　　　也是傘

他愕然站住
把自己緊緊握成傘把
　　而只有天空是傘
　　　雨在傘裏落
　　　傘外無雨

　　　　　　　一九八三年

詩的歲月

—— 給蓉子

要是青鳥不來
春日照耀的林野
　如何飛入明麗的四月

踩一路的繽紛與燦爛
要不是六月在燃燒中
　已焚化成那隻火鳳凰
夏日怎會一張翅
　便紅遍了兩山的楓樹
把輝煌全美給秋日
那隻天鵝在入暮的靜野上
　留下最後的一朵潔白
　　去點亮溫馨的冬日
　　　隨便抓一把雪
　　　　一把銀髮
　　　　一把相視的目光
都是流回四月的河水
都是寄回四月的詩

後記：隨著鳴響在妳童時記憶中的鐘聲，在民國四十四年四月十
　　　四日星期四下午四時，我們一同走過教堂的紅毯；踏著燈
　　　屋裏的燈光，走進詩的漫長的歲月，我心底要向你說的都
　　　在這首詩中。

一九八三年

女性快鏡拍攝系列

一　瘦美人

她站著
一根直軸
把眼球與地球一起轉
　　　　直到她走動

她走動
一縷飄煙
把曠野幽美的臥姿
　遠方溫婉的睡態
　　都先描了出來
　　　等著她臥下
她臥下
一條水平線　游在海上
擺盪成曲線　是江
起伏成弧線　是月
伸展成直線　便月湧大江流

二　老牌式主婦

在產房
　廚房
　臥房
她走進走出

乳嘴咬去她三分之一
菜刀切去她三分之一
剩下的　用來繡綉
　　　　愛鳳床單

三　標準型風塵女郎

風來
雨去
花開
鳥鳴
她是最野的
　　　　原野

南來
北往
峰廻
路轉
她是不限速的
　　　　高速公路

其實說甚麼
　　都不是
她只是那野得
　非常危險的
　　　　　原始

四　ＢＢ型單身女祕書

替公司
記下客戶要的貨色
　　　與交貨時間
她把電話掛上
去接另一個電話
聽見總經理說
下班到玫瑰餐廳去

她對鏡
塗一下玫瑰色口紅
忽然發覺自己
也是一種貨色
　　玫瑰色的
　　準時交貨

五　老處女型企業家

把世界存放在銀行裏
用支票支付歲月

她坐在旋轉椅上
把整座玻璃大廈
旋成一隻水晶球
四面八方反射著
　　太陽的笑聲

帶著笑聲回房
脫下名貴的浪琴錶
時間忽然靜下來
　　　浪無聲
　　　琴也無聲
燈熄後
只有那襲綢質透明睡衣
　抱住一個越來越冷感的夜

六　大眾牌情婦

只要那地方
不設門牌戶籍法院與禮堂
即使靠近懸崖
給她一張床
讓她心驚肉跳
她也敢把天翻過來睡

不必向公婆問早問晚
也不必餵乳
她較所有的新娘
都能一次又一次密造出最蜜的
　　　　　　　　蜜月

一九八三年

歲月的兩種樣子

一

天空來到你的額
群山來到你的眉
樹林來到你的髮
江河來到你的手腳
海來到你的眼睛
大地來到你的身體
日月來到你的心

你醒　日出
你睡　月出
在歡躍中　你是春
在狂熱中　你是夏
在深沉中　你是秋
在冷靜中　你是冬
在四季中　你是花

二

高樓來到你的額
招牌來到你的眉
電線來到你的髮
街道來到你的手腳
櫥窗來到你的眼睛
床來到你的身體
她來到你的心

你醒　她在
你睡　她也在

在歡躍中　她是你的春
在狂熱中　她是你的夏
在深沉中　她是你的秋

在冷靜中　她是你的冬
在四季中　她是你的花

香江詩抄

一、漂水花
—— 贈詩人余光中之一

我們蹲下來
天空與山也蹲下來
看我們用石片
　對準海平面
削去半個世紀
一座五十層高的歲月
　倒在遠去的炮聲裏
　　　　　沈下去

六歲的童年
跳著水花來
找到我們
不停的說
石片是鳥翅
　不是彈片
要把海與我們
　都飛起來
　一路飛回去

二、堤上行
—— 贈詩人余光中之二

長堤拉住
　兩邊的水
　兩頭的山
走入風景
水看山高
山看水遠
看到世界
　　　無
　　　邊
　　　無

際
時
鳥飛水去
雲浮山來
叫聲高闊與久遠
風景便順手推開
照相機的快門
走進故宮的
山水畫

一九八四年

活在框裏的照片

大自然不穿衣服
天空　曠野
河流　海洋
便脫的精光
人看到風與鳥的自由
也想裸回去

人一直裸不回去
頭被髮型與銅像
　　　　抓住不放
身體被時裝與制服
　　　　抱住不放
手被抓去　舉起設計好的表決
嘴被抓去　高呼調製好的口號
臉被抓去　複印規劃好的封面
心被抓去　身體空在那裏
人便活生生依計算機量好的尺寸
　　　　　　　　入框
　　　　活成框裏的那張照片

　　　　　　　　　一九八八年

看世界足球賽
—— 給阿根庭世界球王曼拉杜那

全世界的電視
　　都在看他
他帶著球跑
地球與千萬隻眼球
　　　　也跟著跑
他把球停下來
世界也停下來

踢一個高球
阿根庭的天空便一直藍上去
踢一個遠球
阿根庭的原野便一路綠過來
踢一個彎球
山與天空便沿著弧形跑
踢一個短球
將世界拉近
直衝過去
他是黃河之水天上來
　　擋不住的一條急流
　　　　　　隨波逐浪
追住那顆美的落日
　　　　　　進門

其實　曼拉杜那
他的腳也是神來之筆
在眾目中寫著一行行
　　　　空前的好詩

　　　　　　　　一九八八年

「燈屋」光的建築
—— 所有純正超越的生命，都是
光的建築．兼致L．M．

它不是只停在那裏
隔音擋灰的玻璃大廈
而是一不斷燃燒發光的
動體
與太陽同行
以無聲的光波
穿越嘈雜的音波
以無限的光能
焚化所有的煙塵雲霧
在純粹的光之旅中
透明的光境裏
它已昇華成那座
可容進整個天空的
水晶大廈
讓日月星辰親自出來
設計光的版面
進行光的佈置
展示光的作業
至於永恆什麼時候會來
叫詩與藝術站在光裏等

一九八九年三月

先看為快

黎明用一塊發亮的
　　　　玻璃窗
　　　　　圍住我
周圍的黑暗
站在旁邊看
不一會
光衝進來
將我叫出窗外

太陽剛起床
其他的床仍在睡
　　　　愛在睡
　　　　　情在睡
　　　都市在睡
　　　　世界在睡
尚未啟用的天空
是一幅不沾筆墨的禪畫
太陽蓋下第一個圓印
　　　叫我先看為快

　　　　　　　　　　一九九一年一月

詩眼七視

環視　　看不見範圍
注視　　使一切穩住不動
凝視　　焚化所有的焦點
窺視　　點亮所有的奧祕
仰視　　再也高不上去
俯視　　讓整個世界
　　　　　　跪拜下來
無視　　從有看到無
　　　　從無看到有

　　　　　　　　　　　　　　　一九九三年

社會造型藝術

一　電燈開關

明明是白的
往反面一撥
便全黑了

二　麵包店

最先矚目的
是那頂高帽子
戴上去的是光頭
　　　　　　禿頭
帽子才不管
更妙的　是搓來搓去的麵粉
放進一些酵素
送進暗房烤箱
　便膨脹擴大
　　變形走樣
　　美味可口
在人們的嘴中
　　流行起來

三　圓桌與方桌

大家圍著坐
你恭我敬
我謙你讓
杯碰
心不碰

不同的心情筷子與口水
　　同進一個菜盤
通往腸胃的路
一直都不那麼順暢

一個人吃自助餐
靠著方桌坐
桌方人也方

看自己的錢
　自己的心
　自己的口味
三位一體進菜盤
通往腸胃的路
　　順暢多了
只是後來走到咖啡杯的旁邊
　　　　　同誰聊呢

　四　　澡堂

泡在公共澡堂裏
難免臭味相同
細菌感染機會也多
最好每次出浴
　用「蓮蓬」沖洗

一個人到山中洗山泉
　　　　又清又涼
　　　　風來景去
只是當你叫出一聲爽
卻叫來滿山靜

　五　　垃圾事件

A 門前　堆有垃圾
B 門前　堆有垃圾
C 門前　堆有垃圾
D 門前　堆有垃圾
E 門前　堆有垃圾

你說ＡＢＣＤＥ門前
　　　　堆有垃圾
　　　　污染景觀

第二天醒來
所有的垃圾
　都堵在你望著花園的門口
警察問也不問
過來便開罰單

六　鳥與蟑螂

在沒有紅綠燈的情況下
所有的車都衝入黃燈
車頭車尾相對撞
在攪亂的方向裏
　　　　　搶出口

一隻鳥
帶著天空飛過
往下看　是擠滿在菜盤裏的
　　　　　一群蟑螂

　　　　　　　　一九九四年

全人類都在流浪

人在火車裏走
火車在地球裏走
地球在太空裏走
太空在茫茫裏走
誰都下不了車
印在名片上的地址
　　　　全是錯的

一九九八年

詩人作家對號入座

一

真珠　將豪華宴會的鑽石燈點亮
假珠　沿著鬧市叫賣的地攤亮相
玻璃瓶　在一聲爽中　碎成滿地閃爍

二

星空　燦爛在高不可及的光芒裡
噴水池　亮麗到一定位置便下來
煙火　在搶眼的光速裡死去

三

他的腳印　蓋在全世界的風景裡
他的腳印　只蓋一小部分的風景
他的腳印　只蓋那更小部分的風景

四

他在天空裡　看鳥
他在鳥店裡　找鳥
他在鳥籠裡　抓鳥

五

他把地球　看成畫布
他把地球　看成地圖
他把地球　看成地皮

六

他是沒有圓周的圓
他只是圓裏的面
他只是面裏的點

附記：真正的詩人與藝術家，可拿到「上帝」的通行證與信用卡；可
　　　將人類帶進大自然的生命結構，重新溫習風與鳥的自由；詩與
　　　藝術若失去超越中的形而上精神，就會受到框限而不能進入
　　　N度更廣闊且無限的活動空間去作業。

一九九九年

觀念劇場
—— 世紀末終審，地球·人·詩的演出

２０世紀站在絕崖上
滴答一聲　　　　跳
　　　　　　過
　　　　　　去

落點　　在０的位置
　　　　鳥開始飛
　　　　花開始開
　　　　河開始流
人跑回原本　看自己
地球跑回原來
看造型畫面

是誰最初打下第一根樁
長出地圖來
邊緣多是刀鋒劃的
劃下一條條血路
叫世界在彈道裏走
讓炮管用濃煙畫雲
　　槍管用血畫河流
大自然帶著逃亡的風景
一路告到一九九九年
歲月仍在用彈片刻人像
　　　　看導彈導航

廿一世紀開庭宣判
全案交由詩看管（註）

地球跑到城裏來
大自然擋住在城外
建築物圍成街口

把天空與原野吃掉
將煙囪與地下道排泄給
　　　　　青山綠水
回到冰箱裏看冰山冰水
湧進週末的鞋印看落葉
浮在廣告堆上看流雲
追著新潮熱浪找風向
速度趕著整座城在跑
　　　　帶著人車在衝

肩與肩　斷層
臉與臉　重疊
即使斑馬線緩下步來
腳下也不是林蔭道
至於長河落日圓不圓
日光燈早把菜油燈
望成第一波古遠的鄉愁

困在密封陰冷的機器房
世界電解成一大堆數據密碼
　　　虛擬成沒有肌膚的影像
一不留神　人便被電動玩具
　　　　　玩成肉動玩具
一起推上都市文明的貨櫃車
還來不及想起六十年代的稻草人
電腦與機器已預謀
　　將人軀離肉體的故鄉
　　　　製造第二波更遙遠的鄉愁

廿一世紀開特別庭宣判
複製人不能上市
詩在主審

地球跑到聯合國大廈
會場外　鳥飛起海上的

　　　　　自由神像
　會場內　各種條文主張
　　高談闊論大大小小的鳥籠
　　　　　　長長短短的河道
就是看不見天空與大海
世界便一直開闊不出去
仍留在計算機的範圍裏
　困在地圖與槍炮的射程中
自由還是要帶證件
歲月還是要裝鐵門鐵窗

廿一世紀開庭終審
人與地球一致要求宣判
　　　詩是航行的大海
　　　詩是飛行的天空

註：孔子認為「詩是天地之心」；法國詩人阿拉貢更說「詩就是天
　　國」；於我一九九八年參加在華盛頓舉行的世界文學會議時，
　　諾貝爾獎獲主WOLE　SOYINKA也指出未來的廿一世紀，只有詩
　　（與藝術）能確實與澈底的救助人類。的確，我們深信世界上最
　　「美」的人群、社會與國家，在最後應是詩（與藝術）而非單靠
　　機器造的；廿一世紀，應是一個自由和平與美麗的世紀；應讓詩
　　（與藝術）來導航——因為詩（與藝術）不但能美化科學、哲
　　學、政治乃至宗教的世界；而且能全面與澈底美化人類內外的生
　　存空間，尤其是它在「美」中無限地超越的精神境界，最了解自
　　由，最接近真理、完美與永恆。

又寫完此詩，發現這竟是一首以詩來寫詩論——「論詩的高超價值」
的詩。

　　　　　　　　　　　　　一九九九年

颱風眼
—— 給詩人L・大衛

空出來　給萬有
靜下來　給萬動

你盯住天地的心
看狂風暴雨帶著世界
　　四面八方呼嘯而來
你是無聲的回音谷
來自高山絕嶺的
　「尼采」會帶它回孤寂的峯頂
來自翻天覆地的
　「海」會用天地線牽住它不動
　　　　　　回到有無中

究竟是空　　是有
　　　　是靜　是動
你　　一目了然

二〇〇〇年

隕　石
—— 給　詩

在地球未打樁
　也沒有地圖之前
它帶著宇宙
　從茫茫中降落

石面下　坐著山的深度
石面上　坐著天的高度
石周圍坐著地的廣度

看是遠方
聽是回響
摸它成水流
擊它為火光
冷它入冰心
握它進建築的力點
　架構起無邊的透明
望著滿天的繽紛燦爛
　　　墮落在凋謝中
獨留下它堅韌的這一朵
　開放出大過地球與時空的
　　　一座MINIMAL

附記：詩是一種「前進中的永恆」的存在。MINIMAL在藝術創作理念
　　　中，是「極限」與「極小」之意，但對「美」的世界，有極大
　　　與無限的發言權，故它小卻又大過可見的地球與超過茫茫的時
　　　空。

二○○○年

藝術幫助人走出身體看世界

高樓大廈圍攏成街口
　　　把天空吃掉
都市壓縮在天花板下
終日坐在廣告堆上
看是物
碰也是物
物來物去
人也成了追著物在跑的動物
即使當初在荒野睡覺吃喝的地方
　　　已搬到希爾頓豪華的餐廳與套房
菜單天天改
床單夜夜換
人仍是走動在身體裏的
　　　　　文明動物

走不出身體
人變成沒有窗的屋子
　　　　看不出去
　　　　聽不進來
世界便連盲帶啞
　　　在盤碗裏來回打轉
　　　在抽水馬桶裏回響
要是交響樂不穿越
　　　菜市場的雞鴨聲
　　　機械的尖叫聲
　　　議論的爭吵聲
　　　炮彈的爆炸聲
　　　　　　　將
　　　　　　　生
　　　　　　　命
　　　　　　　響
　　　　　　　亮

　　　　　出
　　　　　來
要是舞步不跨過千山萬水
　　帶著藍天碧海與綠野
　　　　　　　　一起飛
要是色彩不將大自然揮灑在
　　　　繽紛燦爛裏
　　　　線條不把風雲鳥的行程
　　　　　　　　　　描出來

人與世界能看
　　　　能聽
　　　　能美到那裏去

走不出身體
雞在雞籠
鳥在鳥籠
如何把天空飛成那隻
　　不停地飛的遠方
把遠方飛成那隻
　　不停地飛的永恆

註：在藝術世界，人不是封閉的體積；而是透明的建築（羅門詩話）

　　　　　　　二〇〇〇年

說話的幾何圖象

第一眼它只是一根線
第二眼它像是天地線
第三眼它已鳴響成宇宙最後的一根弦 　　————
　　　　在茫茫的時空中

它彎彎曲曲
把河流、山、天空、海浪的輪廓
美女腰部、臀部與乳房的輪廓
以及風雲鳥的行程全都彎進來

走動　是棋盤
定靜　是盤石
所謂方方正正直來直往
　　　大概也就是這個樣子

活著　是名片一張
　　　　一路亮相
死後　是棺材一具
　　　　一片陰暗

三角戀愛　三個角都是刀尖
要登峰造極便不能不仰望
　　　　山峰與金字塔的
　　　　　　　頂點

地球‧眼球‧銀圓都是圓的
最後都圓到銀圓裏去
就是看不見心中的渾圓
世界便在輪盤裏打滾

旋上去　到無限超越的頂點
　　　　　可見到尼采
旋下來　到無限的奧秘之底
　　　　　可遇到里爾克
它是開在時空中最美的一朵形而上
也是宇宙萬物上下的螺旋梯

二〇〇〇年

〔註〕
（一）尼采是向思想頂峰超越的哲學家
（二）里爾克是富哲思向內心探視的大詩人

提著世界與永恆的詩人藝術家

為何千山萬水你獨行
是因天　空出來
　　地　遠出去
只留下千山萬水
除非你帶著千山萬水一起走
　　　走到雲深不知處一起停下來
　　　　　　　在不走中仍在走
　　　走成另一條停不下來的河
　　　　　另一座停下來仍在走的山

為何你回首
　　是因擦過車窗的風景太快
　　　　一次又一次揮別車站的手勢
　　　　　　　仍舉著開跑的槍
過去　緊追在後
未來　猛跑在前
你是　停不下來的路
　　　前後都在走的現在
　　　雙腳踩著過去與未來
　　　雙手提著世界與永恆

二○○一年

詩的假期
—— 巴里島之旅

海與天藍在一起
被天地線分開後
　又藍到藍裏去
浪花與沙灘白在一起
被海岸線分開後
　又白到白裏去
除了白
　是藍

沿著天地線
靜　在遠中看
遠　在靜裏望
除了靜
　是遠

沿著海岸線
一排排浪峰在海上叫
一排排乳峰在岸上應
除了波動
　是起伏

世界自由的來
　　自在的去
只留下最純的一條直線在走
　　最美的一條曲線在動
除了風和日麗　波光浪影
是人與自然一起在悠遊渡假

註：最近同蓉子往巴里島旅遊，有一天整個下午躺在海灘的臥椅
　　上，看海景、看來自各國的遊客；景象確較夏威夷靠近都市的
　　威基基海灘，更自然更美，應是我看過所有海灘最美的一個海
　　灘景點；心中也特別有些感想：人活著，有時確像海浪沖激岩
　　壁那樣的急迫，有時應該也像飄遊的雲那樣舒放。的確，人大
　　半生忙著在辦公室用印章蓋公文與支票，不要忘了也用腳印蓋
　　在世界美麗的風景上。

二〇〇一年

夏

夏　推著太陽的大石磨
　　將天空海洋與原野
　　　磨成一個燃燒的火球
　　　在大自然裡
　　　　滾來滾去

除非午後下陣雨
它不會冷靜的停下來

其實　夏雖也是一隻
　　　　　到處放火的火鳥
但它收下翅膀
躲在林中飲綠蔭
藏在山中喝冷泉
傍著涼亭柳色荷香
　　　　　午寐入綺麗
連自己也夢成大自然冷藏室裡
　　　　　那塊潔美的冰
　　　　在涼風與水聲中
　　　　　　飄
　　　　　　流
　　　　　　而
　　　　　　去
　　　　　　二〇〇一年

以電影鏡頭寫《寂》這首詩

　　首先將鏡頭對準炎夏正午日正當中時刻的天空，並停在那裡幾秒鐘不動，直至天空與世界完全進入沉寂的午睡狀態……

　　之後將鏡頭沿著無聲無影的「空闊」移動過去，停留在山頂寺廟一直刺痛「寧靜」的塔尖上，守望著無邊無際的「空茫」與寂靜……

　　之後，將鏡頭移動到廟裡來，沿著靜默無言的廊柱、空靜的殿堂，滑過打坐和尚他空得較天空還空的光頭，沒有任何聲息。讓敲進「空茫」的木魚聲，將「鏡頭」帶到山谷底，去照泉水滴進荒涼的聲音、樹影睡進「深沉」的聲音、林鳥叫空整座山的聲音……

　　之後，將鏡頭沿著那直頂住天空的塔尖照出去，並緩緩移動，把遠方那朵白雲，終於開放成那朵在「美」中發出巨響的孤「寂」。

　　後　記

　　30年前（一九七一年）我在《藍星》年刊，提出以電影鏡頭寫詩（就廣義的「圖象詩」），那是意圖將平面書寫的靜態「圖象詩」，進一步變成立體掃瞄的動態「圖象詩」，必要時尚可加上音響，達到視覺與聽覺雙重的藝術美感效果。它有可能嗎？在基本理念上，應是可以的；因當時台北電影院放映的7又1/2，整部電影可說是以「詩」的鏡頭拍攝的。我們是否可反過來思考，也以電影鏡頭來寫詩？記得當時我腦海中曾浮現過如何以電影鏡頭來寫這首命題為《寂》的詩。

　　　　　　　　　　　　　　　二〇〇一年

二〇〇六年後現代動畫特輯

一

〇是零
由一開始
橫過東西
直通南北
正交成經緯線
　　　座標與
　　　十字架
地球　人與上帝
　才不會失蹤

〇是滾動的
　　　地球
　　　眼睛
　　　輪子
一是直往
　　前衛
　　領先
　永恆便不會停下來

二

地球是沒有岸可靠的船
田園都市　人與上帝
　　　　都坐在船上
　沿著一　向〇直航
　大家口袋裏的旅遊卡
　　　　與名片地址
　　　　一路丟

只有「悲愴奏鳴曲」「歡樂頌」
　　　　　　與一部聖經
　　　　　　放在船頭

一路上
打開電視一頻道
　　　　一插進〇中
　　只能看到直舉過來的
　　　　　　　　陽具
　　　　　　　　槍支
　　　　　　　　旗桿
　　　　　　　　　與
　　　　　　　　麵條
　　　　　　　　金條
至於那條誰都抓不到的天地線
　　　　　　要把人與地球
　　　　　　　牽到那裏
　　　　　　上帝也不知道

打開電視〇頻道
　　　　〇吞沒一
除了可摸到圓圓的
　　　　　　乳房
　　　　　　臀部
　　　　　　陰部
　　　　　　　與
　　　　　　銀圓
　　　　　　金幣
古羅馬與宮殿的圓頂
　　也不過是歷史的胸罩
誰會去想王維坐著江流
　　到天地外去製作什麼渾圓

打開電視一〇頻道
　　　　一插進〇
　　　　〇吞沒一
　　　世界在虛脫中

人口仍在吵
街口仍在吵
槍口仍在吵
教堂裏的禱告聲
　微弱如氧氣管裏的喘息
沒有什麼好聽的
張惠妹順手把所有的耳朵
　　　都低價收買過來
安裝成全方位的擴音器
　讓都市發瘋發狂尖叫
當世界累倒在〇時的打呼聲中
是誰在國家音樂廳
　把過去現在與未來都叫醒
去聽貝多芬音樂中壯麗的雪崩
　　莫札特音樂中的水流花放
　　　　進入波洛克華麗的綠野

打開頻道外的N頻道
視窗　由夢特里安重建
視野　送入康丁斯基的眼睛配音
單純　在布朗庫斯
圓滿　在康利摩爾
絕對　在馬勒維奇
歸一歸〇　在MINIMAL
世界的造型空間畫面
　　　　在完美裏看

神奇的PL
雙目放進海與天
躺成太陽下的大地
讓體內燃燒的火焰
　燒進冰山
　冷凝成金屬的河流
原來浪漫與古典是同一個溫度計

　　　轉化與昇華才會將火光雪與雲
　　　　　都白到白宮裏去

白是空
什麼也不必帶
只帶神奇的PL
獨行到山下
便一腳把平野踩給一去不回的平遠
讓頭頂與山頂天頂
　　頂著整個世界一同到深遠
　　　　　　　　　　　高遠
往下看
一架飛機正飛過嚴重塞車的街口
大家都急著看錶趕路
有些錶急趕在貨櫃車垃圾車的路上
有些錶是飛車
　　　永恆在開
時間也追不上
如果過去是故鄉
　　　　回憶是美麗的後花園
　　　未來是異鄉
　　　　　　前面由夢與想像帶路
　　　現在是汽車旅館
　　　　　　大家便過一天算一天
至於被都市急躁踩過的後現代
　　　是不是已碎掉的薄冰玻璃
　　　　　　讓路在裂縫裏亂跑
並不那麼重要
只要浮在地面上的浮石
　　仍認得地下的鑽石寶石與玉石
漂在水面上的漂木
　　仍忘不了樹林綠野

神奇的PL
他的雙腳
　　是路的雙軌
　　　　便接送始終
　　　　　　載運千山萬水
行到海邊
　　是江河
　　　　便入海
同海站在一起看潮起潮落
　　　　　　　　浪來山更高
　　　　　　　　浪去天更遠
遠方是一隻不停地飛的鳥
眼睛跟不上　便從迷茫中看回來
一群群採完浪花離去的遊客
　　　　只留下滿海灘失蹤的腳印
　　　　　　　　等著潮水來收

日落後
他與海閉上雙目仍在走
走到山窮水盡　又一村
那是地球村外的宇宙村
千萬個春天在那裏造一個花園
　　　　給來去的季節與歲月看
一座高過一〇一與帝國大廈的螺旋塔
　　　　　　從第三自然旋昇到天堂
　　　　　　　　給永恆上下

　　　　　　　　二〇〇六年

Lomen's Vitae

Name: HAN Jen Tsun (Pen Name: Lomen)

Date of Birth: November 20, 1928

Education: Flight School of the Chinese Air Force (1949-1951)
            Aircraft Accident Investigation School of the FAA, USA
            Certificate of Senior Technician granted by the Examination Board of FAA,
            R.O.C. (1959)

Profession: Senior Technician, Civil Aviation Administration, R.O.C. (1959-1974)
            Researcher of the Development Affairs of Civil Aviation Administration
            (1967-1974)

Positions Held: Honorary Member, UPLI International Poetry Association (1966)
            Director, the Blue Star Poetry Club (1975-1999)
            Founder, Laser Association, R.O.C. (1982)
            Judge, National Literature Competition (1985-1986)
            Director, The World Association of Chinese Poets (1989)
            Chairman, Poetry Workshop of the Chinese Literature and Art (1990)

Awards: The Blue Star Prize and the Chinese Poetry Association Prize (1958)
            A Gold Medal from the President of the Philippines for the masterpiece which
                was cited as a great poem by the United Poets Laureate International
                (1966)
            Honorary "Oklahoma Citizenship" from the State Governor (1967)
            A Gold Medal from the President of the Philippines as Distinguished Literary
                Couple at the First World Congress of Poets held in the Philippines
                (1969)
            Crowned with poetess Rongzi (Yungtze) as "Laureate Poets" at the 3rd World
                Congress of Poets held in USA (1976)
            Honorary Prize for "in Praise of Zhong Xin" by Association of Literary
                Renaissance (1978)
            Citation for Poetry Education, conferred by the Ministry of Education of the
                R.O.C. (1987)
            The Major Poetry Prize of the China Times (1988)
            The Dr. Sun Yat-Sen Prize for Literature and Art (1991)
            Certificate of Honorary Researcher (together with Rongzi) of IWP conferred
                by Iowa State University (1992)
            Certificate for "the 20th Century Five Hundred World Leaders" conferred by
                American Biographical Institute (1995)

Name is listed, together with poetess Rongzi, *in International Who's Who in Poetry* (1970), in *Who's Who of R.O.C.* (1991), in *Encyclopedia Americana* (Chinese Ed. 1992), in *The 20th Century Five Hundred Leaders of Influence* by American Biographical Institute, Inc. (1995)

Invited to attend "International Conference on the 21st Century Asian Literatures", "International Conference on the 21st Century Western Literatures", "World Peace Conference on the 21st Century Literatures" (1997)

Cai Yuanhuang, Professor and Critic from Taiwan Universty won the "Gold Pen Prize" for his review on Lomen's poetry (1977)

David Yang, Professor of National Taiwan Normal University, won Research Funding from National Science Foundation for his project on the study of Lomen's poetry (1995)

Publications: *Collections of Poems,* 15 volumes

Essays on Literature and Art, 7 volumes

Collections of Lomen's writings, 10 volumes in series

Collections of Lomen and Rongzi's Poems, 8 volumes in series

Works were cited in College Textbooks of Chinese Literature

Works were translated and cited in more than one hundred anthologies in English, French, Germany, Sweden, Yugoslavia, Japanese, Korean, etc; Works were also cited in *Anthology of Ten Major Contemporary Chinese Poets.*

Four poems were inscribed on stones and set up in public places: Shin-Sheng Park (Taipei 1982), Taipei Zoo (1988), Chang Hua City Green (1992), and Chang Hua Railway Station Square (1992)

Academic Studies on Lomen:

Ph.D. dissertations

"Self" in Poetic Narratives: A Study of Contemporary Long Poem in Taiwan as exemplified by Luo Fu, Lomen, Chen Kehua and Feng Qing by Tang Yuqi (University of Alberta, Canada 2000)

Shifting Ground: Modernist Aesthetics in Taiwanese Poetry since the 1950s by Au Chung-to (Hong Kong University 2003)

MA theses

Study on Lomen's Metropolitan Poems by Chen Dawei (Suzhou University 1997)

On Lomen by Zhang Aigong (Xiamen University 1998)

On Lomen's View of Time and Space by You Chunchun (Nan Hua University 2002)

Speeches abroad:

Traveling extensively to places such as Hong Kong, Thailand, the Philippines, Mainland China and USA to lecture at universities or take part in seminars on art and literature. Seminars were held at Taiwan and Beijing on Lomen and Rongzi Collections of Poems

Comments received: (A Summary)

In the past half century, Lomen has spent his whole life in poetry and art. He has not only formed his own writing style, but also proposed his individual view of artistic aesthetics "Third Nature Spiral Structure". Lomen is also a critique of poetry, painting, sculpture and movie. He is praised as "Apollinaire of Taiwan", "Distinguished Poet", "Poet of Master", "The Giant of War Poems", "Father of Metropolitan Poems", "Poet of Poets" and so on.

文史哲英譯叢刊　　　1

The Collected Poems of LOMEN : A Bilingual Edition

譯　　　者：Au Chung-to, Tom Rendal
出 版 者：文　史　哲　出　版　社
　　　　　http://www.lapen.com.tw
登記證字號：行政院新聞局版臺業字五三三七號
發 行 人：彭　　　　正　　　　雄
發 行 所：文　史　哲　出　版　社
印 刷 者：文　史　哲　出　版　社
　　　　　臺北市羅斯福路一段七十二巷四號
　　　　　郵政劃撥帳號：一六一八○一七五
　　　　　電話886-2-23511028・傳真886-2-23965656
實價新臺幣四八○元
中華民國九十五年（2006）十一月初版

羅 門 簡 歷

◎從事詩創作五十年，曾被名評論家在文章中稱為：「重量級詩人」、「臺灣當代十大詩人」、「現代主義的急先鋒」、「臺灣詩壇孤傲高貴的現代精神掌旗人」、「現代詩的守護神」、「戰爭詩的巨擘」、「都市詩之父」、「都市詩的宗師」、「都市詩國的發言人」、「知性派的思想型詩人」、「大師級詩人」、「詩人中的詩人」……甚至在文章中被稱為台灣詩壇的五大三大支柱……。半世紀來，他不但建立自己獨特的創作風格：也提倡個人特殊創作的藝術美學理念：「第三自然螺旋型架構創作世界」。

◎曾任藍星詩社社長、世界華文詩人協會會長、國家文藝獎評審委員、世界和平文學聯盟顧問……先後曾赴菲律賓、香港、大陸、泰國、馬來西亞與美國等地（或大學、或文藝團體）發表有關詩的專題講演。

◎曾獲中國時報推薦詩獎、中山文藝獎、教育部詩教獎及菲總統金牌與大綬勳章並接受加冕。

◎名列「大美百科全書」。

◎作品選入大專教科書，選入台灣與大陸出版的《新詩300首》。

◎出版有詩集十七種，論文集七種，羅門創作大系書十種，羅門、蓉子系列書八種；並在臺灣與大陸北京大學兩地分別舉辦羅門蓉子系列書研討會。

◎作品選入英、法、德、瑞典、南斯拉夫、羅馬尼亞、日、韓……等外文詩選與中文版「中國當代十大詩人選集」……等超一百種詩選集。

◎作品接受國內外著名學人、評論家及詩人評介文章超出一百萬字，已出版七本評論羅門的專書。

◎因評論羅門作品，國立臺灣大學教授名批評家蔡源煌博士獲「金筆獎」；國立臺灣師範大學教授戴維揚博士獲一九九五年國科會學術研究獎。

◎六位研究生研究羅門分別獲得碩士或博士學位。

◎羅門作品碑刻在臺北新生公園（1982年）、臺北動物園（1988年）、彰化市區廣場（1992年）、彰化火車站廣場（1996年）與臺中清水公共藝術園區（2004年）。

◎羅門除寫詩，尚寫詩論與藝評，有「臺灣阿波里奈爾」與「臺灣現代裝置藝術鼻祖」之稱。

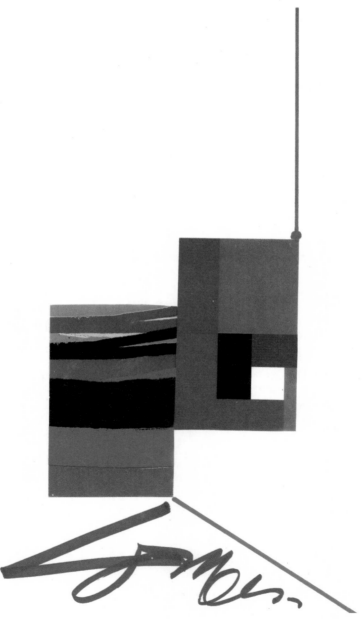

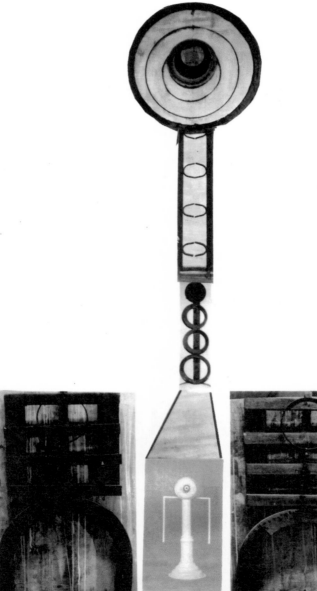

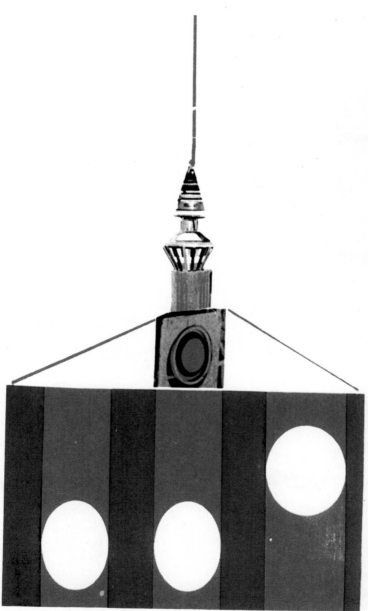

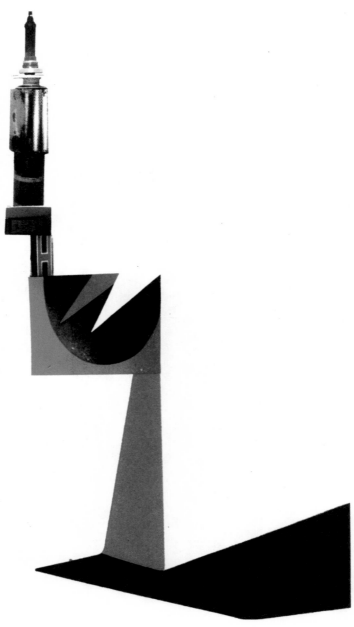

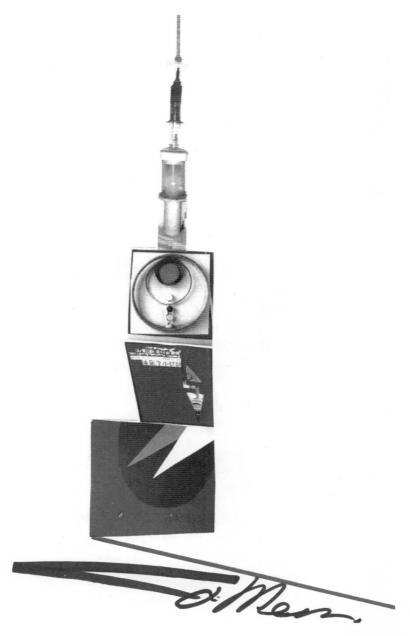

The Collected
Poems of LOMEN
: A Bilingual Edition

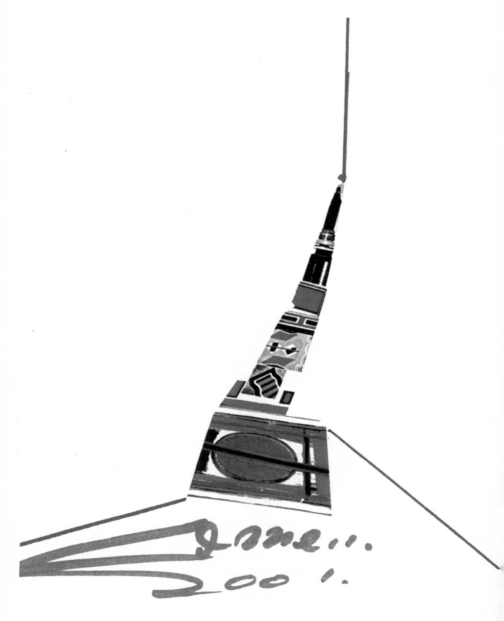

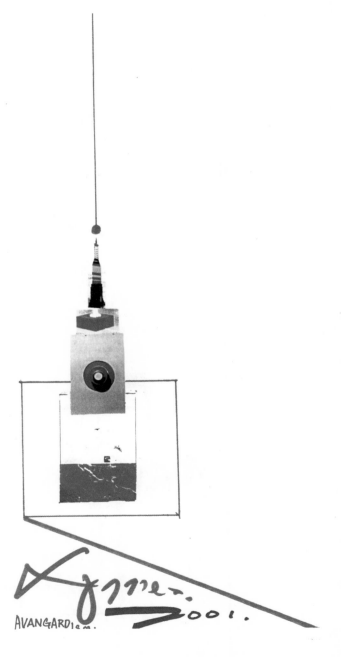

AVANGARDiem.

The Collected
Poems of **LOMEN**
: A Bilingual Edition

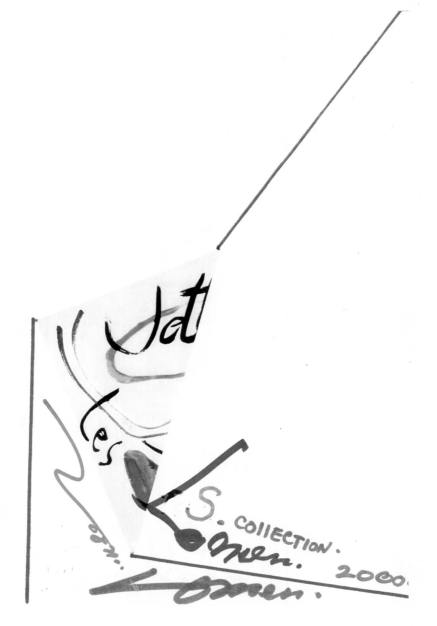

S. COLLECTION.

2000

The eternalness of forging ahead.

POETRY. PAINTING. SCULPTURE.

前進中的永恒‧(羅門)

The Collected
Poems of **LOMEN**
: A Bilingual Edition

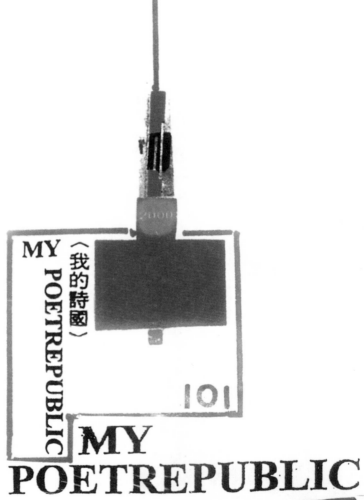

MY
POETREPUBLIC
〈我的詩國〉

101

**MY
POETREPUBLIC**